THE PUBLIC LIBRARY MANAGER'S

FORMS, POLICIES, *and* PROCEDURES HANDBOOK

with CD-ROM

Rebecca Brumley

Neal-Schuman Publishers, Inc.

New York   **London**

Published by Neal-Schuman Publishers, Inc.
100 William Street, Suite 2004
New York, NY 10038

Printed and bound in the United States of America.

The paper used in this publication meets the minimum requirements of American National Standard for Information Sciences—Permanence of Paper for Printed Library Materials, ANSI Z39.48—1992.

Library of Congress Cataloging-in-Publication Data

Brumley, Rebecca R., 1959-
    The public library manager's forms, policies, and procedures manual with CD-Rom /
Rebecca R. Brumley.
    p.cm
    Includes bibliographical references (p 302) and index.
    ISBN 1-55570-488-3 (alk. paper)
    1. Public libraries—Rules and practice. 2. Public libraries—Forms. 3. Library rules and refu-
lations—United States—Case studies. 4. Library rules and regulations—Canada—Case
studies. I. Title.

Z704.B78 2004
025.1'974—dc22

                                                                2003068644

Dedication

For Lisa Lipton who has rescued hundreds of dogs and cats from animal shelters and given them a chance to have a great life

"A civilized society must count animals as worthy of moral consideration and ethical treatment. The question is not, Can they reason? nor Can they talk? but, Can they suffer?"

—Jeremy Bentham

Contents

List of Illustrations

Preface

"Necessity is the mother of invention." This adage resonates with all librarians, whose duties increasingly involve everything—and everything done right now. How often in the librarian's workday would a simple, standardized form, policy or procedure, answer that one question that seemingly has no immediate answer? How often do librarians have to reinvent the wheel, consult a makeshift procedure manual, or shrug their shoulders, every time someone wants to know about Internet use, library card requirements, or any one of the hundreds of everyday questions encountered in library work? *The Public Library Manager Forms, Policies, and Procedures Manual with CD-ROM* is for those librarians who don't want to stop their busy lives, but would rather contribute themselves to meeting their communities' needs.

In my own work as a librarian and a consultant to small libraries, I have seen many libraries operating without a formal, written policy and procedure manual. In countless others, the policy and procedure manual is outdated, poorly organized, or lost. A manual is one of those things that falls by the wayside, due to time constraints, lack of staff, or simply not knowing where to start. This book tackles the questions, of where to start and what types of policies, forms and procedures a library needs.

No one wants to start from scratch and no one wants to adopt unproven policies. The *Public Library Manager Forms, Policies, and Procedures Manual with CD-ROM* compiles forms, policies, and procedures from 114 public libraries, of all sizes, from across the U.S. in a practical format. The companion CD-ROM, which contains all the contents in downloadable versions ready to be adapted or modified, giving every librarian and library manager a seat at the table where they can take the best of what's available and modify it to their own library's needs.

The most timesaving feature is obvious. When creating your library's policies and procedures manual, there's no need to reinvent the wheel. How are other leading libraries handling the problems? This manual gives you multiple versions of each document and careful considerations of the quality of every form, policy, and procedure included in this book. Even libraries with manuals in place can consult the examples to improve their own forms and policies.

ORGANIZATION OF INFORMATION

This work is divided into three parts, for use in three main areas of a public library's operation: public service, administration, and collections. A dozen chapters, each covering a specific area of librarianship, are divided up among the three main topics. Part I, "Public Services Forms and Policies," contains chapters on policies governing circulation, reference service, Internet usage, and miscellaneous public policies. Part II, "Administrative Forms and Policies," covers mission statements; gifts, memorials, and donations; library boards; exhibits, displays, and bulletin boards; meeting rooms; and foundations. Part III, "Collection Forms and Policies," presents chapters on collection maintenance, evaluation, and development.

INSIDE THE CHAPTERS

Part I, "Public Services Forms and Policies," has hundreds of forms and policies that will help establish pleasant and standard relations between your institution and the public it serves.

- Chapter 1, "Circulation," covers borrowing privileges, loan periods, form letters for overdue material, patron conduct, and fines and fees.

- Chapter 2, "Reference Service Policies," provides policies for the types of questions a person in the reference area will respond to, whether to impose a time limit, whether the patron at the reference desk or the one on the telephone comes first, and to what forms of non-face-to-face communication you will respond—telephone, e-mail, mail, or fax. At the end of the chapter, the helpful Daily Desk Count Worksheet not only allows you to track reference statistics to help document your actual workload, but it can also aid in collection development decisions, based on the types of material actually used at the reference desk. Plus, this information can be used to justify budget requests.

- Chapter 3, "Internet Policies," presents diverse policies for Internet usage, the most frequently rewritten policy in libraries today. Some policies prohibit games and chatrooms, others do not. Some libraries employ filters, others do not. Some have short time limits, others do not. Some provide assistance, others do not. In the other eleven chapters, there is a consensus on major issues such as what to do when someone challenges material or what to do if someone seeks confidential patron information, but no such consensus holds sway regarding how to handle problem issues associated with the Internet. This chapter presents wildly diverse policy perspectives.

- Chapter 4, "Miscellaneous Public Policies," contains an assortment of policies that are important to managing the library, but did not fit the subject matter of the other chapters. These policies include copyright, Friends of the library, volunteers, printing/copying fees, fax service, tax forms, continuing education, and other similar services and issues.

Part II, "Administrative Forms and Policies," explains all of the policies, forms, and procedures that help define your institution to both staff and users.

- Chapter 5, "Mission Statements," covers the five important elements of the mission statement—who, what, where, why, and how of library service.

- Chapter 6, "Gifts, Memorials, and Donations," provides policies ranging from acceptance of books to evaluating a piece of donated artwork. Every library receives gifts, memorials, and donations—some wanted, most not. One of the most important factors in accepting a gift is to give the library complete control over the items. These forms and policies will make clear to your patrons how your library accepts gifts and what the roles of donor and recipient will be. There are several types of gift, memorial, and donation forms in the last section of the chapter for you to peruse.

- Chapter 7, "Library Boards," presents policies to perfect your very important work with the library board. Whether you have a governing board or an advisory board, you'll want to look at policies on your duties, the board's duties, the critical elements of a meeting, and committee work.

- Chapter 8, "Exhibits, Displays, and Bulletin Boards," considers display material: duration of a display; suitable types of material; who can post flyers; disclaimers, liability, and damage issues; and exhibit proposal forms. A well-crafted policy can save you many frustrations in this often-used, high-demand area by regulating the public space.

- Chapter 9, "Meeting Rooms," includes three complete policies, two in print and an additional one on the CD-ROM, which are broken down into parts. Some of the policies have fees or deposits, others do not. All of them have damage and liability clauses. Most libraries give the entire policy to the individual or organization when they fill out the meeting room request form. Some policies allow for-profit groups to use their spaces, while others only allow not-for-profits.

- Chapter 10, " Foundations," covers an important asset libraries use to raise, distribute, manage, and coordinate funds. Tax money alone will not support all of the goals a public library wants to achieve. A foundation allows the library to establish endowments, accept bequests in a patron's will, apply for grant money, and accept real estate and other forms of capital. It is important to have a written set of by-laws and coordinate efforts with the Friends group, the director, and the library board. This chapter covers these issues and explains the benefits of foundations.

Part III, "Collection Forms and Policies," examines all the forms and policies to help establish, develop, and maintain your collections, the prized products libraries offer to patrons.

- Chapter 11, "Collection Maintenance and Evaluation," delves into the weeding, mending, and binding process, and how different libraries have chosen to evaluate their collection. Under weeding, mending, and binding you will find helpful slips to fill out as decisions are made about the material. Under the Forms section there are periodical and newspaper check-in, worksheets for counting the titles and number of periodicals and newspapers shelved and reshelved each day, as well as call slips. These keep track of staff productivity and material usage, providing statistics to make subscription and budget decisions.

- Chapter 12, "Collection Development," discusses all facets of selection, including resources, responsibilities, criteria, and children's materials. The type of collection you have depends upon the type of community your serve. Two surveys will help you better understand your community and gauge your customer service efforts. Selection parameters, limited collection efforts, Internet, and electronic resources are treated in this chapter. The policy on controversial material and labeling will help answer patrons' questions on material in the collection. Challenge Forms for print, non-print, and Internet sites are included here.

CHAPTER STRUCTURE AND CD-ROM CONTENTS

I tried to make *Public Library Manager Forms, Policies, and Procedures Manual with CD-ROM* as clear and user-friendly as possible. Each of the twelve chapters begins with a brief overview of the policy area, followed by my reasons for selecting policies for inclusion and the benefits of having these policies. Next come the actual policies then the forms. A checklist with points to consider when writing your policy to fit your individual needs concludes each chapter.

I encourage librarians to modify policies to meet their individual situation, such as a time limit for Internet access or the size of fines you charge for overdue books. All of the nearly 200 different types of policies and forms in the book are located on the CD-ROM. In addition, the CD-ROM contains 22 policies and forms that are not in the book. These offer you more of the same excellent quality resources as those reproduced in the book. The CD-ROM also includes screen captures of policies from the Internet, so you can see how other libraries present their information online.

As you use *Public Library Manager Forms, Policies, and Procedures Manual with CD-ROM*, please remember the importance of sharing in the field of librarianship. Libraries can use the policies of one library, improve it and then pass it on to another library. Shirley Vonderhaar from James Kennedy Public Library said it best on her returned "Permission to Reprint" form: "Like many policies in many libraries, it is the distillation of the wisdom of our peers, if you see your hand in our policy, thank you for your help." If you see your policy or something like it, every librarian who uses it thanks you. I hope we all continue to share what works for us.

Utilize this manual and CD-ROM as a resource to create, rewrite, revise, or add policies and provide easy access to helpful forms. Whether you start with a blank sheet of paper or work from an old policy, with this book you will find the tools you need to create a living document that can change as the library changes. Return to this book again when the inevitable change is necessary. My hope is that *Public Library Manager Forms, Policies, and Procedures Manual with CD-ROM* will help your library operations run smoother, your statistics become more accurate, and that it will help turn the task of creating libraries' policies, procedures and forms manuals and keeping it up-to-date less stressful. You now have access to policy language and forms that have proved useful in libraries across the United States. I trust you will find in *Public Library Manager Forms, Policies, and Procedures Manual with CD-ROM* something that works in your community.

Acknowledgments

I would like to thank Jeri Baker and especially Lisa Lipton for their helpful comments and for reading the manuscript. Thanks to my co-workers at Dallas Public Library Humanities Division, for their constant encouragement and help. Thanks to Kevin Jennings for his help with the forms from Dallas Pubic Library. Special thanks go to my editor Michael Kelley for his guidance, helpful comments, patience, and for getting me on the right track and keeping me on the right track. I would also like to thank Charles Harmon, Director of Publishing at Neal-Schuman, for believing in this book and for help getting it started.

Thank you to my wonderful family and especially my brothers Chester and Paul, also to Janet, Susan, Jack, Charlie, Jason, Patrice, L. E., Jessica, and Barrett for bringing joy to my life. Finally to M. C. Kaufmann for everything that is good.

For all of the library directors, foundations, and board members who graciously allowed me to use their policies (listed below), thanks—there would be no book without them. A special thanks the OWLS (www.ows.lib.wi.us) for a great Web site that got this book rolling and to Dr. Alex Boyd, Director Newark Public Library for liberal use of his policies. I am most grateful to the more than one hundred libraries that gave me permission to reprint their excellent forms, policies, and procedures. Your intelligence and clarity shine on every page. They include the following:

Albert Wisner Public Library
Rosemary Cooper
Warwick, New York
www.albertwisnerlibrary.org

Alhambra Public Library
Stephanie Beverage
Alhambra, California
www.alhambralibrary.org

Anchorage Municipal Libraries
Art Weeks
Anchorage, Alaska
http://lexicon.ci.anchorage.ak.us/aml

Appleton Public Library
Appleton, Wisconsin
www.apl.org

Austin Public Library
Austin, Texas
www.ci.austin.tx.us/library

Beloit Public Library
Peg Bredeson
Beloit, Wisconsin
http://als.lib.wi.us/BPL

Bernardsville Public Library
Bernardsville, New Jersey
http://bernardsville.org

Bettendorf Public Library Information Center
Bettendorf, Iowa
http://rbls.lib.il.us/bpl

Bozeman Public Library
Bozeman, Montana
http://bozemanlibrary.org

Brantford Public Library
Wendy Newman
Brantford, Ontario Canada
www.brantford.library.on.ca

Carrollton Public Library
Lucile Dade, Director of Library Services,

Library Staff, and Library Advisory Board
Carrollton, Texas
www.cityofcarrollton.com/leisure/library

Chapel Hill Public Library Foundation
Robert Woodruff, President
Chapel Hill North Carolina
www.chapelhilllibraryfoundation.org

Charlevoix Public Library
Valerie Meyerson
Charlevoix, Michigan
www.charlevoix.lib.mi.us

Chelmsford Public Library
Becky Herrmann
Chelmsford, Massachusetts
www.chelmsfordlibrary.org

Cleveland Public Library
Cleveland, Ohio
www.cpl.org

Public Library of Cincinnati and Hamilton County
Kimber L. Fender
Cincinnati, Ohio
www.cincinnatilibrary.org

Cook Memorial Public Library District
Cook Memorial Public Library Board of Trustees
Libertyville, Illinois
www.cooklib.org

Cumberland County Public Library and Information Center
Jerry A. Thrasher
Fayetteville, North Carolina
www.cumberland.lib.nc.us

David and Joyce Milne Public Library
Pat McLeod
Williamstown, Massachusetts
www.milnelibrary.org

Dayton Metro Library
Timothy G. Kambitsch

Dayton, Ohio
www.daytonmetrolibrary.org

DeKalb County Public Library
Decatur, Georgia
www.dekalb.public.lib.ga.us

Des Plaines Public Library
Sandra K. Norlin
Des Plaines, Illinois
http://desplaines.lib.il.us

DeSoto Public Library
Mary Musgrave, Director
DeSoto, Texas
www.desotolibrary.org

Delaware County District Library
Delaware, Ohio
http://delaware.lib.oh.us

Ely Public Library
Ely, Minnesota
http://elylibrary.org

Eugene Public Library
Eugene, Oregon
www.ci.eugene.or.us/Library

Fayette County Public Library
Christeen Snell
Fayetteville, Georgia
www.admin.co.fayette.ga.us/public_library

Fort Smith Public Library
P. J. Williams
Fort Smith, Arkansas
http://fspl.lib.ar.us

Fulton County Public Library
Web site design by Bonnie S. Kern, System Administrator of the Fulton County Public Library
Rochester, Indiana
www.fulco.lib.in.us

Gates Public Library
Rochester, New York
www.gateslibrary.org

Grand Island Public Library
Steve Fosselman, Library Director
Grand Island, Nebraska
www.gi.lib.ne.us

Grosse Pointe Public Library
Vickey Bloom
Grosse Pointe Farms, Minnesota
www.gp.lib.mn.us

Henderson County Public Library
Donald Wathen
Henderson, Kentucky
www.hcpl.org

Hershey Public Library
Hershey, Pennsylvania
www.hersheylibrary.org

Hibbing Public Library
Hibbing, Minnesota
www.hibbing.lib.mn.us

Hobbs Public Library
Cris Adams, Director
Hobbs, New Mexico
http://hobbspublib/ea.co.net

Huron Public Library
Anne Hinton
Huron, Ohio
http://library.norweld.lib.oh.us/Huron

Hurt/Battelle Memorial Library
Sharon Shrum and the Board of Trustees
As found on the Web site of the State
Library of Ohio
http://winslo.state.oh.us/publib/policies.htm
l

Indian River County Library System
Vero Beach, Florida
http://indian-river.fl.us/library

Indian Valley Public Library
Linda Beck
Telford, Pennsylvania
www.ivpl.org

Irving Public Library System
Irving, Texas
www.irving.lib.tx.us

Lucius Beebe Memorial Library
Wakefield, Massachusetts
www.nobelnet.org/wakefield

Jackson County Public Library
Julia Aker
Seymour, Indiana
www.japl.lib.in.us

Jacksonville Public Library
Kenneth G. Sivulich, Director
Jacksonville, Florida
www.jplf.org

James Kennedy Public Library
Dyersville, Iowa
http://dyersvillelibrary.org
"This is the policy current as of March 2003 of the
James Kennedy Public Library, Dyersville, Iowa. Like
many policies in many libraries, it is the distillation of the
wisdom of our peers. If you see your hand in our policy—Thank You For Your Help."

Jasper County Public Library
Lynn Daugherty, Director
Rensselaer, Indiana
http://jasperco.lib.in.us

Joplin Public Library
Carolyn Trout
Joplin, Missouri
www.joplinpubliclibrary.org

Kentucky Department for Libraries and Archives
James A. Nelson
Frankfort, Kentucky
www.kdla.net

Kirkwood Public Library
Wicky Sleight
Kirkwood, Missouri
http://kpl.lib.mo.us

Kitsap Regional Library
Bremerton, Washington
www.krl.org

Kokomo-Howard County Public Library
Charles N. Joray, Director
Kokomo, Indiana
www.kokomo.lib.in.us

Laramie County Library System
Cheyenne, Wyoming
www.lclsonline.org

Lawrence Public Library
Bruce Flanders, Director
Lawrence, Kansas
www.lawrencepubliclibrary.org

Liberty Public Library
Marjorie Linko, Library Director
Liberty, New York
www.rcls.org/lib

Lithgow Public Library
Elizabeth L. Pohl
Augusta, Maine
www.lithgow.lib.me.us

Los Angeles Public Library
Los Angeles, California
www.lapl.org

Manitouwadge Public Library
Manitouwadge, Ontario, Canada
www.nwconx.net/~library-man

Marion Public Library
Susan S. Kling
Marion, Iowa
http://community.marion.ia.us/library

Marion County Library
Marion County Library Board of Trustees

Marion, South Carolina
www.marioncountylibrary.org

Marshall Public Library
E. Louise Chavers
Pocatello, Idaho
www.lili.org/marshall

Meadville Public Library
John J. Brice
Meadville, Pennsylvania
http://mplcatl.meadvillelibrary.org

Memorial Hall Library
James E. Sutton
Andover, Massachusetts
www.mhl.org

Miami-Dade Public Library
Miami, Florida
www.mdpls.org

Middleton Public Library
Paul Nelson
Middleton, Wisconsin
www.scls.lib.wi.us/middleton

Middletown Public Library
Douglas J. Bean
Middletown, Ohio
http://middletownlibrary.org

Middletown Thrall Library
Kevin J. Gallagher
Middletown, New York
www.thrall.org

Minneapolis Public Library
Minneapolis, Minnesota
www.mplib.org

Morton Grove Public Library
Morton Grove, Illinois
www.webrary.org

Mt. Lebanon Public Library
Cynthia K. Richey
Pittsburgh, Pennsylvania

http://einetwork.net/ein/mtleb

Muehl Public Library
Seymour, Wisconsin
www.owls.lib.wi.us/sey

Nebraska Library Commission
Rod Wagner
Lincoln, Nebraska
www.nlc.state.ne.us

Neill Public Library
Pullman, Washington
www.neill-lib.org

Neuschafer Community Library
Freemont, Wisconsin
www.owls.lib.wi.us/fpl

New Castle-Henry County Library
Jan Preusz, Director
New Castle, Indiana
www.nchpl.lib.us

New London Public Library
New London, Wisconsin
www.owls.lib.wi.us/npl

Newark Public Library
Alex Boyd, Ph.D.
Newark, New Jersey
www.npl.org

Norfolk Public Library
Yvonne Hilliard-Bradley
Norfolk, Virginia
www.npl.lib.va.us

North Castle Public Library
M. Cristina Ansnes
Armonk, New York
www.northcastlelibrary.org

North Judson-Wayne Township Public Library
Jane Ellen Felchuk
North Judson, Indiana
http://njwt.lib.in.us

Northeast Iowa Library Service Area
Waterloo, Iowa
www.neilsa.org

Oakland Public Library Foundation
Oakland, California
www.oplf.org

Oakville Public Library
Oakville, Ontario, Canada
www.opl.on.ca

Ohio County Public Library
Dottie Thomas
Wheeling, West Virginia
http://wheeling.lib.wv.us

State Library of Ohio
As found on the State Library of Ohio
Web site
Columbus, Ohio
http://winslo.state.oh.us

Oskaloosa Public Library
Nancy Simpson, Director
Oskaloosa, Iowa
www.opl.oskaloosa.org

Outagamie Waupaca System Library
Appleton, Wisconsin
www.owls.lib.wi.us

Park Ridge Public Library
Janet Van De Carr
Park Ridge, Illinois
www.park-ridge.il.us/library

Pasadena Public Library
The Staff of Pasadena Public Library
Pasadena, California
www.ci.pasadena.ca.us/library

Pasadena Public Library
Sheila Ross Henderson
Pasadena, Texas
www.ci.pasadena.ta.us/library

Pend Oreille County Library District
    Janet Lyon
    Newport, Washington
    www.pocld.org

Pikes Peak Library District
    Colorado Springs, Colorado
    http://library.ppld.org

Pittsfield Public Library
    Lyn Smith
    Pittsfield, Maine
    www.pittsfield.lib.me.us

Queens Borough Public Library
    Jamaica, New York
    www.queenslibrary.org

Richland Public Library
    Wayne L. Suggs
    Richland, Washington
    http://richland.lib.wa.us

River Falls Library Foundation, River Falls Public Library
    River Falls, Wisconsin
    www.rfcity.org/library

Rockaway Township Library
    Jeanette Cohn
    Rockaway, New Jersey
    www.gti.net/rocktwp

Salem Public Library Foundation
    Salem, Oregon
    www.splfoundation.org

San Antonio Public Library
    Laura J. Isenstein
    San Antonio, Texas
    www.sanantonio.gov/library

San Francisco Public Library
    Susan Hildertl
    San Francisco, California
    http://sfp14.sfpl.org

Shawnee Library System
    Carterville, Illinois
    www.shawls.lib.il.us

Sno-Isle Regional Library
    Mary Kelly
    Snohomish Island Counties, Washington
    www.sno-isle.org

Stratford Public Library
    Stratford Public Library Board
    Stratford, Ontario Canada
    www.stratford.library.on.ca

Tempe Public Library
    Teri Metros
    Tempe, Arizona
    www.tempe.gov/library

Tiffin-Seneca Public Library
    Patricia Hillmer
    Tiffin, Ohio
    http://tiffinsen.lib.oh.us

Tippecanoe County Public Library
    Jos N. Holman
    Lafayette, Indiana
    www.tcpl.lib.in.us

Tuscarawas County Public Library
    Susan B. Hagloch
    New Philadelphia, Ohio
    www.tusc.lib.oh.us

Vancouver Public Library
    Vancouver Public Library Board
    Vancouver, British Columbia Canada
    www.vpl.vancouver.bc.ca

Villa Park Public Library
    Villa Park, Illinois
    www.villapark.lib.il.us/library

Wadsworth Public Library
    Ella M. Everhand
    Wadsworth, Ohio
    www.wadsworth.lib.oh.us

Washoe County Library System
    Reno, Nevada
    www.washoe.lib.nv.us

Waverly Public Library
    Patricia Coffie
    Waverly, Iowa
    www.neilsa.org/policy_manual/trustees.html
    As found on the Northeast Iowa Library Service Area's
    Web site

West Hartford Public Library
    West Hartford, Connecticut
    http://west-hartford.com/library

Westerville Public Library
    Westerville, Ohio

www.wpl.lib.oh.us

Winnetka-Northfield Public Library District
    Barbara J. Aron
    Winnetka, Illinois
    www.wpld.alibrary.com

Wood Place Public Library
    Lisa Marshall
    California, Missouri
    http://woodplacelibrary.org

Woodbridge Town Library
    Woodbridge, Connecticut
    http://woodbridge.lioninc.org

Part I:
Public Services Forms and Policies

Chapter 1

CIRCULATION

OVERVIEW

The circulation desk is the most frequent point of contact between patrons and staff. Library decisions made about residency requirements, fines and fees, renewal and loan periods, overdue materials, lost or damaged material, reserves, conduct rules, and borrowing privileges will directly impact your community when a patron asks a staff person a question. Because of the wide variety of issues encountered at the circulation desk, this chapter has the greatest diversity in policies of any in the book. The wide variation allows you to craft a policy that addresses your special local needs.

Ideally, forms will make managing the library easier by allowing you to keep track of important details and to maintain written records for future reference. Form letters for overdue materials, materials claimed returned, and for lost and/or damaged material are effective ways to inform patrons about problems. Circulation statistics, in-house use worksheets and monthly use worksheets track the types of material patrons are using. It is important not only for collection development purposes, but also to justify budget requests.

This chapter covers policies and forms in the following areas:

- Residency Requirements
- Borrowing Privileges
- Loan Periods and Renewals
- Lost and Forgotten Cards
- Book Returns
- Overdue Material, Fees, and Fines
- Lost and Damaged Material

- Loaning Reference Material
- Reserving Material
- Patron Rights
- Staff Rights
- Patron Responsibilities
- Unattended Children
- Complaints Concerning Library Staff

Clear consistent rules, regulations, and procedures in your policy and consistent enforcement of the rules make managing your circulation responsibility much easier than if you simply go on a problem-by-problem basis without written guidelines. Having written guidelines makes it easier on you and the staff. In addition, these guidelines may serve to discourage inappropriate behavior by patrons.

ADMINISTRATIVE POLICIES

Features of an Effective Policy

- Empowers the library to offer a choice of residency requirements (e.g., granting privileges to citizens of their county or city only, granting privileges to citizens in neighboring communities, and granting privileges to students who attend school in the city/county or tax-paying business owners in the city/county);
- Places shorter circulation periods for high demand material;
- Sets shorter borrowing limits for high-demand items, such as CD-ROMs and DVDs;
- Allows telephone and/or Internet renewals;
- Covers loaning of audiovisual equipment;
- Limits the number of items that can be on an "on search"/"claimed returned" list requested by a patron;
- Limits the number of reserves and the number of days an item will be held at the desk;
- Lists reasons for not loaning reference material;
- Has flexible policies and rules, always taking into account that there will be exceptions;
- Suspends borrowing privileges for unpaid fines and fees and for disruptive behavior;
- Gives reasons for the need and purpose of fines and fees;
- Sets fees for such things as putting videos in the book drop box and losing a library card;
- States that the library can ask patrons for current address and identification at anytime;
- Has written notification procedures for overdue material and fines;
- Reviews cases where library privileges have been suspended.

Benefits of an Effective Policy

- Requires written rules and procedures to make it easier to enforce such things as reserves, borrowing privileges, loan periods, renewals, and fines and fees, and in some cases even makes it possible;
- Operates on a first come, first served reserve system, making it an equitable way to manage high-demand items;
- Promotes good public relations, by being clear, fair, and understandable;
- Explains why there are fines and fees, in order to make patrons aware of the rules;
- Allows staff to help a higher number of patrons, by limiting the number of reserves and the number of items per subject area (class assignments);
- Ensures that items are enjoyed and used by a wider readership in an equitable way, by having borrowing limits;
- Benefits patrons who may not be able to afford equipment, such as VHS players, by loaning audiovisual equipment;

- Allows you to use your discretion when exceptions occur, based on the policy's flexibility on the rules and procedures.

Policies

Residency Requirements

Los Angeles Public Library   **Los Angeles, California**

Library Cards are free! There are no residency requirements! You must, however, have identification with your name and current address. Identification can be a driver's license or an ID card issued by the DMV. The Mexican Consulate ID card, Certificado de Matrícula Consular, issued by the Mexican Consulate can be used as the sole ID requirement for obtaining a library card.

If you don't have a driver's license or ID card, then present two of the following, one of which must have your current address: Printed personal check, credit card, rental or property tax receipt, or business mail with current postmark. If you are under the age of eighteen, identification is not required. Your parent or guardian's signature on the library card application is accepted instead of identification.

Tempe Public Library   **Tempe, Arizona**

Applicants for Tempe Public Library cards must show identification with a current residential address. Identification with only a post office box number or with a motel or hotel address is not considered valid. Although not required, applicants are requested to provide a Social Security number at the time of registration. All cards are valid for one year, at the end of which time applicants will be asked to present an acceptable form of identification for address verification.

The Library may, at any time before the expiration date, require that current address identification be shown; so borrowers should bring appropriate identification in addition to their Tempe Public Library card.

For applicants under the age of sixteen (16), a parent or legal guardian must be present with the applicant and sign the application. Young people between sixteen (16) and eighteen (18) years of age will be issued a Tempe Public Library card upon presentation of acceptable identification; the Library will provide written notification to the parents or legal guardians of children within this age group that their child has been issued a Tempe Public Library card. Parents or guardians will be responsible for all items checked out on their children's cards.

Notifying parents they are responsible for books checked out on their children's card is a very effective tool to assign responsibility for lost or damaged material checked out by the child. Also, there are occasions where you know a patron has moved to another town or outside of your service area. Here, Tempe notifies patrons that proper and current identification can be requested at any time. This is an effective means of controlling former residents who continue to use library resources.

Pittsfield Public Library   **Pittsfield, Maine**

Anyone can use the resources of the Pittsfield Public Library. Only registered patrons may borrow library materials. People living in or owning property in Pittsfield will be extended borrowing privileges. Others may borrow materials upon payment of a non-fundable annual fee. The fee is currently $25.00 per family, $20.00 for an individual. The towns of Burnham, Palmyra and Detroit will reimburse their residents the annual cost of the annual fee.

Children and young adults of any age are eligible for a library card. The youth or parent/guardian must provide proof of identification. The parent/guardian must sign the child's registration card. If parent/guardian is not present, the registration card may be taken home, signed and returned.

How can I get a library card?

To obtain a library card, personal identification with current address must be presented.

One of the following is acceptable:

        Maine driver's license

        Picture identification card with name, current address and signature

        Dwelling lease less than one year old

        Checkbook with address

        Automobile registration

        Recently postmarked mail that is not hand-addressed

        Unacceptable forms of identification:

        ID with post office box as address

        Social Security card

        Expired driver's or out-of-state driver's license

Borrowing Privileges

Marion Public Library   **Marion, Iowa**

Cardholders are responsible for all items checked out on their cards. Patrons are encouraged to present their cards at the circulation desk for the most efficient service. Library staff may ask to see some identification before checkout of materials to a person who has forgotten his/her library card if that person is not known personally.

Patrons are responsible for notifying the Library of any change of name, address, phone number, or place of employment. Many of the patrons are known to the staff and there is not a problem with out-of-area users.

Beloit Public Library   **Beloit, Wisconsin**

Elementary and Secondary School libraries within Beloit city limits.

1) The private or parochial school / public school district must complete the application forms. The application must be signed by:

(a) The school principal for private and parochial schools.

(b) The school district Director of Curriculum and Support Services for the Beloit public schools.

2) The private or parochial school /public school district must agree to accept all financial responsibility for charges against the institution's card including overdue charges, and replacement cost plus service charges for all lost or damaged materials.

3) School library cards are covered by the same Library policies as individual cards, except that the person desiring to check out must have the card in hand.

Businesses in Rock County and City of Beloit Departments/Divisions:

1) The owner or head of the business/heads of the City of Beloit Department and Division must complete and sign the business card application form.

2) By signing the application form, the business acknowledges that the sole purpose of a business card is to allow employees to check out items from the Library for business purposes and have the company take full responsibility for such use.

3) The business agrees to accept all financial responsibility for use of the card by its employees. This includes responsibility for charges against the business card including overdue charges, and replacement cost plus service charges for all lost or damaged materials.

4) Business library cards are covered by the same Library policies as individual cards, with the following exceptions:

   - Fines would be charged on juvenile materials.

   - One library card will be issued per business. The card's use is solely monitored by the business. The person desiring to check out must have the card in hand.

   - The Library will assume its use was authorized by the business. The Library must be notified if the library business card is lost or stolen.

   - The card will expire in one year and can be renewed by the owner or the head of the business/heads of City of Beloit Department and Division signing a new application form.

5) Proofs for getting a business card:

   - One of the following four proofs is mandatory for application or renewal and must show: the name of the business, the Rock County address, and the name of the owner or the head business.) In the case of City of Beloit Departments or Divisions, this proof is not necessary.

      a) A current (annual) A Wisconsin Sellers' Permit@ with a Wisconsin sellers' number.

      b) A copy of an official A Employer Registration Certificate@ with a Wisconsin Employer Identification number.

c) A current (annual) paid property tax receipt.

d) A current lease agreement.

(Any of the additional, following proofs can be submitted to connect the name of the owner or head of business with the name of the business:)

a) An Official certificate off incorporation or foundation.

b) An insurance bill for the business

A signed letter from the owner/head of a business on a company letterhead stating that they are that person and will take responsibility for a business library card.

Albert Wisner Public Library   **Warwick, New York**

Customers are responsible for materials checked out on their library cards whether the card is used by the owner of the card or anyone else. For this reason, the library restricts the use of a library card to only the person who applied for and signed for the card.

Customers are limited to a total of thirty (30) library items checked out on his library card at a time. Any materials borrowed from the Library are subject to a due date and the customer is expected to respect that date; a late fine will be imposed if materials are returned to the Library after the due date.

The customer must have his library card with him at the time he checks out or renews materials either in the Library or by telephone. The Library card and its number is the means by which customers are identified in our records.

Most materials may be renewed and this can be done either in the Library, by the telephone or on the Library's home page on the Internet.

Loan Periods and Renewals

Tempe Public Library   **Tempe, Arizona**

The following loan periods and limits have been established to provide library users with an adequate amount of time to both use library materials and return them so that they are available in a reasonable amount of time for other users.

LOAN LIMITS:

A library user may have up to 30 items checked out at any time.

LOAN PERIODS:

The majority of items within the library's collection may be borrowed for twenty-eight days. If the due date falls on a holiday when the library is closed, the loan period will be extended until the next day that the library is open. Special loan periods have been established for the following library materials:

1. Rental Books: Seven (7) days

2. Videos and DVDs: Seven (7) days

3. Compact Discs: Seven (7) days

4. High Demand Items: Library materials that are in high demand by library users

may be temporarily assigned a fourteen (14) day loan period.

5. Circulating Periodicals: Fourteen (14) days

RENEWALS:

One twenty-eight (28) day renewal of items with standard loan periods is permitted, if the item is not reserved for another library user. One fourteen-day (14) renewal of High Demand items is permitted, if the item is not reserved for another library user. One seven (7) day renewal of videos is permitted if the item is not reserved by another library user. Items may be renewed in the library, by telephoning the Customer Services Desk, or via the Library's Web-based online catalog or in-house online catalog. In order to renew via the in-house or Web-based online catalog, library users must request a personal password from the Customer Services Desk. Library users who wish to renew by phone or via the online catalog are advised to do so in advance of the due date in case their items cannot be renewed. Rental Books and circulating periodicals may not be renewed.

Muehl Public Library   **Seymour, Wisconsin**

Loan periods for library materials are:

1. Most books and audio books: 21 days.

2. Magazines: 7 days. (Current issues do not circulate).

3. High demand short loan: 7 days (Some newly released books).

4. Videocassettes: 3 days.

5. Circulation encyclopedias: 7 days.

6. Circulating CD-ROM programs: 7 days.

Renewals:

1. All items may be renewed twice except popular items with short loan designation.

2. Persons must renew items in one of these ways:

    (1) Present the materials and borrower's card at the library service desk.

    (2). Present the printed receipt for the borrowed item(s) at the service desk.

    (3). Telephone the library and give the library employee the patron's name and barcode number on his/her borrower's card, and the title and barcode number(s) of the item(s) to be renewed.

Lost and Forgotten Cards

Tempe Public Library   **Tempe, Arizona**

Library users must present a valid City of Tempe Community Service card for check-out of all library materials. If they forget to bring their cards to the library, they may show proper identification to the Customer Services staff. If the staff can verify the validity of their cards on the computer system, check-out will be permitted.

Library users who have lost their Tempe Public Library cards may apply for new ones by showing valid identification (see section I.A above) and paying a non-refundable $2.00 replacement charge. If they later find their first card, it must be destroyed or returned to the library for disposal.

Neuschafer Community Library   Fremont, Wisconsin

If a patron loses his/her library card, there is a $3.00 charge for replacement. Any patron, adult or juvenile, who presents material for checkout but cannot present a library card because it has been forgotten, will only be allowed to checkout materials with the proper picture ID such as a driver's license.

Book Returns

Meadville Public Library   Meadville, Pennsylvania

BOOK RETURN:

All materials, except videos, may be returned to the book drop in front of the Library. There is a $1 charge for each video returned in the book drop, as temperature changes can damage the video tape. We encourage you to return materials inside when the Library is open, to help reduce wear and tear.

Overdue Material, Fees, and Fines

North Judson Wayne Township Public Library   North Judson, Indiana

Philosophy & Responsibilities

It is the responsibility of the Library to maintain a collection of materials to be shared by persons living within the service district—i.e., persons paying taxes within the legal service area. It is also the responsibility of the Library to govern the use of such materials shared with, or borrowed from, other libraries. The goal of the Library is to recover materials held beyond the agreed loan period, in good condition, for further use by the community. The Library does not want to resort to punitive action to recover items. Fines and fees are used solely to remind offenders of their responsibility to the other community members who fund and support the Library.

Written Notice Procedures for All Library Materials Except Video Tapes

1. A notice listing the overdue materials will be sent, as a courtesy reminder, to the patron the first week following the date due. Overdue materials are automatically highlighted on the computerized circulation system.

2. A second notice will be sent, to re-notify the patron of overdue materials, approximately 2 weeks after the first card. Borrowing privileges will be suspended at this time with a notice posted on the automated circulation system.

3. A registered letter will be sent 2 weeks after the second card explaining the

responsibilities and legal actions available to the library if the overdue patron has not made contact with the Library.

4. A complaint to the prosecuting attorney for conversion will be initiated one month from the date of sending the registered letter. The course of action will be at the discretion of the staff and legal system. Should such legal action be necessary the negligent patron will be responsible for all court costs.

Fines & Fees for All Library Materials Except Video Tapes

A charge of three cents ($.03) per day (excluding Sundays, holidays and days the library is closed unexpectedly) for each overdue item will be applied up to a maximum fine of five dollars ($5.00) per item. A one-day "grace" period without fines exists for print, audio and related materials but not videotapes. Any patron with overdue materials will be held responsible for all fines, postage costs, and legal costs involved in the recovery of the materials. If the materials are not returned, the patron will be responsible for the cost of replacement materials and the cost of processing the new materials.

Inter-library loan materials overdue by more than 1 week will be subject to fines. These fines may be those imposed by the lending institution, the Library or both.

Notice Procedures For Video Materials

Videocassettes (both the Library and the Indiana Visual and Audio Network collections) become over due the day after the due date (excluding Sundays, holidays and days the library is closed unexpectedly). Patrons with videos more than 2 days over due will be notified by telephone, informed of their responsibility and requested to return the videos. After two telephone calls, a letter requesting the return of the videos will be sent. If necessary, a Library staff member may be sent individually, or in the company of a law enforcement official, to the patron's residence to retrieve the overdue videos. Legal action in Small Claims Court, or by filing with the prosecuting attorney for conversion, may be initiated. The course of action will be at the discretion of the staff and legal system.

Fines & Fees For Video Materials

Fines and fees for regular collection and IVAN videos are as follows:

- $1.00 per day per overdue video

- $.50 per video returned in wrong box

- $5.00 deposit is forfeit for videos returned in book drop

- Videos overdue more than 10 days will be assessed the cost of the video plus daily fines plus a $10 processing charge per tape.

Marion Public Library   **Marion, Iowa**

Overdue materials/fines:

General: a "library day" is a day that the library is open.

Fines:

1. Adult materials: on the first library day after the due date a charge of $.15 per item per day will begin to accumulate.

2. Children's materials: on the first library day after the due date, a charge of $.10 per item per day will begin to accumulate.

3. CDs and videos: on the first day after the due date, a charge of $.15 will begin to accumulate.

4. Interlibrary loans (I.L.L.) will accrue fines of $1.00 per day up to a maximum of $15.00.

A courtesy phone call or written reminder about overdue materials will be made after materials are 7 days past the due date but the responsibility to return materials rests with the borrower. The amount of fine assessed is determined by whether an item is in the adult or the children's collection, not by the type of card an individual holds (a child checking out adult materials would be charged $.15 per day and an adult checking out children's materials would be charged $.10 per day).

A patron's borrowing privileges will be temporarily suspended when the fines owed either the Marion Library or the Cedar Rapids Public Library reach $3.00, or when notice of non-return of materials from either library is registered in the borrower's account. Borrowing may resume when fines are paid or reduced below the $3.00 maximum.

Fine limits for substantially overdue materials:

If an item is overdue more than six months it may be withdrawn from the collection and the patron charged the appropriate fee. If the item is returned to the library in good condition after it has been withdrawn, the Library Director or Assistant Library Director will make a determination as to the fees to be charged. Value of the items to the collection and whether it has already been replaced will be considered in this evaluation.

If an item which has been overdue up to six months is returned in good condition, the fine will be limited to a maximum of $6.00 for each adult trade soft cover or hardcover item; $2.00 for each mass market paperback; $4.00 for each children's item; $2.00 for each magazine; and $6.00 for each audio cassette, video cassette or CD.

Non-returned library materials:

- Borrowers who have non-returned materials whose value totals $25 or more may receive up to two phone call reminders and a written notice. If they do not respond to the library's requests for return of materials, they will be subject to action by Unique National Collections.

- Borrowers who have fines totaling $25 ore more will receive a written request for payment from the library. If they do not respond to the library's request for payment of the fines, they will be subject to action by Unique National Collections.

- It is possible that fines totaling $25 or more could be a combination of non-returned materials and fines. Similar procedures will be used.

- Borrowers who are turned over to Unique National Collections will be assessed a $10 collection fee in addition to any replacement costs and/or fines.

The Unique National Collections program will include up to three written demands and two phone calls before borrowers are reported to credit agencies.

Lost and Damaged Material

Beloit Public Library   **Beloit, Wisconsin**

LOST OR DAMAGED MATERIALS:

Replacement Costs:

Full replacement cost, including a service charge of $4, will be charged for any periodicals or cataloged materials that are lost or damaged so badly that they have to be replaced. Audiovisual equipment—full cost of repairs will be charged, (or replacement cost if not repairable

Claims Returned:

A customer can have a maximum of two "claim returned" items in active status. Any items "claim returned" over that limit will be billed.

Damaged Materials:

The borrower may keep any damaged materials for which full replacement cost has been paid.

Lost Item Found:

If a lost item is found and returned to the Library within four months after payment, the customer will get a refund from the City if the item is in useable condition. The $4 service fee will be subtracted from the amount refunded.

Minor Damage:

The charge for minor damage and missing parts is as follows:

1. $4 for a plastic bag for Juvenile kits (including the barcode and labels);

2. $4 for video, CD-ROM, DVD, audio tape, or compact disc case (including the barcode and labels);

3. $4 for Book jacket (including the barcode and labels);

4. $4 for DVD, CDROM, or compact disc guide;

5. $4 for mending an audio tape or videotape.

6. $2 for a missing or damaged security strip or barcode.

7. Cleaning items that are too dirty/sticky to circulate—amount determined by staff.

Continued Delinquency:

Persons failing to return materials and/or pay for damaged materials may be subject to prosecution under section 18.03 of the Beloit City Ordinances or may be referred to the City Attorney's office for Court action. When judgments are found in favor of the Library, the person will be assessed court costs, plus an additional $10 Library handling charge. The Library may also choose to use a collection agency to retrieve delinquent materials. Any costs to the Library may be passed on to the customer.

Loaning Reference Material

Tempe Public Library   **Tempe, Arizona**

Selected magazine and newspaper titles to which the Tempe Public Library subscribes may not be taken out of the building as their physical format is very susceptible to damage; they are often impossible to replace in case of loss; and they are frequently used as reference sources. In addition, books that have been designated for reference use do not circulate. In general, these are titles that are not designed to be read from cover to cover but are used to find answers to specific questions, and must be available at all times to the Reference staff in order to respond to requests for information from the public as efficiently as possible. The Library Director or a Library Supervisor may grant exceptions to this rule.

Not Loaning Reference Material

Kentucky Department for Libraries and Archives   **Frankfort, Kentucky**

Reference materials do not circulate but may be used in the library. Kentucky vertical file materials do not circulate. A coin-operated copier is available for making copies.

Reserving Material

Los Angles Public Library   **Los Angeles, California**

1. You can place a HOLD on an item free of charge from any library terminal, or over the Web by clicking "Catalog" on the Library's Web Page. After searching for the title you want to reserve, select the library location to which you want the item sent and we will notify you by a computer-generated telephone call or a postcard when it is available for pick up. If you need help with the Hold service, library staff will guide you through the process or place the hold for you. The maximum number of holds on a patron record at any time is 30.

Pittsfield Public Library   **Pittsfield, Maine**

Reserves may be placed on any circulating item.

A reserve is a hold placed for an item in the circulating collection that is checked out or otherwise unavailable at the time of the hold. A reserve may be made by contacting a library member in person, by mail, by phone, or by e-mail. Because of the demands for reserve items, reserve items will be held for three (3) days only. When more than one reserve is placed on an item, a queue will be established, and each request will be filled in the order in which it was received

Indian River County Library   **Indian River, Florida**

Items verified by our staff to be in our collection may be reserved for 25 cents each. Reserves are placed and paid for at the circulation desk.

PUBLIC SERVICE POLICIES

Features of an Effective Policy

Everyone has rights in the library—patrons and staff. Conduct rules try to ensure that everyone has a pleasant experience at the library. One disruptive patron can destroy that experience for everyone. You also may face a child being left alone in the library. Rules and procedures for dealing with disruptive patrons and unattended children give you the means to enforce rules to maintain a safe and comfortable environment for research, reading, listening, learning, and working.

- Acknowledges that staff, as well as patrons, have rights;
- Lists unacceptable behavior, and adds a clause that it "is not limited to"—giving you the right to address any problem, even if it is not specifically listed in the rules;
- Includes in the rules that unpaid fines are also not acceptable;
- Suspends library privileges for either a set period of time, or it allows you to set an indefinite period of time;
- Sends notification, by certified mail, to tell the patron that their library privileges have been suspended to ensure the patron is informed;
- Grants the patrons the right of appeal;
- Requires caregivers to monitor those under their supervision while in the library;
- Has written procedures to follow when a child is left unattended, including what to do when it is closing time and when to call the police.

Benefits of Effective Policies

- Makes enforcing the rules easier, because they are in writing;
- Takes the bias out of enforcement;
- Clarifies and makes it unambiguous when to notify the authorities;
- Protects you against accusations and perhaps formal charges of unfairness and prejudice against a patron;

Policies

Patron Rights

Kentucky Department for Libraries and Archives   **Frankfort, Kentucky**

KDLA customers have a right to expect certain behaviors from staff when they are requesting or using resources:

- The right to equal treatment regardless of race, color or national origin.

- The right to reasonable accommodation based on disability.

- The right to be treated politely.

- The right to conduct research in a safe environment.

- The right to request reasonable research assistance.

- The right to expect confidentiality when asking for research assistance.

- The right to submit a Suggestion Form.

Staff Rights

Kentucky Department of Libraries and Archives   Frankfort, Kentucky

KDLA employees have rights that should not put them in conflict with the rights of customers:

- The right to be treated politely.

- The right to work in a safe environment.

- The right to ask the customer to abide by rules posted in public service areas.

- The right to ask the customer to abide by the rules on the Archives Research Room Registration Form.

- The right to ask customers to abide by the written policies and procedures for using Archival materials.

- The right to offer options when a customer's request exceeds agency resources.

Patron Responsibilities

Huron Public Library   Huron, Ohio

The Huron Public Library seeks to provide quality library service to all patrons. The following code of conduct has been adopted for the comfort and protection of the rights of all those using and working in the Huron Public Library. The library staff will enforce this code in a courteous but firm manner. We ask your cooperation in helping us provide a safe and pleasant environment for all our patrons and staff.

Unacceptable behavior is not permitted. Unacceptable behavior includes, but is not limited to:

- Loud talking or other noise

- Physical threats or abuse

- Running and roaming

- Abusive or foul language

- Abuse or misuse of Library furnishings, equipment or materials

- Congregating in or around entrances or stairways, inside or out

- Commission of an illegal or unauthorized act on Library property against the patrons, personnel or property of the Library, i.e., theft, trespass, assault, arson, etc.

- Failure t• pay fines or proper Library costs when due.

- Use of alcohol or mood-altering drugs on library property.

- Sexual conduct which is considered a violation of Chapter 2907 of the Ohio Revised Code.

The following are not permitted:

- Solicitation

- Smoking

- Eating or drinking

- Loitering

- Weapons

- Possession of alcohol; possession of illegal drugs.

Radios, tape-players, walk-mans and cellular phones may not be used in the Library.

Patrons will be warned once and requested to leave if the unacceptable behavior continues. Suspension of library privileges for a determinate or indeterminate period of time may occur if a patron is found to have engaged in unacceptable behavior on library property. Notice of suspension will be mailed by certified mail, return receipt requested, to the last known address of the patron or, in the case of a minor child, his parents or guardian.

Appeal of the suspension may be made, in writing, to the Board of Trustees, within ten (10) days of receipt of notice of suspension.

The patron, or in the case of a minor child, the parents or guardian, will be notified by the Board of the date and time of the hearing on the notice of appeal.

Adult patrons or a minor child patron may be prosecuted under Title 29 of the Ohio Revised Code for acts against other Patrons, Library personnel or property.

Violators may be prosecuted for a fourth degree misdemeanor under Ohio Revised Code 2911.21.

Cleveland Public Library   Cleveland, Ohio

The Cleveland Public Library encourages the use of its facilities for reading, study, research, and the legitimate use of the Library's resources and services. The Library pledges to provide an atmosphere conducive to delivering library services to its patrons.

To further this goal, Library patrons are asked to conduct themselves in an orderly and considerate manner. Any behavior that disrupts the orderly use of the Library is prohibited. This includes, without limitation, behavior that constitutes a nuisance, or presents a safety and/or security hazard or affects the ability of the Library staff to provide service to its patrons.

Smoking is prohibited in all Cleveland Public Library buildings. Other prohibited behaviors include, without limitation, soliciting; sleeping; intoxication; card playing; littering; excessive noise; and abusive, profane, or offensive language and/or behavior which unreasonably interferes with other patrons' use of the Library. Eating and drinking are prohibited, except in designated areas.

Patrons are asked to dress appropriately; shoes and shirts are required. Battery operated radios, CD players, televisions, tape recorders, etc., may be used only with ear phones and only in such a manner that does not disturb other patrons or Library staff.

Defacing or intentionally damaging Library property is prohibited, as is the theft and/or attempted theft of Library property or the property of patrons and staff, and may be subject to prosecution.

Bundles, packages, backpacks, briefcases, purses, and other containers may be subject to search upon entering or leaving Library buildings in order to protect and preserve the safety and security of property and people using the Library. Patrons are asked not to bring large bundles into the Library.

Carts, dollies, bicycles, and skateboards are prohibited in all Library buildings, without prior approval of Library staff.

Animals are not permitted in Library facilities with the exception of guide dogs, assistance dogs, and animals brought in for special programs.

Patrons who violate any of these guidelines will be given notice of this policy. A violation may result in a patron's expulsion from the Library, suspension of Library privileges, or criminal prosecution or other legal action, as appropriate.

Cumberland Public Library   **Fayetteville, North Carolina**

- Rearranging or soiling of library furniture or use of furniture outside its intended purpose.

- Extreme body odor or other strong or offensive smells which unreasonably disturb others.

- Sleeping in the library.

- Bringing bedrolls, blankets, suitcases, duffel bags, or other large bags or other containers into the library. Unauthorized items may be subject to search upon departure.

- Board games, gambling, card playing, games of chance or skill except during library sponsored events.

- Skateboarding, roller-blading, roller-skating, etc., on library property.

Unattended Children

Grand Island Public Library   **Grand Island, Nebraska**

Children are welcome in our library and we are concerned about their safety and welfare. However, parents and caregivers are responsible for monitoring the activities and regulating the behavior of their children while the children are in the library.

- All children 7 years and under shall be adequately supervised by a responsible parent or caregiver at all times for the sake of their own well being.

- Children may be left unattended during scheduled library programs and the responsible person may choose to leave the building, but he/she should plan to be at the library when the program is scheduled to conclude. However, persons responsible for children who have special needs related to physical or mental ability, disruptive behavior, emotional problems, lack of adequate attention span, incomplete social skills, etc., shall remain with their children at all times.

- Children 8 years and older may use the library unattended, subject to the rules and regulations of this library.

If a child is left unattended, the following procedure will be enacted:

- Staff will notify a supervisor and will stay with the child as they try to locate the responsible person by searching nearby area or paging on library intercom. If no name is known, page using the child's name or physical appearance.

- When such person is located, explain the library policy in regard to children, give them a handout, etc.

- If the responsible person is not located within a half-hour, or if the library is closing within a half-hour, the police will be notified and asked to pick up the child. Staff will remain with the child in the building until parent or police arrives.

- If a child is reported missing, obtain name, age, and a description of child. Check all possible areas (restrooms, etc.) within the library. Page child on intercom. Notify responsible person of your extensive search.

- If child is not found, recommend that the police be notified.

Cleveland Public Library   Cleveland, Ohio

Children are encouraged to use the Library as a place of study and inquiry. The Library encourages parents, guardians, and caregivers to use the Library with their children. Children six and under must be accompanied at all times by a responsible party. Pre-teens and any child not able to travel alone must be picked up prior to closing. Disruptive juveniles may be asked to disperse at the librarian's discretion. Parents are responsible for the behavior of their children; guardians and caregivers are responsible for the behavior of the children in their care. The Library is not responsible for the safety or security of children left unattended.

Complaints Concerning Library Staff

Wood Place Public Library   California, Missouri

Personnel and Library Service Complaint Procedure For a Patron Criticisms of the library service, librarian, or the library staff, which are brought to the attention of the Board of Directors, shall be handled in the following manner:

- Complainant will be asked to submit a formal complaint form to the Library Board of Directors.

- Complainant will mail the form to the Board President who will provide copies to the remaining Board of Directors.

- Upon review of the complaint, the Board of Directors will determine whether a special meeting needs to be called or whether the matter may be handled at the next scheduled library board meeting.

- The complainant will be informed within 15 days of the Board's decision and whether further audience from the complainant will be necessary.

- The complainant will be contacted within seven days of said meeting regarding the Board's decision regarding the complaint.

FORMS

Benefits of Written Forms

- Using Circulation Statistics and the Monthly Circulation Report helps to justify budget requests and aid collection development;

- Establishes a history and pattern of behavior with disruptive patrons that can justify suspension of library privileges or legal action, if necessary;

- Uses letters for overdue, lost/damaged, and claimed return material as an effective way to communicate problems to your patrons;

- Uses worksheets to compare and contrast usage of days, months, and years;

- Uses worksheets to track in-house usage of material versus material that circulates;

- Uses a Special Reference Loan sheet on those rare occasions when the library permits a patron to check out reference material;

Date

Our records indicate the following items are overdue:

Title:

Author:

Date Due:

Fines for over due the material are as follows:

Number of days overdue:

Fine per day:

Fines must be paid before other material can be checked out. Your prompt attention is appreciated. The books can either be returned to the book return box located on the west side of the building or it can be brought directly into the library.

21 day items: 25 cents per day
10 day items: .$1.00 per day
Interlibrary Loan items: $2.00 per day
Maximum fines are $10.00
Charges are assessed for damaged items.

Fees for lost material will be the cost of the item plus a $5.00 processing fee. Payments can be paid with cash, local check or MasterCard or Visa.

Two letters will be sent for overdue material. The third letter will be for replacement costs. Fourteen days after the third letter, it will be turned over to a collection agency. A $10.00 non-refundable charge will be accessed.

Failure to receive notice or delays in the mail will not be considered grounds for waiving the fees and fines.

Sincerely,

Library Manager

Figure 1.1 Overdue Letter

Response Letter to Request for a Search in the Library for Overdue Material

(Today's date)

Author and Title:

Date item was due:

Dear

In response to your request, the above mentioned material charged to your card at the Oak Grove Public Library on the date indicated is in the process of an overdue search of 60 days ending. A overdue search is simply a suspension of the normal overdue notification process and a suspension of the hold on your card for a 60 day period. This allows the library staff and you, the patron, the time to conduct a thorough search for the materials in question. It also allows continued checkout privileges. It does not suspend fine accumulation nor does it remove liability for payment of replacement costs if the material is not found. Currently, our maximum fine for a book or book-on-tape is $5.00 and $10.00 for videos.

Please understand that the primary aim in this process, as well as that of all Circulation policies, is the return of materials so that others may use them. If the material in question is located during the 60-day period, your record will be cleared. If at the end of the 60-day period, the material is not located, you will be assessed replacement costs of the material plus a processing fee.

Sincerely,

Library Manager

Figure 1.2 Search for Material Letter

Dear _____

At the time a library patron borrows materials from the public library collection, the patron assumes the responsibility for the care and timely return of the materials. Recently materials checked out on your library card were returned to the library damaged beyond the point of being usable in the Library's collection. The titles and costs of these materials are listed below:

$ _____

$ _____

$ _____

Your assistance in clearing this matter promptly will be appreciated and will be necessary in order to retain your borrowing privileges.

Thank you in advance for your prompt response to this matter.

Sincerely,

Library Manager

Figure 1.3 Damaged Material Letter

Circulating Material

Date:_____

Books-on-tape:_____

Fiction:_____

Youth Non-Fiction_____

Childrens_____

Biography:_____

CDs_____DVDs_____

Easy Readers:_____

Non-Fiction:_____

Youth Fiction:_____

Videos:_____

Newspapers_____

Magazines:_____

Cassettes: _____

Total number of items :_____

Figure 1.4 Circulation Statistics

In House Usage

Date: _____

Reference Books: _____

Books: _____   Maps: _____

Magazines: _____   CDs: _____

Videos: _____   DVDs: _____

Easy Readers: _____   Childrens Books: _____

Youth: _____   Vertical Files: _____

Newspapers: _____ Local Historical Material: _____

Genealogy Material: _____

Microfilm: _____

Total Items: _____   Date: _____

Figure 1.5 In-House Use Statistics

Monthly Report

For the month of:_____

Year:_____

	This Month	This month last year:	Percent Change
Number of items which circulated:	_____	_____	_____
Number of in-house use items:	_____	_____	_____
Number of fiction items:	_____	_____	_____
Number of non-fiction items:	_____	_____	_____
Number of videos:	_____	_____	_____
Number of CDs:	_____	_____	_____
Number of DVDs:	_____	_____	_____
Number of audiocassettes:	_____	_____	_____
Number of overdue material:	_____	_____	_____
Number of items declared lost:	_____	_____	_____
Internet Assistance:	_____	_____	_____
Money Collected:	_____	_____	_____
Number of Patrons:	_____	_____	_____
Number of items missing:	_____	_____	_____
Number of items withdrawn:	_____	_____	_____
Number of reference questions answered:_____		_____	_____

Figure 1.6 Monthly Circulation Report

Special Reference Loan

Date:_____

Title:_____

Author:_____

Accession number:_____

Number of days or hours item may be loaned:_____

Name:_____

Patron record number:_____

Day time phone:_____

Staff member approval:_____

Date Due: _____

Returned:_____

Staff Member:_____

Figure 1.7 Special Reference Loan

Kentucky Department for Libraries and Archives   **Frankfort, Kentucky**

Patron Complaint Form Concerning Library/Librarian

1. Your complaint concerns which of the following:

Librarian

Library Services

Library Staff

2. Describe the situation that led to your formal complaint.

3. Briefly, what is your specific complaint?

   What attempt have you made to resolve this situation with the librarian?

   Do you think the librarian has made a fair attempt to explain policy/procedure if applicable and/or work with you to come to a fair resolution of the complaint?

6. What course of action would you like the Board of Directors to take in this matter?

Name: _____

Phone: _____

Mail to the library: _____

_____

Figure 1.8 Patron Complaint Form Concerning Library Staff

Kentucky Department for Libraries and Archives   **Frankfort, Kentucky**

Date of Incident:_____   Time of Incident_____

Name (if known):_____

Address (if known):_____

City:_____ State:_____

Physical Description

Male:_____ Female:_____

Race/NationalOrigin:

Caucasian _____ African American_____ Hispanic_____
Asian _____Other_____

Height_____ Weight_____ Hair Color_____ Eye Color_____

Any Identifying Features: (Beard, Scars, Tattoos, Mustache, etc.):

Clothing: Hat:_____   Coat:_____   Shirt:_____   Pants:_____
Skirt:_____Dress:_____ Shoes:_____ Glasses _____

Other Witnesses:

Name:_____

Address: _____

_____

Telephone:_____

Name:_____

Address: _____

_____

Telephone:_____

Staff Action: (Notification of Supervisor, Console, Call Security, Outside Help)

Figure 1.9 Incident Form for Disruptive Patrons

Kentucky Department for Libraries and Archives　　　　**Frankfort, Kentucky**

Type of Incident: Accident/Injury Disturbance Theft Vandalism

Date: _____

Time: _____

Name of Employee Filing Report: _____

Department: _____

Address: _____

_____

Telephone: _____

Description of Incident:

Figure 1.10 Incident Report for Unusual Situations

CHECKLIST

- Make it a simple fair process for patrons to complain about staff members.
- Leave yourself latitude to make exceptions.
- Have a system for those rare occasions when you want to check out reference materials that are neither critical to the reference desk, nor high-use items.
- If you choose not to circulate reference material, have a policy you can show patrons.
- Use the size of the collection to determine circulation periods, renewals, and residency requirements.
- Create a fair process when suspending library privileges.
- Uses a complaint form to help you identify potential staff problems, and to give patrons an effective way to express their frustration or anger.

Chapter 2

REFERENCE SERVICE POLICIES

OVERVIEW

The goal of reference service is to provide fair, accurate, unbiased, factual information to anyone who seeks it for any reason. The purpose of a written policy is to state your objectives, provide a framework that describes your staff responsibilities, the types of questions you will and will not answer, and what levels and types of services you will provide. Finding, organizing, analyzing, and delivering information puts you in a powerful position. Therefore, librarians in all phases of operations shoulder a tremendous responsibility. Librarians who control a community information resource center are bound by a code of ethics established by the American Library Association and must maintain the high professional standards of that professional organization. The guidelines below will shape your service. Since small libraries cannot provide all the resources that large libraries do, you will need to select the policies pertaining to what you are able to do.

On the CD-ROM you will find many excellent policy examples. Tempe Public Library, in Tempe, Arizona, has a very good interlibrary loan policy explaining the process and what is and is not allowed for patrons. The policy is too long to have included it in the book, but is worth examining.

This chapter covers policies and forms in the following areas:

- Reference Service Objectives and Philosophy
- Children's Reference Service Policy
- Reference Resources
- Reference Staff
- Types of Reference Questions Answered
  - Medical, Legal, Financial, and Tax
  - School Assignments
  - Contest Questions
  - Books and Collectibles
  - Translations
  - Criss-Cross
  - Consumer Information
  - Mathematical Calculations
  - Referrals
- Patron Priorities
  - In-person
  - Patron Backup
  - Time Limits
  - Extensive Research
  - Telephone, E-mail, Fax, and Mail
- Fee-based Services
- Patron Confidentiality, the Librarian Code of Ethics, and the Patriot Act
- Services Provided

- Service to the Homebound
- Notary Public
- Proctoring Exams
- Interlibrary Loan

- Daily Desk Count Sheet
- Fee-based Charge Sheets
- Patron Agreement

PUBLIC SERVICE POLICIES

Establishing objectives, defining services, describing staff responsibilities, outlining resources, and providing equal service to all patrons, are all functions of these policies. One of the advantages to having a policy is the ability to tailor it to match your individual financial and staff resources. Another advantage is to advertise library services—clearly communicate to your community what information resources and services the library offers. Relying upon tradition instead of a written guidelines and criteria causes your service to vacillate from encounter to encounter leaving you and your patron unsure of what you really can offer, what you really can do, and why you do it.

Features of an Effective Policy

- Seeks to provide the best service possible through all available internal and external resources;
- Provides equal information services to all individuals regardless of age, gender, ethnicity, disability, sexual preference, English language proficiency, or national origin;
- Outlines the external and internal resources available;
- Specifies a separate policy for the children's area;
- States the types of questions that will and will not be answered, such as contest questions, appraisals, school assignments, and consumer information;
- Establishes patron priorities, such as in-house patrons and telephone callers and first come, first served;
- Gives the option of having no time limits or imposing time limits on each patron;
- Provides a fee-based service option for questions involving extensive research;
- Communicates to the community what services the library is able to provide;
- Provides special services, such as proctoring exams, having a notary, or a speaker's bureau.

Benefits of an Effective Policy

- Makes it possible to tailor reference services to maximize use of individual library resources and work within the constraints of staff availability;
- Increases comfort level of patrons knowing they can ask any question, for any reason, and it will be treated confidentially;
- Establishing service parameters allows libraries to reach their collection goals;
- Permits the library to set limits, accompanied by an explanation, on what it can and will do;
- Raises staff confidence about the reference service you offer and why;
- Enables staff to show a dissatisfied patrons in writing why you do or do not have certain

services, such as refusal to appraise a book or coin or translate a passage in a foreign language you do not speak;

- Removes questions about whose request comes first—in-house, or first come, first served;

- Places clear time limits, or no time limits, on how much time a staff person will devote to any given question;

- Dictates the forms of non-face-to-face communication to which you will respond, such as e-mail, fax, mail, telephone;

- Explains to patrons the rules and regulations of the interlibrary loan process;

- Gives the library publicity and fills a need in the community through efforts such as proctoring exams, providing services to the home bound, and creating a speaker's bureau;

- Assures the community that the librarians are highly skilled information professionals.Policies

Policies

Reference Service Objectives and Philosophy

Newark Public Library   **Newark, New Jersey**

Reference service at The Newark Public Library is one of the most vital and visible expressions of the Library's purpose and mission and is key to each of the Library's four primary service roles: to serve as a center for information, formal education, research and independent learning.

Reference service is defined in this document as personal assistance provided to users and potential users of information. Reference service takes a variety of forms including direct personal assistance, directories or signs, exchange of information culled from a reference source, readers' advisory assistance, dissemination of information in anticipation of user needs or interests, and direct end-user access to an information system via telecommunication hardware and software.

The Library shall actively publicize the scope, nature, and availability of the information services it offers. It shall employ those media most effective in reaching its entire clientele or selected segments of that clientele.

The Library shall survey and assess the information needs of its community and create local information products to fulfill those needs not met by published materials.

The Library shall serve its community by collecting and creating information and referral files to provide access to the services and resources of local, regional, and state organizations.

Based on its clients' known needs and interests, the Library shall provide information even if it has not been explicitly requested.

The Library's building shall not be a boundary to its information services. It shall identify and employ external databases, agencies, and services to help meet the information needs of its community.

The Library shall participate in consortia and networks to obtain access to information sources and services it cannot provide on its own.

When the Library is not able to provide a client with needed information, it shall refer either the client or the client's question to some other agency, an expert, or another library which can provide the needed information.

The Library shall use or provide access to information systems outside the Library when these systems meet information needs more effectively and efficiently than internal resources can.

It is the policy of the Library to consider each individual information query to be of equal merit regardless of the age, gender, ethnicity, disability, sexual preference, English language proficiency or status of the inquirer. The Library's intention is to accord equal attention and effort to each inquiry, although the time spent by staff on a question may vary in response to the perceived needs of the patron, the information resources (both staff and collections) available and the method of receipt of the inquiry.

Westerville Public Library   **Westerville, Ohio**

Users of all ages and circumstances are to be treated with equal attention particular needs.

All requests for public information are legitimate

All questions must be either answered or redirected.

The basic function of the Reference staff is to provide information, not opinions. Questions should not be answered on the basis of personal experience. It is the staff's responsibility to provide information in an impartial and businesslike manner even when contrary to personal beliefs.

Children's Reference Service Policy

Beloit Public Library   **Beloit, Wisconsin**

The Children's Services function of the Beloit Public Library provides library service to children and adults working with children in order to promote a more literate public.

To fulfill this goal the Beloit Public Library's Children's Services:

Provides a collection of materials that meets children's interests and information needs, stimulates their curiosity, and challenges them to greater achievement.

Provides access to this collection with a physical facility that accommodates the size and capabilities of children and a reference staff who have training in, knowledge of and enthusiasm for children's literature and the interests and abilities of children in different age groups.

Promotes reading and library use by:

Providing a pleasant, stimulating atmosphere at the library including a knowledgeable staff who make children feel their requests are significant and their presence is welcome.

Offering programs and tours that encourage children and their families to come to the library.

REFERENCE SERVICE POLICIES

Cooperating with individuals and groups with similar goals. Extending library services (small collections and reading promotion programs) into the community emphasizing contact with children who need literacy support.

Reference Resources

Newark Public Library   **Newark, New Jersey**

The Library shall collect or provide access to information resources germane to its mission and reflecting the interests of the full spectrum of the population it serves. These information resources shall satisfy, through content, currency, format, organization, and quantity a diversity of user needs.

The Library shall provide access to the most current reference sources available in order to assure the accuracy of information.

As appropriate, reference services staff shall reach beyond reference collections to tap the resources of the Library as a whole. To provide the information their users need, they shall also reach beyond in-house collections and in-house expertise by drawing on the resources of other organizations that collect and provide information, by consulting individual experts, by tapping external information sources regardless of their medium, and by accessing the world of information accessible via the Internet.

The Library shall acquire appropriate materials in medical, legal, and business subject areas that meet the needs of the community served. The reference librarian shall direct the user to possible sources, both in and out of the library, where the information the user requires will be provided. These materials might include books, pamphlets, journals, electronic services, service agencies, and professionals in the appropriate field. When helping a user, librarians must be careful to avoid using technical terms. Under no circumstances shall information be withheld from a user.

Reference Staff

Memorial Hall Library   **Andover, Massachusetts**

Reference staff members serve as the link between resources and the patron. As such, it is important that staff members be:

- Highly knowledgeable about traditional reference sources and proficient with electronic resources and the technology needed to access those resources.

- Knowledgeable about the town of Andover and its government.

- Open and approachable; friendly but professional.

- Able to communicate effectively with all library users.

- Discreet in the handling of questions that might be confidential or sensitive.

- Impartial in dealing with all patrons.

- Able to exercise good judgment both in the interpretation of policy and in the handling of exceptional situations.

- Able to instruct the public in the use of print and electronic resources.

- Able to evaluate the Internet for authority, accuracy, currency, and content.

- Skilled in the interviewing process in order to help the patron formulate their specific question and make the patron comfortable in the transaction so they will return for further help if their specific need has not been met.

- Take the responsibility to seek continuing education opportunities especially workshops provided by the Merrimack Valley Library Consortium, Northeast Massachusetts Library System, Board of Library Commissioners, and any other workshops and conferences approved by the Library Director.

New staff members will receive orientation to Memorial Hall Library and to the Northeast Massachusetts Regional Library System. Continual training is necessary in order to provide the highest level of service. Participation in workshops and attendance at meetings on a local, state, and national level is encouraged.

Newark Public Library   Newark, New Jersey

Reference service staff members shall communicate easily and effectively with the full range of the Library's clientele regardless of a client's age, gender, ethnicity, disability, sexual preference, or English-language proficiency.

Reference services staff shall have knowledge and preparation appropriate to meet the information needs of the clientele the Library serves. Staff responsible for the services shall be thoroughly familiar with and competent in using information sources, retrieval techniques, telecommunication methods, and interpersonal communications skills.

Continuing education of reference service staff is essential to professional growth. It is the responsibility of the individual to seek continuing education and of the employing institution to support its staff's continuing education efforts and, when possible, to provide continuing education programs.

The conduct of all Library staff, including those who provide reference services shall be governed by the American Library Association's Code of Ethics

Types of Reference Questions Answered

Medical, Legal, Financial, and Tax

DeKalb County Public Library   Atlanta, Georgia

Definitions of terms will be read, but no interpretation of the information will be given as staff are not qualified Doctors, Lawyers, or Accountants.

DeKalb County Public Library   Atlanta, Georgia

Stock and bond quotations and other financial information related to personal investment cannot be given over the phone

Memorial Hall Library   Andover, Massachusetts

The library does not provide advice in the areas of medicine, law, and taxes. Under no circumstances will a staff member offer advice in medical, legal, or tax areas, no matter how commonplace the question seems to be. Complicated legal searches will not be undertaken nor will personal interpretations of legal matters be offered. Referrals will be made to the Lawrence Law Library in its role as the NMRLS Legal Reference Center.

Brief definitions and descriptions from authoritative sources will be provided in response to requests for medical information. These sources will be quoted verbatim with no personal interpretation. The patron will be informed of the sources from which the information is taken. Every effort will be made to use authoritative, current online sources when using the Internet.

Specific tax forms and publications will not be suggested. Patrons need to know the number of the forms they need. If more information is required, the patron will be encouraged to examine the library's collections or be referred to another source.

School Assignments

Westerville Public Library   Westerville, Ohio

These questions are handled in the same manner as any other reference question, i.e., same amount of time spent on questions. With complex school assignment questions, librarians should make tactful suggestions to telephone callers or to parents of students, that the students come into the library for personal assistance and do their own in-depth research.

DeKalb County Public Library   Atlanta, Georgia

Answers to questions which can be answered in five minutes or less will be given; students requiring more extensive information are urged to come to the library.

Memorial Hall Library   Andover, Massachusetts

Questions related to school assignments will be treated like any other request for reference assistance. Every effort will be made to satisfactorily answer a student's questions and provide the sources for information and the instruction needed to use those sources. If a student has a printed school assignment, it is helpful to ask permission to copy the assignment and pass it on to the Young Adult librarians so that they can set some books aside for the assignment or contact the teacher for further explanation

Contest Questions

Westerville Public Library   Westerville, Ohio

No effort is to be made to screen out contest or puzzle questions. They are to be treated in the same manner and within the same time limits as other questions.

Memorial Hall Library   Andover, Massachusetts

Contest questions will be approached with the same guidelines and time limits as any other type of reference question. However, contest questions are often designed to be interpreted in more than one way and have more than one answer that seems to be correct. The staff will not interpret contest rules.

Books and Collectibles

Memorial Hall Library   **Andover, Massachusetts**

Patrons will be referred to appropriate reference sources or to consultants or experts. Staff members will never give a personal appraisal of the value of an object.

Newark Public Library   **Newark, New Jersey**

Financial appraisals of collectibles (antiques, rare books, coins, stamps, etc.) and fine arts are not within the purview of the Library's reference service. Values as they are stated in published price guides are provided. For additional information patrons may pursue further research on their own at the Library or be referred to appropriate professional services.

Translations

DeKalb County Public Library   **Atlanta, Georgia**

Basic translations of foreign words or phrases will be attempted using basic dictionaries; for more extensive translations referrals will be made to agencies and individuals who perform these services.

Memorial Hall Library   **Andover, Massachusetts**

Brief translations may be provided only if a person on the staff with appropriate expertise is available. Otherwise, referrals from the Community Information Database will be given.

Criss-Cross Directory

DeKalb County Public Library   **Atlanta, Georgia**

Information from these sources is intended for in-library use and cannot be provided over the phone.

Memorial Hall Library   **Andover, Massachusetts**

Criss-Cross and city directory inquiries will be answered only for the name or street provided. No more than three listings will be provided per patron at any one time. Staff members will not give "nearby" listings.

Consumer Information

Westerville Public Library   **Westerville, Ohio**

The 3–5 minute time limit applies for telephone requests for consumer information. No attempt will be made to interpret ratings. The librarian will not recommend a brand of product nor relate personal preference or experience. The librarian should always recommend that the caller come to the library to read the entire rating article in order to make an informed purchase.

DeKalb County Public Library   **Atlanta, Georgia**

Evaluation of consumer products requires interpretation and background reading; consumer product evaluations will not be provided over the phone, but a search will be done to determine if a product has been rated.

Mathematical Calculations

DeKalb County Public Library   **Atlanta, Georgia**

Statistical figures such as the consumer price index or population figures will be given; figures requiring compilation or calculations will not be attempted; similarly mathematical formulas or measurement equivalents will be provided, but calculations based on these formulas will not be performed.

Memorial Hall Library   **Andover, Massachusetts**

Mathematical calculations will be provided only if a person on the staff with appropriate expertise is available. Otherwise patrons are referred to sources containing the formulas or tables necessary for them to complete their calculations.

Referrals

Newark Public Library   **Newark, New Jersey**

Referrals shall be made only if the librarian expects that the agency, service, individual, or other source can and will provide the information needed. Librarians shall be prepared to refer questions to human as well as to written sources. Awareness of community, state, and private services outside of the Library proper is important. Reference librarians may provide access to biographical and other information that is available in directories and other sources. They may not make recommendations to specific lawyers, legal firms, doctors, other medical care providers, or financial professionals. Users shall be referred to county or state professional associations for additional information.

Patron Priorities

Westerville Public Library   **Westerville, Ohio**

Priorities of Service

1. All users, adults and children, are to be treated with attention and care.

2. Requests from individuals acting in their official capacity [elected officials, county government staff, etc.] are priority requests.

3. Handicapped individuals may require additional assistance, within available resources.

Although good judgment should prevail, take phone questions and walk-ins in the order in which they occur. If you are on the phone when a user approaches the desk, acknowledge their presence but complete at least the phone question negotiation before dealing with the walk-in. If there is a mob of people at the desk and the phone starts ringing with no other staff available, you should immediately inform the telephone caller that you will need to put them on hold, or if preferred, take the name and phone number, indicating that you will call back as soon aspossible. Callers should not be left on hold more than two minutes without an explanation and their consent.

Memorial Hall Library   **Andover, Massachusetts**

The public is served on a first come, first served basis. People calling the library are helped in sequence. Callers will be asked if they would like to wait, to call back, or to be called back before being put on hold. Patrons approaching the desk will be informed that they will be helped as soon as possible.

Priority—If a patron has a time-consuming request, it may be necessary to get him/her started and make sure a follow-up is done to continue the patron in the process. Additional staff will be summoned if necessary or during break time.

In-person

Memorial Hall   **Andover, Massachusetts**

Basic Assistance—Reference staff members will assist patrons at every level of the Reference transaction, if the patron so desires. This may require accompanying the patron to the computer catalog to explain its use, or physically locating the materials for the patron. In the event that the staff member is unable to accompany the patron to the stacks area, it is important to remind the patron to check back with the reference desk if the material cannot be located.

Patron Backup

Westerville Public Library   **Westerville, Ohio**

First priority is given to the person who has been waiting the longest. Questions which can be answered quickly may be dealt with first, if this is agreeable to the first person. If it is apparent to the librarian that persons in line for service may have to wait longer than three to five minutes, additional help should be obtained, if it is available. Although all requests for assistance will be provided on a first-come, first-served basis, priority will be given to in-person inquiries over other kinds of inquiries in event of a tie.

Time Limits on Questions

Westerville Public Library   **Westerville, Ohio**

Ten minutes is a reasonable amount of time to spend with one person. Three to five minutes is appropriate when others are waiting. Additional time may be spent with users who have special difficulties in using library resources. (Examples: the very old, the very young, visually impaired, non-English speaking.)

Memorial Hall Library   **Andover, Massachusetts**

No two reference questions are alike; therefore, no special time limits can be placed on an actual question. The amount of time devoted to a question is at the discretion of the reference librarian. When questions from member libraries cannot be answered in-house within a day's time, they will be referred to another source.

Extensive Research

Memorial Hall Library   **Andover, Massachusetts**

Requests for and/or completion of lengthy research are not considered a traditional role of the public reference librarian. Patrons needing extensive bibliographies, lists, statistics, or research will be directed to the appropriate resources and offered as much assistance as staff time allows.

It is the library's practice to respond to all reasonable reference inquiries received by mail, fax or E-mail. If the question becomes too involved or time-consuming, the staff member will explain the limitations of the service and suggest that the patron visit the library or their own library for further assistance. Suggestions of Internet sites, which maybe helpful in answering a patron's question, can be a good referral especially when dealing with email requests.

Telephone, E-mail, Fax, and Mail Questions

Westerville Public Library   **Westerville, Ohio**

It is the library's policy to respond to all reference inquiries received by mail. These requests fall under the same guidelines as in-house and telephone requests for information.

DeKalb County Public Library   **Atlanta, Georgia**

In general, any question that has a short answer can be given over the phone. Answers to telephone reference questions can include: definitions; reading short poems, quotations or passages; statistics, figures and dates.

In general, more complex questions that may require interpretation or extensive research are not appropriate for telephone reference. For these questions, reference staff can determine if there is a body of material available for further research that would warrant a trip to the Library.

Memorial Hall Library   **Andover, Massachusetts**

It is the library's practice to respond to all reasonable reference inquiries received by mail, fax or E-mail. If the question becomes too involved or time-consuming, the staff member will explain the limitations of the service and suggest that the patron visit the library or their own library for further assistance. Suggestions of Internet sites, which maybe helpful in answering a patron's question can be a good referral especially when dealing with email requests.

Email and fax requests from member libraries are treated the same as telephone calls. Email requests will be moved to a "Questions In Progress" folder while being worked on and transferred to a Completed folder when done.

Appleton Public Library   **Appleton, Wisconsin**

The reference interview is a vital part of reference or reader's advisory transactions. Because telephone, fax, e-mail and mail do not allow face to face interaction and follow-up, misinterpretation is always a possibility. Therefore, only brief definitions or descriptions can be read over the telephone or sent via mail, e-mail or fax. Sources are always quoted verbatim without interpretation.

Fee-based Services

Newark Public Library   **Newark, New Jersey**

Access to today's complex world of information is as simple as one telephone call to The Newark Public Library.

Requests for fast facts and quick answers—anything that can be handled in a 5-minute call—is still free for the asking.

But if your research needs are more extensive or if time or distance prevent you from conducting your own research, let Newark Public Library's specialists supply you with the information or material you need.

Gateway Service Provides Access to:

- Business information: company profiles, product, and industry information, price quotations, rankings, financial data
- United States patents from 1790 to the present
- Government publications: the largest collection of Federal and New Jersey publications in the state
- Census data from 1790 to the present
- New Jersey state and local history and genealogy
- Words and music to more than 100,000 songs
- The largest public library visual and performing arts collection in New Jersey
- American history, culture, and biography, with extensive resources on women, African-Americans, and Latinos
- Literary quotations, poetry, criticism, and reviews
- Online databases and the Internet

Fees for Research

$75.00 per hour charged in 1/4 hour increments with 1/2 hour minimum; plus any additional costs for online searches, photocopying, etc. Rush surcharge for same day service (request received by 11:00 a.m., sent by 5:00 p.m.)

Charges are as follows: (See Figure 6.2)

Research Charged in ¼ hour increments with a ½ hour minimum	$75 per hour
Ten photocopied pages	$.15
Eleven plus photocopied pages	$.75 per page
Fax	$.75 per page
Postage and handling	At cost
Same day service	$20 per item

Payment is required in advance by credit card or check. Frequent customers are invited to open a deposit account.

Payment is required in advance by credit card or check. Frequent customers are invited to open a deposit account.

Henderson County Public Library   Henderson, Kentucky

Due to the increasing demand of Reference Services via telephone, mail and electronic mail, the Library has set in place a schedule of fees to be charged for these services. Fees will be charged for the Librarian's research time as well as for any copies, faxes, or postage expenses. Charges for research time will include the time it takes to find the information, make copies, send faxes, and/or prepare items for mailing.

Realizing that many reference questions can be answered in less than 15 minutes, fees will not be charged for the Librarian's research time if it takes 15 minutes or less for the answer to be found. However, a patron who requests photocopies, faxes, and/or mailed information must be charged at the rates listed below. All applicable fees must be paid in advance by the patron before the results of the Librarian's research are released.

Research fees will not be charged to Henderson County residents or patrons who come into the Library and request information.

Cleveland Public Library   Cleveland, Ohio

The comprehensive information service of the Cleveland Public Library:

The Cleveland Research Center (CRC) is a fee-based research service of the Cleveland Public Library. CRC is staffed with information professionals trained to retrieve the data you need, when you need it, cost-effectively. Cleveland Research Center specializes in custom research. Projects are tailored to fit your goals and your budget.

Services Include:

- Prospect And Mailing Lists: Locate and contact prospective clients

- Industry And Market Research: Identify potential markets. Utilize industry trends and forecasts for proactive marketing strategies

- Competitive Intelligence: Get the "skinny" on your competition

- Tracking Service: Stay on top of topics of interest with information updates at regularly scheduled intervals

- Patent/Trademark Searches: Ensure the thoroughness of your investigations. Guard against infringement

- Grants/Federal Assistance Searches: Match your needs and goals with available public and private funding sources

- Scientific/Technical Searches: Keep up with the latest R&D advances and trends

Cleveland Research Center is staffed with information professionals who specialize in searching and have access to the vast electronic and print collections of the Cleveland Public Library including:

- Lexis-Nexis

- Dialog DataStar

- Dun & Bradstreet

- Dow Jones News Retrieval

- Investment house reports

45

- United Nations' documents

- Patents

- Industry standards

- Just to name a few!

In addition CRC can help you with Research Road Maps: Want to do your own research but need a little guidance? Our "Research Road Map" can help you successfully navigate the maze of information sources by recommending appropriate resources* and providing search tips and research advice. Maps are tailored to your research skill level.

Research Time Frame: Most research requests are completed within three to five days. CRC makes every effort to accommodate deadlines and we offer "Rush Service" for same or next day delivery.

Rate Schedule: Research Rate:

$60.00 per hour; 15-minute minimum. Rush service $90.00 per hour.

Online Searches:

Rates vary with database used

Long-distance Telephone Charges:

$2.00 per call

Photocopies:

$.10 per page plus 7% sales tax

Method:

- MasterCard

- Purchase Order

- Cash/Check

Delivery Options:

- Fax

- E-mail

- Regular Mail

- Courier

- Federal Express

- UPS

*All suggested electronic and hard copy resources are available free at the Cleveland Public Library

Services Provided

Service to the Homebound

Pasadena Public Library   **Pasadena, California**

This program is designed to provide library materials to anyone who is a resident of Pasadena and is confined to their home or a convalescent center due to illness, injury or disability. Each homebound patron is individually profiled and matched with a volunteer on a one-to-one basis, with the exception of patrons in retirement and convalescent homes that receive services from a volunteer. The volunteer will visit the library and select reading and other materials for a homebound person. Materials include large-type books, books-on-tape and music cassettes. Reference desk personnel are available to assist in filling the patron's special requests. Once library materials have been selected and checked out using the patron's own library card, volunteers will then contact their patron and deliver the books.

Notary Public

Lucius Beebe Memorial Library   **Wakefield, Massachusetts**

The library has notaries public that will notarize documents at no charge. It is advisable to call ahead to verify when the notary will be available.

Proctoring Exams

Lucius Beebe Memorial Library   **Wakefield, Massachusetts**

Reference Librarians will provide proctor service for tests. A written request and instructions should be received by the library from the testing agency and an appointment set up well in advance of the test date.

Interlibrary Loan

Fort Smith Pubic Library   **Fort Smith, Arkansas**

To obtain books outside of the library's collection, patrons must come in person to the library (or any of the branches) and fill out an interlibrary loan request. If the request is for an article, the library may be able to have it faxed. Please note: Library patrons with non-resident out-of-town cards are charged a nominal, non-refundable fee of $2.50 for each request. The library has several database sources that list books not available at this library, such as OCLC FirstSearch.

Patrons must have a valid Fort Smith Public Library card and be 16 or older in order to use the Interlibrary Loan service. Patrons cannot use Westark cards. No more than three requests per patron will be accepted at any one time.

Pittsfield Public Library   **Pittsfield Maine**

Items not available in our collection can usually be obtained from other libraries through Interlibrary Loan.

Patrons wishing to retrieve sources using Interlibrary Loan must be in good standing with the library as far as fines and overdues. You request an item through interlibrary loan by asking a staff member. Please provide the title, author, publisher, and date of publication, along with your name and phone number.

Once we receive your ILL request, it generally takes from several days to three weeks for you to get the materials. Any charges from the loaning institution will be passed on to the library user. The lending library that loans us the item to loan to you sets a due date on the materials. The items are due back to our library in time to return them to the lending library.

ADMINISTRATIVE POLICIES

Patrons should feel free to ask you anything for any reason and know the interaction will be kept private. The American Library Association established a librarian's code of ethics that should be followed by every staff member, including circulation staff. Your state may also have laws that govern certain aspects of library and reference service. The federal government may institute laws governing confidentiality of patron records. For information on how your library can respond to the Patriot Act, go to the American Library Association's Web site. Several complete policies are given below to give you one that suits your library's needs.

Features of an Effective Policy

- Includes any state law pertaining to privacy and confidentiality, such as the Queens Borough, New York, (example on the CD-ROM) and Wadsworth, Ohio (here);
- Defines your duties and responsibilities as a professional;
- Reminds patrons they have a fundamental right to privacy;
- Extends the confidentiality responsibilities to include all library staff;
- Follows the American Library Association's "Statement on Professional Ethics";
- Conforms to the American Library Association's "Policy Concerning Confidentiality of Personally Identifiable Information about Library Users";
- Extends the policy to protect children's privacy;
- Responds to the Patriot Act.

Benefits of Effective Policies

- Develops a high level of trust between you and the public;
- Show in writing to patrons what the policy says about their right to privacy;
- Articulates to governmental officials the policy on privacy;
- Emphasizes privacy as a fundamental right.

Policies

Patron Confidentiality, the Librarian Code of Ethics, and the Patriot Act

Tiffin-Seneca Public Library   **Tiffin, Ohio**

HR-3162 became Public Law 107–56 in response to the events of 9/11/01. The full title of the law is: Uniting and Strengthening America by Providing Appropriate Tools Required to Intercept and Obstruct Terrorism Act of 2001.

The Act may provide law enforcement broader boundaries when investigating information accessed and transmitted by patrons with regards to national security concerns.

Access to patron information may include but not be limited to:

- Database Search Records

- Circulation Records

- Computer Use Records

- Interlibrary Loan Records

- Reference Interviews

The T-SPL Policy & Procedures Regarding Information Access and Confidentiality

> Database Search Records: These records refer to the searches of the collection a patron may conduct on the Online Public Access Terminals (OPAC). These searches are conducted by utilizing the library's automated circulation system, Spydus. Once a search is conducted, the software does not retain a copy of the search. Any records of the search will not exist.

> Circulation Records: Patron material is circulated via the Spydus system. The circulation software tracks materials currently checked out, automatically erasing a reader's borrowing record once a book is returned and all fines are paid.

> Computer Use Records: The library system is equipped with public computers.

> Patrons use their library card to access the computers. The library does not assign a computer to a patron and no paper record with the patron's information printed is generated. When the patron logs off, the software erases all history of his research and activity.

> Interlibrary Loan Records: Patrons may borrow items not owned by T-SPL from other libraries worldwide via Inter-Library Loan (ILL). T-SPL tracks items currently being borrowed and generates a paper record with patron information. Once the materials are returned and all appropriate fines and/or fees are paid, the paper record is destroyed.

> Reference Interviews: A reference interview occurs when a patron looking for information approaches a library staff member. The staff member questions or interviews the patron in order to narrow down the specific information needed.

No paper record is kept during the interview that has any patron information on it. If a patron name and number is taken by phone, and patron information is written down, as soon as the requested information is delivered, the paper record is destroyed.

T-SPL Policy & Procedures for Complying with Law Enforcement

T-SPL administration will comply with law enforcement when supplied with legal subpoena or warrant.

Wadsworth Public Library   Wadsworth, Ohio

The Wadsworth Public Library specifically recognizes that library records and patron information are confidential. Library records are defined as a record in any form that is maintained by the Library and that contains any of the following types of information:

- Information an individual is required to provide in order to be eligible to use Library services or borrow materials

- Information that identifies an individual as having requested or obtained specific materials or materials on a specific subject

- Information that is provided by an individual to assist a staff member to answer a specific question or provide information on a particular subject

Information that does not identify an individual and that is retained for the purpose of studying or evaluating the use of the Library is not considered confidential and is not subject to this policy.

Under Ohio law, library records shall not be made available to any agency of federal, state, or local government, or to any spouse or other individual, except as pursuant to the following:

- For the records of minor children when requested by parents, guardians, or custodians

- In accordance with a subpoena, search warrant, or other court order, or to a law enforcement officer who is investigating a matter involving public safety in exigent circumstances

- At the written request or with the written consent of the individual who is the subject of the record or information

- For library administrative purposes as defined by Ohio Revised Code § 149.432

Mt. Lebanon Public Library   Pittsburgh, Pennsylvania

The Board of Trustees of the Mt. Lebanon Public Library specifically recognizes the confidentiality of records related to circulation of Library materials that contain the names or other personally identifying details regarding the users of the Library in accordance with Pennsylvania law: 24 Pa. Cons. Stat. Sec. 4428.

The Board of Trustees supports the concept of intellectual freedom and the right of each citizen, regardless of age, to free access to information without fear of intimidation or recrimination. The Library's confidentiality policy safeguards the first amendment and privacy rights of Library users. The Library advises employees, volunteers, and patrons that all Library records that contain names or other personally identifying details regarding the users of the Library are confidential.

The Board of Trustees of the Mt. Lebanon Public Library further subscribes to the American Library Association Library Code of Ethics, Section III, which states, "We protect each Library user's right to privacy and confidentiality with respect to information sought or received and materials consulted, borrowed, acquired, or transmitted."

In all instances and regardless of circumstances, Mt. Lebanon Public Library safeguards access to patron Library records and restricts access to that information to only the patron who owns the Library card and provides that card or to the parent/legal guardian of a minor child with the stipulations and exceptions specified below.

No patron records will be made available to federal, state, or local law enforcement agencies except by a court order as required by law.

- Court orders from law enforcement officers will be referred to the Library Director who will consult legal counsel. Other Library employees will not provide any patron records to law enforcement agencies under any circumstances.

- The Library will take such action as is necessary to determine that any court order or process issued by any court or pursuant to any court rule or any agency of government requires that such records be made available.

When Library employees or volunteers speak either in person or on the telephone to anybody other than the patron, or to persons who cannot produce their Library card numbers and provide other identification, information regarding items charged out, items overdue, fines, holds will be restricted as to information that does not reveal the content, such as number of items or figures for fines owed. Addresses, phone numbers, or any other personal information from patron's records will not be given out under the above circumstances. When a patron is unable to confirm his or her identify as required, a printout of the requested information may be mailed to the patron using the mailing address provided in the Library's registration records.

The Library record of a child has the same confidentiality protection under Library policy as that of any other patrons with the following exceptions.

- Parents or legal guardians are permitted access to the records of their minor children under the age of 13 (thirteen). The parent/legal guardian must be accompanied by the child, provide the child's Library card, and/or provide other acceptable identification. In the case of telephone inquiries, Library card number and verification of the child's address, telephone number, and date of birth are required.

- Parents or legal guardians of minor children ages 13 through 17 are permitted to know only the number of items, not titles, authors, or subjects, charged out on their children's Library cards, unless the child accompanies the parent or legal guardian to the Library and grants permission for access. The parent or legal guardian must provide the children's Library card or, in the case of telephone inquires, Library card number and verification of the child's address, telephone number, and date of birth.

- Mt. Lebanon Public Library recognizes that parents or legal guardians who have signed their minor children's applications have assumed the financial responsibility for materials charged out to their children's cards; therefore, parents or legal guardians will be provided with specific information about their minor children's Library records when materials are overdue or lost.

FORMS

Benefits of Written Forms

- Documents your workload with the Daily Desk Count Sheet;
- Provides statistics so local governmental officials can see what you do;
- Justifies budget requests for materials and staff when actual work load is shown;
- Gives an indication of fee structures other libraries use;
- Deploys staffing to meet workload;
- Identifies the type of resources you use the most at the reference desk to aid patrons;
- Notifies patrons of their rights and responsibilities in their signed Patron Agreement Regarding Confidentiality.

Daily Desk Count Sheet

Date: _____

Department: _____

Reference Questions Asked:

Reference Questions Answered:

Questions referred to another source:

Reference Questions Unable to Answer:

Reference Books Used:

Circulating Books Used:

Periodicals, Newspapers, and Microfilm and Micro Fiche:

Gave Directions:

Referred to the Children's/Adult department:

Internet Assistance Given:

Charged at the rates listed below.

Figure 2.1 Daily Desk Count Sheet

Cleveland Public Library   **Cleveland, Ohio**

Fee-based Services Cost Sheet

Due to the increasing demand of Reference Services via telephone, mail and electronic mail, the Library has set in place a schedule of fees to be charged for these services. Fees will be charged for the Librarian's research time as well as for any copies, faxes, or postage expenses. Charges for research time will include the time it takes to find the information, make copies, send faxes, and/or prepare items for mailing.

Research Charged in ? hour increments with a ? hour minimum	$____
Ten photocopied pages	$____
Eleven plus photocopied pages	$____ per page
Fax	$____ per page
Postage and handling	$____
Same day service	$____ per item

Payment is required in advance by credit card or check. Frequent customers are invited to open a deposit account.

Realizing that many reference questions can be answered in less than 15 minutes, fees will not be charged for the Librarian's research time if it takes 15 minutes or less for the answer to be found. However, a patron who requests photocopies, faxes, and/or mailed information must be charged at the rates listed below.

Figure 2.2 Fee-based Charge Sheet

Newark Public Library **Newark, New Jersey**
Fee-based Service Cost Sheet

Access to today's complex world of information is as simple as one telephone call to XYZ Public Library.

Requests for fast facts and quick answers—anything that can be handled in a 5-minute call— is still free for the asking.

But if your research needs are more extensive or if time or distance prevent you from conducting your own research, let XYZ specialists supply you with the information or material you need.

Rate Schedule:

Research Rate:	$60 per hour; 15-minute minimum.
Rush Service:	$90.00 per hour.
Online Searches:	Rates vary with database used
Long-distance Telephone Charges:	$2.00 per call
Photocopies:	$.10 per page plus 7% sales tax

Method of payments that are accepted

- MasterCard
- Purchase Order
- Cash/Check

Delivery Options:

- Fax
- E-mail
- Regular Mail
- Courier
- Federal Express
- UPS

Note: This will give you a cost comparison for your library. The form on the

CD-ROM will be blank so you can fill in the amounts for your service.

Figure 2.3 Fee-based Charge Sheet

Mt. Lebanon Public Library   **Pittsburgh, Pennsylvania**

Patron Agreement

A Library card permits the borrowing of valuable material that is public property and must be returned. The cardholder is financially responsible for Library property charged out to his/her card. The parent/legal guardian who endorses a child's application is financially responsible for materials charged out to the minor (under the age of 18) child.

Parents or legal guardians assume responsibility for deciding what Library resources are appropriate for their children, including information accessible through the Internet.

The confidentiality of Library records is protected by law and the administrative policies of the XYZ Public Library. This safeguards your rights to free speech and privacy. In order to safeguard access to Library records, only the patron who owns the Library card, or in the case of overdue or lost books, the parent/legal guardian of a minor, will have access to his/her record upon verification of the Library card number. All other information will be restricted to that which does not reveal the content.

Cardholder's signature _____ Date _____

Parent/guardian signature if applicant is a minor _____

Print Parent's name _____

A XYZ Public Library card is your key to a universe of information and entertainment. Cherish it, guard it, and use it wisely.

Figure 2.4 Patron Agreement

CHECKLIST

- Make your Reference Services Objectives and Philosophy compatible with the Mission Statement.
- Look at staff, resources, and available time to determine the type and range of questions you can answer.
- Determine which patron is first, the one on the telephone or the one in person, or is it first come, first served.
- Have a list of referral agencies, or experts in your area, who can answer reference questions you are unable to answer.
- How extensive is your research and will you charge a fee for in-depth research?
- Do you want to have a time limit you will spend on a reference question?
- Are you able provide services to the homebound or disabled patron?
- Are you able to proctor exams or provide notary services?
- Will you answer homework questions over the phone, or must the student come into the library?

Chapter 3

INTERNET POLICIES

OVERVIEW

The Internet has revolutionized how information is disseminated. No longer bound by physical media, such as print, tape, and film, libraries offer a virtually unlimited fountain of information. One truism is that the "best thing about the Internet is everyone can publish. The worst thing about the Internet is everyone can publish." The problem is not that we disagree about some of the information on the Web, or that we personally disagree with some of the books we select. The problem is inaccuracy or misinformation, out-of-date or simply wrong information; and new content we never before had in libraries presents unanticipated problems. Selection criteria, publishing houses, and standard review sources serve as a filter with print material, but now we also face pornography, hate sites, and illegal activity within the library with no real effective means of control. Filtering software throws a wide net and desirable information gets excluded along with the undesirable. Every librarian must figure out how to handle the problem in one way or another. But you may not be the one who decides on filtering software or whether children can search the Internet. Your library board, your community, your county or city commissioners, a legislature, or a court may decide for you. Libraries have always been at the forefront in supporting the right to read and view anything for any purpose, but this seems somehow different to many librarians. Because the type of information available is different than ever before, many librarians feel it requires a different solution than those we found for print resources. I see no really effective solution even on the horizon. The policies below reflect the different ways libraries are treating this ocean of access. Choose the ones that make sense for your library.

This chapter covers information on policies and forms for the following areas:

- General Policies
- Rules of Conduct
- Patron Rights
- Library Rights
- Children and the Internet

- Termination of Internet Privileges
- Filters
- Internet Assistance
- Chat Rooms, E-mail, Headphones, Pornography, Conducting Commercial Business, and Playing Games

- Time Limits
- Printing Fees and Diskettes
- Access Priorities

- Library Links
- Internet Users Agreement
- Liability Issues

PUBLIC SERVICE POLICIES

Features of an Effective Policy

- Holds parents ultimately responsible for their children's Internet activity;
- Warns patrons that information may be inaccurate, misleading, incomplete, or out-of-date;
- Prohibits illegal activity;
- Addresses how much and what types of commercial activity are permitted;
- Addresses tampering with the library's network and software and using the library computer to release viruses;
- Prohibits vandalism;
- Addresses copyright issues;
- Stipulates the length of time- a user may be online sessions;
- Outlines clearly a patron's right to confidentiality and privacy;
- Allows library staff to terminate sessions for rules violations;
- Gives librarians the right to bar repeat violators;
- Grants the patron barred from use a right to appeal;
- Makes parents sign a permission slip for their child to use the Internet;
- Requires each patron to accept the user agreement before continuing the session.

POLICIES

General Policies

Alhambra Public Library,   **Alhambra, California**

The Alhambra Public Library is dedicated to providing the community with a wide variety of information on all topics. In keeping with the mission and vision of the Library, free limited use of the Internet is available to all library users, upon signature of the "Acceptable Internet Use Policy" agreement.

The library offers both unblocked and blocked access to the Internet. Full (unblocked, unfiltered) access is available to Adults. Adults use the Internet at their own discretion, and the Library has no control over and is not responsible for the content on the Internet. Not all sites provide accurate, complete, or current information. Some access points carry information that a user might find controversial or inappropriate. We encourage our patrons to be sensitive to the fact that they are in a public setting.

Minors (up to age 18) can have full (unblocked, unfiltered) access to the Internet, with the signed permission of a parent or guardian. (The parental permission form will be kept on file, and a child's library card will contain information about their permitted access.) Limited Internet access is also available for minors on machines with commercially available blocking software that is intended to prevent access to visual materials of an obscene or sexually explicit nature that would be considered legally "Harmful to Minors" under the California Penal Code (Section 313.3). The Library cannot guarantee the effectiveness of the software in use, nor can the Library be responsible for any failure on the part of the software to block offensive or inappropriate materials. The Library is also not responsible for the inadvertent restriction of access to desirable, necessary or appropriate information that may result from use of the blocking software. With or without blocking software, children who use the Internet without parental guidance may encounter material that is beyond their maturity level or otherwise unsuitable. We strongly urge parents to discuss the use of the Internet with their children, to determine the most appropriate use of this new medium.

Old Town Public Library   **Old Town, Maine**

The mission of the Old Town Public Library is to ensure that the people of the City of Old Town have the right and means to free and open access to ideas and information that are fundamental to a democracy. The Library will protect intellectual freedom, promote literacy, encourage lifelong learning, and provide library materials and information services.

Throughout its history the Old Town Public Library has made information available in a variety of formats, from print to audiovisual materials. The Library's computer system provides the opportunity to integrate electronic resources from information networks around the world with the Library's other resources.

The Internet, as an information resource, enables the Library to provide information beyond the confines of its own collection. It allows access to ideas, information and commentary from around the globe. Currently, however, it is an unregulated medium. As such, while it offers access to a wealth of material that is personally, professionally, and culturally enriching to individuals of all ages, it also enables access to some material that may be offensive, disturbing and/or illegal.

The Internet is a global entity with a highly diverse user population and information content. Library patrons use it at their own risk. The Library cannot censor access to materials or protect users from materials they may find offensive. In choosing sources to link our home page, we follow generally accepted library practices. Beyond this, we do not monitor or control information accessible through the Internet and do not accept responsibility for its content. We are not responsible for changes in content of the sources to which we link, nor for the content of sources accessed through secondary links.

As with printed information, not all sources on the Internet provide accurate, complete, or current information. Users should evaluate Internet sources just as they do printed publications, questioning the validity of the information provided.

The Library upholds and affirms the right of each individual to have access to constitutionally protected material. The Library also affirms the right and responsibility of parents to determine and monitor their children's use of Library materials and resources.

Rules of Conduct

San Francisco Public Library   **San Francisco, California**

Guidelines for Use of Computer Terminals

Purpose:

3. To provide all interested Library users with access to the Library catalog, various databases and Internet connections.

4. To discourage a few individuals from monopolizing computer workstations thereby hindering the ability of others to make use of these resources.

5. To provide staff with a method to modify consistently and equitably individuals' inappropriate behavior.

Application:

1. Individuals may use a public workstation for a period of time (for example, thirty minutes) specified by the Branch/Floor Manager.

2. Library Staff may make exceptions to time limits when demand is light or heavy. Terminals, which access only the Library catalog, may be exempted from any time limit.

3. At some Library workstations, a printer is available. A Branch/Floor Manager may limit use of such stations to patrons who are ready to print. There is a charge for printing.

4. Access to the Internet or to particular kinds of activity (for example, e-mail, chat rooms, game playing) may be limited or prohibited at the discretion of a Branch/Floor Manager to allow for easier access to the Library's catalog and other databases.

5. More than one individual may use the same workstation so long as this does not disrupt others in the library.

6. After an individual has occupied a workstation for the time limit, s/he must relinquish the workstation.

7. Users of computer workstations are expected to be alert to others who may wish to use the equipment. Individuals will lose their Library privileges if they intimidate or otherwise discourage others from exercising their right to use the computer.

8. Downloading is available at some stations. Files downloaded from the Internet may contain a virus; neither the San Francisco Public Library nor any of its vendors shall be held responsible for any loss of data, damage or liability that may occur from an individual's use of a Library computer.

Procedures:

1. Any limit or sign-up requirement shall be clearly posted.

2. Any individual who violates these guidelines (for example, using a false name or signature or otherwise trying to circumvent limits) may lose his/her Library privileges.

Old Town Public Library   **Old Town, Maine**

- Internet computers will not be used for illegal activity, to access illegal materials, or to access materials which by local community standards would be obscene.

- Library staff may limit use of computer equipment which has been purchased from grant funds, according to the terms or intent of the grant agreement.

- Installation, downloading, or modification of software is prohibited.

- Users will respect copyright laws and licensing agreements.

- Users will not make any attempt to gain unauthorized access to restricted files or networks, or to damage or modify computer equipment or software.

- Prompt payment is required by users who incur charges for printing or other authorized fees.

- Users must sign up to use the Internet on a next-available-terminal basis. Terminals will not be "reserved" for persons who are not in the immediate vicinity when their name is called, and telephone reservations will not be taken.

- Access sessions will be limited to thirty minutes, unless otherwise authorized by the Librarian in Charge.

- Users must end their session and leave the terminal when asked to do so by authorized Library staff.

- Upon completion of an Internet access session, a user may be required to wait 30 minutes before signing up for another session.

- The number of access sessions available per day, per user, may be established by the Librarian in Charge: such limitations will be dependent on facility-specific demand in order to provide access for the majority of users.

- Users will respect the privacy of other users, and will refrain from attempting to view or read material being used by others.

- By mutual agreement, two persons may share one access session as long as their behavior or conversation does not disturb other users or Library staff.

Patron Rights

Vancouver Public Library   **Vancouver, British Columbia Canada**

Library patrons have the right to confidentiality and privacy in the use of electronic information networks to the extent possible given certain constraints such as proximity of other patrons and staff in public access settings. Please note, for legal reasons complaints from patrons that a user is accessing legally prohibited material may result in a VPL staff member intervening.

The same confidentiality standards and procedures that apply to other library/public transactions will apply to the use of Internet resources. VPL does not store any individual information on patron Internet use or other VPL electronic information sources except for cumulative, generic statistics used for assuring equitable access or to provide statistics for measuring service utilization and directing information subscription purchases. Library patrons have the right to equitable access to electronic information networks. Library patrons have the right to access and read this document and discuss questions with appropriate staff.

Winnetka-Northfield Public Library District   **Winnetka, Illinois**

Library patrons have certain rights with respect to use of electronic information networks such as the Internet. The Winnetka-Northfield Public Library District will work with other libraries in the Illinois Library and Information Network to preserve and protect these rights, subject to limitations imposed by licensing and payment agreements with database providers.

- Library patrons have the right to confidentiality and privacy in the use of electronic information networks to the extent possible given certain constraints such as proximity of other patrons and staff in public access settings.

- Library patrons have the right to equitable access to electronic information networks.

- Library patrons have the right to access and read all library service policies and discuss questions with appropriate library staff.

Library Rights

New London Public Library   **New London, Wisconsin**

- To terminate the user's session, without notice.

- To limit the amount of computer time at any one sitting.

- To erase any and all users files stored on library equipment, without notice.

- To immediately suspend persons from computer use for violating these rules and regulations.

- To limit the software available to users to library owned resources and to deny the loading of user provided software.

Children and the Internet

Winnetka-Northfield Public Library District   **Winnetka, Illinois**

The Winnetka-Northfield Public Library District supports the right of all library users to access information and will not deny access to electronic information networks based solely on age.

The Winnetka-Northfield Public Library District recognizes that the electronic information networks such as the Internet may contain material that is inappropriate for children. Parents are expected to monitor and supervise their children's use of the Internet. Library staff are unable to monitor children's use. Parents are encouraged to discuss with their children issues of appropriate use and electronic information network safety.

Liberty Public Library   Liberty, New York

Parents and legal guardians of children under 18 are responsible for their children's use of the Internet. We encourage parents to take an active role in their children's use of the Internet, and to talk about their personal values and expectations of their children's use of this resource. Parents should be aware that children will have full access our computer programs and to the Internet. The only way to monitor their children's search is for the adult to be present at the keyboard.

Queens Borough Public Library   New York, New York

Parents or legal guardians must assume responsibility for deciding which library resources are appropriate for their own children. Parents or legal guardians should guide their children in use of the Internet and inform them about materials they should not use. While the Library affirms and acknowledges the rights and responsibilities of parents and guardians to monitor and determine their children's access to Library materials and resources, including those available through the Internet, the Library has taken certain measures designed to assist in the safe and effective use of these resources by all minors.

A. To address the issue of access by minors to inappropriate material on the Internet, including material that is harmful to minors, the Library:

  i. Develops and maintains special web sites for children and teens;

  ii. Develops and provides training programs on safe and effective Internet use;

  ii. Encourages staff to guide minors away from materials that may be inappropriate; and,

  iv. Distributes a publication entitled "A Message to Parents: Surfing the Internet".

B. To address the issue of the safety and security of minors when using electronic mail, chat rooms and other forms of direct electronic communications, as well as the unauthorized disclosure, use and dissemination of personal identification information regarding minors, the Library provides training programs and also urges minors to keep in mind the following safety guidelines:

  i. Never give out identifying information such as home address, school name, or telephone number.

  ii. Let parents or guardians decide whether personal information such as age, marital status, or financial information should be revealed.

  iii. Never arrange a face to face meeting with someone via the computer without parents' or guardians' approval.

iv. Never respond to messages that are suggestive, obscene, threatening, or make one uncomfortable.

v. Have parents or guardians report an incident to the National Center for Missing and Exploited Children at 1–800–843–5678 if one becomes aware of the transmission of child pornography.

vi. Remember that people online may not be who they say they are.

vii. Remember that everything one reads may not be true.

C. To address the issue of unauthorized access, including so called "hacking," and other unlawful activities by minors online, minors and all other Library users are hereby advised that use of the Library's computers for hacking or any other unlawful activity is strictly prohibited.

Termination of Internet Privileges

Carrollton Public Library   **Carrollton, Texas**

When library employees observe that a user has failed to comply with the ER/Internet policy, they are authorized to terminate that users access session or to prohibit that user from future sessions for up to two weeks from the date of informing the user of that action. After a meeting with the library's administrative authority, the customer may be permanently barred from Internet access from the library.

Internet users whose access session has been terminated or prohibited will be given information concerning the process to protest the action and/or request that Internet access privileges be reinstated. Temporary or permanent denial of Internet privileges at any Carrollton Public Library facility will be effective at all Carrollton Public Library facilities.

- First inappropriate behavior incident will result in termination of the session and formal warning. Note is placed in user's personal library account.

- Second inappropriate behavior incident will result in termination of the session and prohibition of access to library computers for two weeks. This incident will be noted in user's personal library account. The customer must make an appointment with Library Administrative Authority to request a hearing to reinstate computer privileges.

- This meeting will determine whether access to Internet will be reinstated or permanently denied.

San Antonio Public Library   **San Antonio, Texas**

Public Library employees are authorized to terminate any user's access session, or to prohibit a user from subsequent access sessions for up to two weeks from the date of informing the user of that action, given cause to believe that the user has failed to comply with the Internet Acceptable Use Policy and/or Rules.

Internet users whose access session has been terminated or prohibited will be given information concerning the process to protest the action and/or request that Internet access privileges be reinstated. Temporary or permanent denial of Internet privileges at any San Antonio Public Library facility will be effective at all San Antonio Library facilities.

Filters

James Kennedy Public Library   Dyersville, Iowa

Just as the library does not restrict access to other material forms and formats, we cannot refuse access to Internet content that someone else may deem objectionable. The principles of intellectual freedom that apply to the traditional monographic library also apply to the modern electronic access library. All patrons using the Internet must read and sign the Internet Users Agreement before use. Patrons under the age of 18 must have a parent or legal guardian sign the agreement.

San Antonio Public Library   San Antonio, Texas

The San Antonio Public Library supports the right and responsibility of parents to direct use of the Internet by their own children, and provides convenient access to filtered search engines on all Internet terminals. Filtered search engines (which are not under the control of the Library) may restrict access to sites that could be deemed objectionable, but may also limit access to sites which have legitimate research value. No filtering system is completely effective or efficient. Access to filtered search engines has been provided, but Library staff will not require that children utilize Filtered Search Engines for their research.

Pasadena Public Library   Pasadena, Texas

The library has recently implemented Internet filtering in order to ensure that the Internet is used responsibly.

The library filters the following sites for the computers designated as the Children's OPACs

1 Chat

2. E-mail

3. Criminal Skills

4. Dating

5. Extreme or Obscene

6. Games

7. Hate Speech

8. Sex

The library filters the following sites in the computers designated as the adult OPACs at both the Main Library and the Fairmont Branch Library

1. Chat

2. E-mail

3. Extreme or Obscene

4. Games

5. Sex

Choice of Filtered or Not Filtered

Pikes Peak Library District   **Colorado Springs, Colorado**

The library provides a choice for patrons searching on the Internet. The library's web site contains a list of filtered and unfiltered search engines. Library patrons may select the search engine that best fits their information needs. Using filtered search engines does not guarantee the exclusion of objectionable material.

No Filters

Neill Public Library   **Pullman, Washington**

The library provides full Internet access and does not limit or filter out information. Parents are ultimately responsible for children's access on Internet stations (some content is of a mature nature). Unattended children are responsible for their actions in the library.

Internet Assistance

Basic

Carrollton Public Library   **Carrollton, Texas**

Library employees provide basic introductory training concerning Internet or personal computer use as time permits but do not provide in-depth Internet assistance. Staff can locate books and other library resources dealing with computer-related topics and can provide referrals to area computer classes.

Winnetka-Northfield Public Library District   **Winnetka, Illinois**

The Winnetka-Northfield Public Library District's staff may provide assistance to patrons in the use of electronic information networks as time and staff knowledge permit. Printed reference tools are available at or near the reference desk.

Individualized instruction in particular aspects of the electronic information network is available upon request as time permits.

Fee for Individual or Small Group Instruction

Vancouver Public Library   **Vancouver, British Columbia Canada**

VPL will provide free large group introductory training sessions to the Internet as VPL resources permit.

VPL will provide small, hands-on training sessions for the public at a cost which will cover both the large training sessions and hands-on training sessions as well as provide revenue to the library for other public information resource training. The objective is to break-even on our Internet training program.

Self-help Internet training sheets will be provided to the public as well as bibliographies of training materials.

No Assistance

James Kennedy Public Library   **Dyersville, Iowa**

No individual instruction will be given to patrons using the computer. The library's purpose in having computers for public use is to provide the service, not to educate in the use of computers. Librarians will help patrons get started on the computers, and assist with troubleshooting, but cannot devote the time needed for one-on-one instruction.

Chat Rooms, E-mail, Headphones, Pornography, Conducting Commercial Business, and Playing Games

Carrollton Public Library   **Carrollton, Texas**

Internet access computers may be used to access games.

Manitouwadge Public Library   **Manitouwadge, Ontario Canada**

The Library's Internet access is intended primarily as an information resource. Terminals DO NOT have access to e-mail, chat rooms, news or discussion groups or other forms of online communication.

Pasadena Public Library   **Pasadena, Texas**

Users may not access chat-rooms or e-mail on the library computers.

Hobbs Public Library   **Hobbs, New Mexico**

Headphones must be checked out and returned to the Circulation Desk.

James Kennedy Public Library   **Dyersville, Iowa**

While it may not be illegal under Iowa law for an adult to view material that "might be harmful to minors", it is a violation of the James Kennedy Public Library Internet Use Policy and of common correct behavior in the library; where someone may be offended and sue under other Iowa & United States laws. It is one of the adult privileges to view pornography, but not obscenity, it is NOT however, one of the acceptable uses in the library. Librarians have and will defend adults' rights under the United States Constitution, but we expect you to exercise those rights appropriately. If you violate the rules of the James Kennedy Public Library, you may be asked to leave, or may lose your use privileges—be it because of pornography, damaging or not returning materials.

James Kennedy Public Library   **Dyersville, Iowa**

The library's Internet resources are intended for educational, informational, and recreational purposes only. Therefore, conducting any commercial activity or enterprise or distributing advertisements using these resources in not permitted.

Time Limits

Carrollton Public Library   **Carrollton, Texas**

Access sessions are limited to a maximum of 2 hours in length with a 30-minute timeout period between sessions. During the timeout period the user is denied access to library computers except for the "catalog and database only" workstations.

Manitouwadge Public Library   **Manitouwadge, Ontario Canada**

You may sign-up for half-hour blocks of usage. You will be allowed additional time if no one is waiting. Please remember to sign-out before leaving the library.

Pasadena Public Library   **Pasadena, Texas**

A 30-minute time limit will be enforced when others are waiting to use a terminal. No extra time will be added for restarting the computer

Brantford Public Library   **Brantford, Ontario Canada**

The Internet is a very popular resource. You are welcome to search the Internet for a maximum of one hour per day, including time required to print pages. Please plan time accordingly. You must sign in with the Reference staff before using the Internet computers. You can book in advance, either in person or by telephone. We hold your spot for 10 minutes only if others are waiting.

ADMINISTRATIVE POLICIES

Benefits of Effective Policies

- Provides a common foundation for discussions with patrons and the community;
- Treats violators with a known standard procedure;
- Applies written standards so each violation is dealt with equitability;
- Lets patrons know the rules before they begin searching the Internet, with a written Acceptable Use Agreement;
- Assigns responsibility to parents, by making them sign an Internet Use statement before their child can access the Internet;
- Informs patrons of printing charges;
- Teaches the entire staff the library's set of rules so they can enforce those rules equitably.

Policies

Printing Fees and Diskettes

Carrollton Public Library   **Carrollton, Texas**

The Carrollton Public Library runs its printing on the 'honor system'. You may make 3 prints free of charge per person per session. After the 3 free pages, we ask that you keep track of the pages you print and voluntarily give the Access Services Staff (at the Circulation Desk) ten cents for each page after three.

Manitouwadge Public Library   Manitouwadge, Ontario Canada

Please ask for staff assistance before printing. Printing costs are clearly posted as they vary. It is thirty cents for text only black and white up to fifty cents per page for colored graphics. If you wish to save your document, you must purchase a diskette from the Circulation Desk for $2. If you wish to update your document in the future, leave this diskette at the library to be retrieved by you at a late date. You may not use or load your own diskette or CD-ROM onto the library computers. Patrons may not bring their own software or blank disks for downloading from library workstations. Blank formatted disks can be purchased at the library.

Pasadena Public Library   Pasadena, Texas

The library can provide fifteen sheets of paper for printing research or academic information from the Internet.

Hobbs Public Library   Hobbs, New Mexico

Charge for printing is 10¢ per page. Black and white printing only is available. All printing will be picked up at the Circulation Desk and paid for at that time. Patrons must pay for all pages printed.

Diskettes are available at the Circulation Desk for a minimal charge or you may bring diskettes from home to download.

Access Priorities

Pasadena Public Library   Pasadena, Texas

Priority on the use of the Internet is given to those using it for academic or research purposes; these users will receive priority access over those using the Internet for entertainment purposes.

Handicapped users will be given priority to spaces designated for handicapped individuals. There shall be appropriate signage indicating which workstations are so designated.

Hobbs Public Library   Hobbs, New Mexico

Access will be determined on a first come, first served basis. Public computers cannot be reserved for specific times.

Library Links

San Antonio Public Library   San Antonio, Texas

The staff of the San Antonio Public Library has developed a variety of Web pages with recommended links in order to facilitate use of the Internet. Users should recognize, however, that the Library is not responsible for changes to the content of linked sites, nor for the content of sources accessed through subsequent links. Staff will provide assistance to Internet users to the extent that time and patron demands allow.

Internet Users Agreement

Marion County Library   **Marion, South Carolina**

Internet Acceptable Use Agreement

Please read the Public Internet Access Policy and this document carefully before signing the Agreement.

This document is given to all users of the Internet at Marion County Libraries. All users must sign it, and if under 15 years of age, must be accompanied by a parent or guardian to be allowed access to the Internet.

The Library retains the right to ask for proof of identification/proof of age.

Providing access to the Internet is in keeping with the Library's mission statement to continually identify, evaluate, and respond to the informational, educational, cultural, and recreational needs of all residents of Marion County. The Internet allows users to connect to vast networks of information, resources, and ideas outside the library. Marion County Library has no control over these resources nor does the Library have complete knowledge of what is on the Internet. Information on the Internet may be reliable and current or it may be inaccurate, out-of-date, or unavailable at times. The Internet and its resources are always changing. Some material on the Internet may contain items that are illegal, inaccurate, defamatory, and potentially offensive and/or disturbing to some people.

Warning! Internet use will be managed in a manner consistent with the Library's Code of Conduct. The following actions will not be allowed: sending or displaying obscene (as defined by S.C. Code 16–15–305) or disruptive messages, files or images; changing or adding files to the network; harassing, insulting, or attacking others; violating copyright laws or software license restrictions.

Staff will take appropriate action as they become aware of violations. Violations of these rules may result in a loss of access as well as appropriate legal action.

User Agreement: As a user of Marion County Library's public access to the Internet, I understand and will abide by the Acceptable Use Agreement. I hereby agree to comply with the above stated rules.

Signature   _____

Date of Birth   _____

Date Phone Number   _____

Print Name   _____

Address   _____

                             _____

Parental Permission Agreement: As the parent or legal guardian of the minor child named below, I have read and agree to the Acceptable Use Agreement. I understand that some material on the Internet may be objectionable, and I accept the responsibility to directly supervise the Internet access of my child under the age of 15.

The undersigned parent or guardian expressly assumes all responsibility for the use of the Internet by his or her child and agrees to hold Marion County Library harmless from any and all liability that may occur from the use.

(Please print all requested information in the area provided below.)

Parent's Name   _____

Address   _____

                       _____

Parent's Signature   _____

Date   _____

Child's Name   _____

Child's Age   _____

Child's Birth date   _____

Child's Address if different _____

James Kennedy Public Library   **Dyersville, Iowa**

I have read the policies concerning the use of the James Kennedy Public Library's Internet computers and agree to abide by the policies. I also understand that failure to observe such rules or failure to observe other library policies may result in the suspension of my use of the library's Internet access computers as follows: First offense—verbal warning; Second offense—loss of computer and library privileges for the day; Third offense—loss of computer privileges with reinstatement of privileges only after safety conference, which will include the Library Director, the patron, and the patron's parent or guardian, if patron is a minor. The "Safety Conference" will cover such material as is needed to correct the problem; Fourth offense—loss of privileges for one year and Safety Conference; Fifth offense—loss of privileges while a minor, or, for adults permanent loss of privileges.

Signature:_____   Date:_____

Name (Please Print):_____

Birthdate:_____

FOR PARENTS OF MINORS: I have read the policies pertaining to the Internet usage and hereby grant my permission for my son/daughter/legal ward to use the Internet access computers in the James Kennedy Public Library. I also understand that the same above rules apply to my ward and that I will be held responsible for any damages incurred by the minor. I am aware that the library will NOT limit my child's access to the Internet.

Parent/Guardian

Signature:_____

Parent/Guardian Name

(Please Print)_____

Date:_____ Signature of Witness:_____

Liability Issues

James Kennedy Public Library   Dyersville, Iowa

Patron, and parent or guardian if patron is a minor, whose signature appears on the Internet Users Agreement agrees to indemnify and hold harmless the James Kennedy Public Library, its agents, employees or any other person against loss or expense including attorneys' fees, by reason of the liability imposed by law upon the James Kennedy Public Library, for damage because of bodily injury, including death at any time resulting there from, sustained by any person or persons, or an account of damage to property arising out of or in consequence of this agreement, whether such injuries to persons or damage to property are due or claim to be due to any passive negligence of the James Kennedy Public Library, its employees or agents or any other person. It is further understood and agreed that the parent or guardian shall (at the sole option of the James Kennedy Public Library) defend the James Kennedy Public Library with appropriate counsel and shall further bear all costs and expenses, including the expense of counsel, in the defense of any suit arising hereunder.

CHECKLIST

- In light of the recent Supreme Court decision on Internet filters, will you add filters?
- If you choose to install filters, will you require parents to sign a responsibility form?
- Will you charge for printouts?
- Determine if you want to exclude certain behavior, such as games and chatrooms.
- What level of assistance will you give patrons—such as basic, full, or none?
- Do you want to teach a formal Internet training class; if so, will you charge patrons to take the class?
- What time limits do you want to place on computer use?

Chapter 4

MISCELLANEOUS PUBLIC POLICIES

OVERVIEW

Some policies do not fit neatly into categories usually associated with library work, such as reference, collection development, or circulation, but are essential to day-to-day operations. Important policies, such as those that govern volunteers and the Friends group, copyright, printing fees, and other patron activities are essential components to managing the library.

This chapter discusses a wide array of policies, including those mentioned above.

More specifically, this chapter covers information on policies and forms in the following areas:

- Tax Forms
- Activities with Fees
- Printing, Copying Fees, and Diskettes
- Faxes
- Microfilm Reader/Printer
- Word Processing
- Surplus Furniture and Equipment
- Petitions and Solicitations
- Photographing and Videotaping
- Public Phones
- Programming

- Volunteers Orientation, Rights, and Responsibilities
- Friends of the Library
- Continuing Education and Professional Organizations
- Copyright
- Friends Application
- Volunteer Applications
- Volunteer Hours Report
- Literacy Tutoring Worksheet
- Program Evaluation
- Tour Request

ADMINISTRATIVE POLICIES

Features of an Effective Policy

Many library operations policies directly impact patrons and the service they receive. Some libraries are forced to recoup printing, copying, and diskette costs, while others absorb all of it, or only a portion. Cost is also a factor in licensing fees for word processing and other software packages. Because public libraries are tax-supported institutions, questions arise over whether people can solicit, sign petitions, photograph or videotape in the library, and the use of library telephones.

Also at issue is the disposal of surplus furniture and equipment. Your local or state government may have laws or procedures for this. Including them in your manual or adding some of these policies will save you many headaches and conflicts with members of the community.

Librarians need to make patrons continually aware of copyright laws, when they download and copy information from electronic databases, the Internet, and all print material.

Volunteers and the Friends group are vital components in a thriving library. They provide needed extra help and fundraising to support all aspects of library services and programs. Volunteers provide clerical work, literacy tutoring, assist with income tax questions, and many other duties. The Friends raise needed money and garner community support for the library's projects and programming.

Programming is a great tool to reach the community and brings citizens into the library. It is an outgrowth of the library's overall mission. This policy serves as a framework and guide when you design programs for different groups in the community.

Internal policies are also important. Every staff member can benefit from additional training. Reference staff need training just to keep up with changing electronic resources, software, and hardware. As the policies demonstrate, training is an essential feature in a progressive thriving library.

- Discusses the distribution of tax forms;
- Gives examples of costs for printing from different libraries;
- Provides guidelines for staff and patron use of the fax machine;
- Discusses the proper use and printing fees for microform readers and printers;
- Addresses the proper use, care, and treatment of word processing software;
- Details procedures for the disposal of surplus equipment and furniture;
- Discusses the use of library telephones by patrons;
- Discusses the rules on photographing and videotaping in the library;
- Recognizes the importance of providing specialized programs;
- Gives specific procedures for conducting programs;
- Supports keeping statistical data to gauge the effectiveness of programs;
- Requires a length of stay time commitment from volunteers;
- Outlines guidelines for volunteers and staff to follow;
- Requires an orientation for volunteers;
- Discusses the role of the Friends of the Library;
- Describes the activities of the Friends of the Library;
- Stresses the importance of formal and informal continuing education for staff;
- Stresses the need to belong to a professional association;
- Advises patrons and staff of copyright laws.

Benefits of an Effective Policy

- Ensures equal application of the rules and procedures;
- Clarifies the rules when a question arises;
- Explains to patrons charges and procedures related to certain activities.

Policies

Tax Forms

Grand Island Public Library   **Grand Island, Nebraska**

The Grand Island Public Library provides a convenient location for distribution of many tax forms and publications. This distribution service does not replace the services of the Internal Revenue Service, however. There may be times that the tax form distribution services of the library are not sufficient to meet the public's need for certain forms or publications. Information about how to request items from the Internal Revenue Service and other distribution locations, including the State Department of Revenue office, will be made available to the public. In addition, Library staff members are not authorized to issue tax advice.

Activities with Fees

Printing, Copying Fees, and Diskettes

Hobbs Public Library   **Hobbs New Mexico**

- Charge for printing is 10¢ per page.
- Black and white printing only is available.
- All printing will be picked up at the Circulation Desk and paid for at that time.
- Patrons must pay for all pages printed.
- Diskettes are available at the Circulation Desk for a minimal charge or you may bring diskettes from home to download.

Fax

Westerville Public Library   **Westerville, Ohio**

Westerville Public Library will use FAX for Interlibrary loans, for monograph or journal articles to local and out-of-state libraries. The library will comply with copyright law and ALA Interlibrary loan procedures. Transmittals are not limited in length. Patrons are charged 10 per page excluding the cover letter.

The FAX machine may also be used by Administration and staff. There is no fee to administration or staff. However, staff members will be charged for long distance telephone calls when the transmittal is for personal use. The Business Manager will notify the staff member of the exact cost of the call after the library receives its monthly telephone bill. Staff members must complete the long-distance phone call slip and turn it into the Business Manager. Mark "FAX" clearly on the slip.

Jasper County Public Library   **Rensselaer, Indiana**

The FAX machine will be used by staff when they need to communicate quickly with each other. It will also be used when a patron from one branch needs information available at another branch and does not wish to wait for it to be sent by transport.

Library Materials Faxed Between Libraries for Patrons:

> There will be no charge for the first five pages of library materials faxed for a patron. If more than five pages are needed, the charge is 20 cents per page for the additional pages.

Patron Requests to Use Fax Service:

> Library materials faxed to patrons' homes or businesses

> JCPL patrons in good standing will be charged 30 cents per page to receive library materials by FAX. No flat fee will be charged.

> Non-Library materials faxed at patron request

> The Library does not fax non-library materials for patrons.

> Staff and Board members will be charged 20 cents per page for personal use of the FAX machine.

Microfilm Reader/Printer

Jasper County Public Library   **Rensselaer, Indiana**

Only persons in 6th grade or older may use the reader/printers. Younger persons must have assistance with the usage of the machine. If a parent or staff member is not available to assist, patrons not yet in 6th grade will not be permitted to use the machine. Loss or damage to the reader/printer or to microforms due to abusive handling will be paid for by the user.

Print copies are 30 cents per page.

Availability of the reader/printer is first come, first served, with a two hour limit. If no one is waiting, patron may continue use.

Library staff have the right to restrict usage for those people who cannot abide by the regulations of the library and the specific rules for use of the reader/printer.

Word Processing

Richland Public Library   **Richland, Washington**

In order to effectively meet the personal computer needs of library patrons, this policy has been established by the Richland public Library Board to govern the use of the on-site word processing personal computers.

1. All users must sign in to use the word processing computers.

2. The user must read and sign the Library's Word Processing Computer Use Agreement (see page two of this policy.) The endorsement shall be attached to the library patron's record.

3. A fee of $.05 per page will be charged for all pages printed. The patron must report to the Circulation Desk upon completion of use to pay charges. Failure to do so shall result in a charge being assessed to the patron's account.

4. Word processing computers will be available on a first come first served basis. Computer time cannot be reserved. Word processing computers may be used a maximum of three hours per day on any one day. Patrons will not be able to connect their own equipment, such as lap top computers, to library equipment.

5. Patrons using the word processing computers are responsible for complying with all copyright laws. Patrons violating this rule will lose their word processing computer use privileges. Illegal acts involving library computing resources may also be subject to prosecution by local, state, or federal authorities.

6. Patrons are responsible for proper use, care, and treatment of the word processing computers and software. Repair/replacement charges will be assessed to the user for any damage caused by careless or malicious misuse based on current City of Richland, Information Services, rates.

7. Any difficulties with the word processing computers must be reported immediately to the Reference Desk.

8. Users must be familiar with, and be able to use on their own, the programs available on the Library's word processing computers.

9. Users are expressly forbidden to copy Library owned commercial software.

10. Children under the age of 10 must have parent or guardian supervision.

Surplus Furniture and Equipment

Worthington Public Library   **Worthington, Ohio**

It is the policy of Worthington Public Library to dispose of library materials, furniture and equipment that is no longer functional or useful. The Clerk-Treasurer shall be responsible for the sale or disposal of all library furniture and equipment that is no longer of any use to the Library. Department Managers will be responsible for reporting to the Clerk-Treasurer any items needing to be disposed of and for filling out the appropriate forms. When an item no longer has value to the Library, it will be removed from inventory and disposed of:

6. Books and other materials, no longer deemed appropriate for the collection, will be donated to the Friends of Worthington Libraries for disposal through their regular book sales.

7. Computer equipment, no longer of use to the Library, may be donated directly to a local school district for use in their educational programs. Computer equipment

may be sold to a technology recycling company if local school districts do not accept donations.*

8. Furniture, no longer of use to the library, the value of which is less than $300.00, may be donated by the library to a non-profit, charitable organization.

9. Items not covered by the above will be sold through auction or publicly advertised sale with any proceeds from such sale being deposited to the General Fund of the Library. Prior to such sale, the Clerk-Treasurer will prepare a list of those items to be included in the sale for approval by the Board of Trustees.*

10. If an item is determined by the Clerk-Treasurer to have marginal or no resale value, or it does not sell through auction or publicly advertised sale, it may be sold or discarded in the best interest of the Library.

11. The Clerk-Treasurer is authorized to accept trade-in allowances on any item of equipment being replaced or upgraded for which a trade-in allowance is offered.

In an instance where an item of surplus inventory is determined by the Director or Clerk-Treasurer to have unusual, historic or artistic value such items may be referred to the Board for determination of value which determination may include the services of a professional appraiser or outside expert opinion.

Petitions and Solicitations

Public Library of Cincinnati and Hamilton County   **Cincinnati, Ohio**

Solicitation of the public or the staff is not permitted on Public Library property or property under the control of the Public Library by the public or members of the Library staff. By soliciting is meant the sale or distribution of merchandise, sales materials, tickets, insurance, coupons, magazine subscriptions, political campaign material, or anything not connected with the work of the Library.

The only exceptions to the non-solicitation policy are the following:

12. those authorized and directed by the Library Administration including the annual United Way Campaign and the Fine Arts Fund Campaign, which benefit the entire community,

13. those for fundraising projects conducted by the Friends of the Public Library or the Anderson Library Committee, and

14. those solicitation and fundraising projects sponsored by the Library Staff Association with the approval of the Library Director (i.e., walk-a-thon teams, food drives, etc.)

*The Department Manager and Library Manager who declare an item to be surplus, the Director, Clerk-Treasurer, Associate Directors, Finance staff, members of the Board of Trustees and immediate family members of the above, are not permitted to purchase that item(s).

Middleton Public Library   **Middleton, Wisconsin**

Canvassing—for example, soliciting signatures for a petition, nomination papers, and the like—is not allowed on library property.

Photographing and Videotaping in the Library

Public Library of Cincinnati and Hamilton County   **Cincinnati, Ohio**

Photography or videography is generally permitted if it is for general Public Library promotion by the media, student projects, and/or strictly for personal use.

In order to protect the rights of individual Library patrons and to reduce distractions, photographing and videotaping on Library property are restricted as follows:

- Under no circumstances may the public, members of the media, or Library staff take photographs or videotape without the express permission of any Library patrons who would be prominently included within the composition.

Requests to photograph or videotape for commercial purposes are not permitted without approval by the Library Director. Requests for permission to photograph or videotape for commercial purposes must be submitted in writing for review by the Library Director.

Public Use of Telephones

Cumberland County Library and Info Center   **Fayetteville, North Carolina**

Library telephones shall be used by library patrons in emergency situations only. Emergency calls shall be limited to no more than three minutes.

Programming

Sno-Isle Regional Library System   **Marysville, Washington**

Each library, regardless of size, should offer programs that support people in their home lives, their learning, and their leisure activities. In planning programs, the library should consider:

1. The library's Long-Range-Plan

2. Regional needs

3. Purpose of the program

4. Quality of the presentation

5. Appropriateness of content to the audience

6. Other programs available in the community.

Attendance statistics, and evaluations are kept to determine the impact of the program on the audience, to help in preparing budgets, and to aid in future planning. Parades, festivals, fairs and other mass-audience events may have an estimated audience in the Monthly Statistical Report, but that estimate is not carried over to the official summary.

A consistent effort is made to represent diverse cultures in programming rather than replicating local holiday observances such as Christmas. Sign language interpreters are available.

Quality programs form an integral part of library service. Therefore, Sno-Isle will provide staff, materials, and training to maintain quality programming.

In addition to program time for the presenter, there may be other staff requirements. Programs with anticipated large attendance may require additional staff or volunteer help to assist with the program. It is important that ample staff be available to provide assistance to library audiences before, during, and after the program.

Tours are given at the request of a group or individual. Tours may be considered a program if there is preparation of materials and information involved.

BABY/TODDLER programs may be presented as a series of 4–6 week sessions for the public or individually at the request of a community group.

PRESCHOOL STORYTIME most often consists of 4–6 week series in Fall, Winter, and Spring plus monthly storytimes in Summer for the public or individually at the request of a community group.

Elementary Programs may be scheduled more frequently in Summer and during other school vacations. These guidelines include programs presented to the public, to groups, and to schools. The programs may take place in the library or in the community.

ELEMENTARY SCHOOL PROGRAMS include those programs presented in conjunction with a public or private school.

TEEN PROGRAMS include both programs scheduled for the public and those presented in conjunction with schools. Again the programs may take place in the library or in the community.

ADULT PROGRAMS include both programs scheduled for the public and those presented in conjunction with other community organizations. These programs may take place in the library or elsewhere in the community.

MOBILE SERVICES provides programming through their Childcare service. Programs are presented to preschoolers in the childcare facilities served.

SERVICE CENTER staff may provide programming on request. Children' Services office personnel staff community booths, speak to community groups, and substitute for library staff at scheduled programs. Adult and Teen Services staff are available to speak to community groups, assist with library programs, or substitute for library staff at scheduled programs.

Volunteers—Orientation, Rights, and Responsibilities

Middletown Public Library   **Middletown, Ohio**

The Middletown Public Library Volunteer Program is designed to expand and enhance public service to the community. Volunteers generally provide support services to paid staff and/or work on special projects. Volunteers learn more about the library and its place in the community and observe first hand the way the library serves the community's needs.

1. Volunteers are required to make a commitment of at least 6 months.

2. Volunteers are required to wear identification badges when working in the library and to return them to the coordinator when you resign.

3. Volunteer performance will be evaluated by the volunteer coordinator once a year.

4. If you are going to be absent from your assignment, need to change your work schedule, or if you are going to take a vacation, please advise your volunteer coordinator as soon as possible.

5. If you are going to leave your volunteer position, please notify your volunteer coordinator as soon as possible, so that a replacement can be sought.

6. Please bring any concern, problem or suggestion to your volunteer coordinator. Ask him/her for any information you need to do your job more effectively.

7. If, for any reason, you are not happy with your volunteer assignment, please talk it over with your volunteer coordinator. If you want to consider a change in your assignment, please talk it over with your volunteer coordinator.

8. An important requirement of your volunteer position is the Volunteer Quarterly Report form. Please keep an accurate record of the hours you work, record them on the form and give it to your volunteer coordinator by the last working day of the quarter.

9. Expenses directly related to volunteer service are generally deductible from state and federal income taxes. Therefore volunteers may wish to keep an on-going record of transportation, parking and other relevant expenses. (For more specific information see IRS Publication 526, Charitable Contributions.)

10. The volunteer coordinator will ask you for an evaluation of the volunteer program periodically and also when you leave. Your comments are welcome at other times as well.

11. Volunteers are expected to operate within the stated policies and procedures of the M.P.L.

12. Volunteers are expected to have a good knowledge of the goals and purpose of

Pend Oreille County Library District   Newport, Washington

The Library District welcomes members of the community serving as volunteers in any of the community libraries in Pend Oreille County. The services volunteers perform are valued and valuable.

Volunteering is a serious business. To the public, a volunteer is part of the Library's staff and represents the Library. The Library makes an investment in the training and experiences of the volunteer so that the services offered meet the needs of the public.

Volunteers are viewed as the most valuable resource of this agency, its staff, and its clients. Volunteers have the right to be given meaningful assignments, the right to be treated as equal co-workers, and the right to effective supervision. Volunteers have the right to full involvement and participation, and the right to recognition for work done. In return, volunteers shall agree to perform their duties to the best of their abilities. They will remain loyal to the goals of the agency and operate according to its policies and procedures.

The following guidelines have been established to provide consistent information to volunteers in all community libraries and to assure that volunteers fully understand the commitment they are making:

1. A volunteer represents the Library District to the community while actively serving as a volunteer.

2. A volunteer is expected to follow approved policies and procedures of the Library District during the time of volunteering within library buildings and at library events elsewhere;

3. A volunteer is oriented, trained, supervised, and evaluated on a continual basis concerning those policies and procedures necessary for the activities carried out;

4. Of special importance in carrying out volunteer activities is observance of the Library Bill of Rights, adopted by the Library District Board of Trustees. Under the Library Bill of Rights, the Library District must protect the confidentiality of each library user, and assure equal access and the freedom to read and inquire of each user regardless of age, religion, race, nation of origin, background and views;

In carrying out the requirements of the Library Bill of Rights, volunteers actively working in a community library may not express their religious, political, social or other personal views to members of the public. They must protect the confidentiality of each library user. Violation of these special trusts, policies, or procedures is reason to discontinue the volunteer services.

5. In light of the time and expense involved in training and supervising volunteers, the Library may decide to discontinue or change a volunteer's service assignment, which it determines is not beneficial;

6. Volunteer fill out an information form, which is used by the Library to assure that the volunteers are involved in activities appropriate to their skills, experience, and interests;

7. The Library will pay labor and industry costs according to Washington State Law as pertains to volunteers—RCW 51.12.035.

Labor and Industry requires a monthly time sheet be turned in to the branch manager where volunteering.

ORIENTATION FOR VOLUNTEERS

1. Introduction of person doing orientation and introduce volunteers.

2. Review volunteer policy, Library Bill of Rights, and confidentiality.

3. Discuss specific job description and parameters of that job.

4. Pass out time sheets for volunteers, review time sheet and indicate where and to whom it is to be turned in.

5. Inform volunteers of dress code.

6. Inform volunteers about breaks.

7. Discuss with volunteers the seriousness about the Library Bill of Rights, confidentiality, and policies and procedures and what constitutes dismissal.

Example of dismissal:

7a. Giving out a patron's address or phone number to another person.

7b. Not letting a person check out a book of their choice (it does not matter what the volunteer thinks about the book).

7c. Discussing with anyone what someone else has checked out.

7d. Violating Library policies.

8. Hand out volunteer badge.

9. Be sure volunteer has filled out Volunteer Information Form, has been given Library Bill of Rights, has been given the procedures for the job they are to do.

RIGHTS AND RESPONSIBILITIES OF STAFF WORKING WITH VOLUNTEERS

RESPONSIBILITIES

1. To provide an accurate job description.

2. To prepare professional staff.

3. To prepare all participants—through an orientation.

4. To offer a well-planned program of training and supervision.

5. To be ready to place the volunteer.

6. To treat volunteers as co-workers with acceptance and trust.

7. To avoid confusing jargon.

8. To give the volunteer a significant task.

9. To continue to inform the volunteer.

10. To give the volunteer proper recognition.

11. To evaluate with the volunteer.

12. To provide opportunities for the volunteer's personal growth.

13. Annual all-county appreciation day.

Friends of the Library

Fulton County Public Library   **Fulton, Indiana**

Friends of the Library is a group of people who have joined together to form a Non-Profit support organization for the Fulton County Public Library.

Purposes:

1. To improve the services & resources of the libraries;

2. To promote citizen involvement in library activities;

3. Services: funding for library programs, helpers for various Children's & Adult programs, provision of refreshments for said programs, fundraising, bringing in authors, etc.

4. To act as an advisory group to the library administration.

The aim of the Friends of the Library is to allow our libraries the opportunity to offer programs and services that could otherwise not be attempted.

Who can be a Friend? Anyone with a desire to see the Fulton County Public Library thrive and grow; who has a willingness to be a part of that growth.

How does one join? Attend a meeting or send in an application. To find out when the next meeting will be held, call the Rochester Library, or watch the Rochester Sentinel. Meetings are always posted in advance, and are always open to the public.

Cost? The annual cost for membership in the Friends is minimal. Currently dues are collected annually. Anyone who feels they cannot join due to financial restraints should let the President know. We do not want anyone to feel they cannot join due to finances. We gladly accept physical presence and help over money! Gifts and donations made to the Friends of the Library are deductible to the extent allowable by law to a 501 (c)(3) organization.

Friends of the Library—Annual Membership Application

You can follow the above link and print the page, fill out application and mail to address at bottom of page.

Programs:

Summer Reading Club—Each year the Friends group helps

Children's Dept. with the Summer Reading Program through acting as volunteer helpers during activities; funding programs; and hiring authors to visit the libraries. Opportunities to work with children, books, crafts, games, etc., abound during this time.

Jail Program—The Friends help the library bring books and magazines to inmates at the Fulton County Jail. This collection stays at the jail.

Hospital Program—They provide used magazines & books to the waiting rooms & patients of Woodlawn Hospital. These materials may be taken home by those readers.

Literacy Coalition—The Friends help fund programs & support this library service which offers free reading help to county citizens.

Christmas Open House—In December, the Friends host an evening of fun where library patrons can come in to visit, hear a concert by local musicians, see a puppet show; let the children tell Santa their wishes, and have light refreshments. The Friends plan this event, and provide helpers, refreshments, Santa's stipend, and entertainment.

Puppet Shows and Author visits—The Friends provide financial help, refreshments, and helpers.

County Fair Booth—The Friends staff the Library's County Fair Booth in the Commercial Building and provide giveaway items for the nightly drawings held at the booth.

Copier Supplies—are paid for by the Friends

Book Sale—Each year the Friends gather together discarded books & other items from the Library, add gift donations from the public, and hold a Book Sale, the profits of which go toward funding more programs for the library.

Continuing Education and Professional Organizations

Pend Oreille County Library District   **Newport, Washington**

If funding is available, paid library employees who work _ time or more may apply for a continuing education tuition grant from the district to cover tuition for all classes required for a library degree, or any other library related, credit bearing classes.

The Library District will budget a minimum of $2500 per year for tuition for such courses. Classes may be taken at any accredited college, university or trade school. This budget item will not include conferences or workshops, which do not carry credit, as this is covered under another budget line item.

Books, supplies, food, and lodging will be the responsibility of the student. Transportation may be paid if several staff members are involved in the same class, at the discretion of the Board.

Application for a tuition grant must be made at least 30 days prior to enrollment. More advanced notice will improve the chance of Board approval, especially if funds are low.

In special cases where there is not sufficient time for Board approval, the Director may approve a tuition grant, to be confirmed by the Board at the next regular monthly Board meeting.

New London Public Library   **New London, Wisconsin**

The Board of Trustees recognizes that a well-trained and educated staff is essential to the provision of quality library service.

Workshops, Meetings:

1. Employees may be allowed to be absent from duty for the purpose of attending seminars and workshops, professional and business meetings, or visiting other libraries and museums. The Directors shall authorize attendance in accordance with scheduling needs and budget.

2. Budget funds permitting, the directors may authorize actual travel expenses at a mileage rate to conform to the City of New London's mileage allowances and including reasonable expenses for meals, lodging, and other necessary expenses.

3. Employees and Trustees are encouraged to apply for scholarship money for workshops (if available) for expenses incurred.

4. First preference for workshop or professional meeting attendance will be given to the personnel who must maintain their minimum professional certification.

Educational Development:

1. Staff members shall be encouraged to take appropriate college courses, vocational courses, or workshops to improve their competencies in library or museum work.

2. Whenever possible, the Directors shall authorize changes in work schedules, providing that time is "made up" and that normal library or museum services are not disrupted.

3. The Library and Museum budget shall include an amount, to be determined by the Board, to defray tuition and fee expenses for employees.

4. Employees should request permission as far in advance as possible, and date of application may be considered in the decision to grant the request. Application should include a description of coursework, schedules, a list of fees, and a statement concerning the benefit to the library or museum. Primary consideration will be given by the Board to those applications which offers a direct benefit to the Library or Museum.

5. Grants will be given only to employees with at least one year of service. The employee shall agree to return any tuition grant to the Library or Museum if he/she leaves employment within one year after course completion.

6. The board will approve applications for any request more than $75 cost to the Library or Museum. Approval is discretionary and the Board will not be obligated to expend all budgeted funds.

7. The Board may request an employee to enroll for outside coursework, in which case the Library or Museum will pay all legitimate expenses and allow paid time off to attend classes.

Professional Associations:

1. The Library recognizes the value of library professional associations and encourages employees to participate in them, especially the Wisconsin Library Association and the American Library Association. Attendance at their conferences is to be encouraged. Within reason and subject of the scheduling needs of the library, the Director may permit attendance on library time. "Time off" will be limited to the number of work hours missed, not the number of hours in attendance.

2. Volunteer work as an officer or committee member on behalf of a professional association is encouraged, but is secondary to the employee's responsibilities to this library. Employees nominated or appointed to positions, which would require significant time away from the library, should discuss the matter with the Director (or Board of Trustees) in advance.

3. The library will further support membership by paying for basic dues in The Wisconsin OR American Library Association.

4. Expenses for attendance at professional conventions and/or conference may be reimbursed partially within budgetary limitations. Employees will be asked to seek further assistance in the form of scholarship money.

Copyright

Hurt/Battelle Memorial Library of West Jefferson　　　　　**West Jefferson, Ohio**

Under the 1976 Copyright Act, Libraries may provide limited copying services for their patrons. The following guidelines must be followed for the Library to comply:

- The copied material must display the following information: "NOTICE": This material may be protected by copyright law. (Title 17 U.S. Code)

- The material must become the property of the patron, and the Library must have no notice that the material will be used for anything but "private study, scholarship, or research."

- Materials may not be copied in large quantities nor should it substitute for subscription to or purchase of materials.

Tuscarawas County Public Library　　　　　**New Philadelphia, Ohio**

It is the intent of the Tuscarawas County Public Library to comply with Title 17 of the United States Code, titled "Copyrights," and other federal legislation related to the duplication, retention and use of copyrighted materials. A notice of copyright will be prominently placed on the library's photocopiers. Library staff will refuse to duplicate any materials if doing so would violate copyright. Library patrons copying any materials on library machines are solely and fully responsible for using the materials in compliance with relevant copyright law.

Audiovisual materials for which the library has purchased public performance rights are so labeled. Items without public performance rights are for personal and home use only.

Library staff will follow copyright law in selecting and using materials for public performance. Original or copyright-free art will be used to produce library publicity items or for creating displays and decorations

Pikes Peak Library District   **Colorado Springs, Colorado**

Librarians have an ethical responsibility to keep abreast of copyright and fair use rights. This responsibility applies to:

- The library's own online publications,

- Contractual obligations with authors and publishers,

- Informing library users of copyright laws which apply to their use of electronic information.

FORMS

Benefits of Written Forms

- Create continuity;
- Ensure equal application of the rules and procedures;
- Show, in writing, to patrons the need to comply with all copyright laws;
- Create a more professional atmosphere, by giving volunteers written procedures and responsibilities.

Name:

Address: _____

City _____

State: _____

Zip Code: _____

Telephone: _____

I wish to join the Friends at this rate:

_____Basic $10.00

_____Sustaining $25.00

_____Benefactor $100.00

_____Life Member $250.00

_____Business $500.00

_____Additional amount_____

New Member:_____   Renewal Membership:_____

Friends can help in many ways: fundraising, tutoring, clerical, events

Which activities would you like more information about?

Figure 4.1 Friends of the Library Application

Name: _____

Address: _____

City: _____

State:_____ Zip Code:_____

Telephone:_____E-Mail:_____

Emergency Contact:_____

Highest Education Level:

1–8 grade:_____ 9–12_____ HS Diploma:_____ College:_____

Special Skills/Interests:

Volunteer Placement Information:

Please check all the programs you would like to join:

Clerical:_____ Outreach:_____ Computer Tutor:_____ Homework Helper:_____
Literacy Volunteer:_____ Programs:_____ Book Sale: _____

What days would you be available:

Monday:_____ Tuesday:_____ Wednesday:_____ Thursday:_____

Friday:_____ Saturday:_____

Have you ever been convicted of a crime?: Yes_____ No:_____

I authorize the library to conduct a background check: All statements made are true.

Signature:_____ Social Security Number:_____

Figure 4.2 Volunteer Application

Pend Oreille County Library District
VOLUNTEER INFORMATION FORM

1.Date: _____

2.Name: _____

(Last)(First)(Middle)

3.Current address: _____

4.City:_____ 5. State_____ 6. Zip_____

7.Home/message phone: _____8.Do you have a current driver's license and use of an automobile?

Yes_____ No_____

9.Have you been convicted, or have you served time in a correctional institution within the past seven (7) years, for any crime, which might have some bearing on your fitness to serve as a library volunteer?

Yes_____ No _____ if yes give details on a separate sheet.

10.List the days and hours you are available for volunteering.

11.Indicate the kinds of activities or tasks you think you might be able to do or would like to learn to do in the library:

_____

_____

12.Previous volunteer/work experience, education, special training and/or hobbies:

_____

_____

13.I certify that all statements above and attached to this Information Form are true and complete to the best of my knowledge. I understand that false statements shall be sufficient cause for my volunteer activities to be discontinued by the Library.

I have read and understand the Volunteer Policy of Pend Oreille County Library District as well as the Library Bill of Rights.

Signature of volunteer _____

Date_____

Figure 4.3 Volunteer Application

Volunteer Report

Date:_____

Number of new volunteers:_____

Number of volunteers who left:_____

Total number of hours:_____

Duties performed:_____

Figure 4.4 Volunteer Hours Report

Literacy Volunteers Worksheet

Name of Pair Tutor/Student BR/ESL:

	Week 1	Week 2	Week 3	Week 4

Comments: (How is Student Progressing)

Figure 4.5 Literacy Tutoring Worksheet

Program Evaluation
Dallas Public Library   **Dallas, Texas**

EVALUATION FORM

1. Overall Rating

Excellent Good Fair Needs Work Poor

     5   4   3   2   1

2. Presentation

    a. Informative and helpful   5 4 3 2 1

    b. Clear and understandable   5 4 3 2 1

    c. Well paced   5 4 3 2 1

3. Content

    a. Usefulness to my situation 5 4 3 2 1

    b. Ease of understanding   5 4 3 2 1

4. Please expand on any of the above ratings:

5. What was the best part of the Workshop?

6. What part would you change or improve?

Thanks for your participation and feedback!

Figure 4.6 Program Evaluation

I am interested in scheduling a

Library program or tour for my

Group or Organization

Name:_____

Organization:_____

Address: _____

           _____

Telephone:_____

If you have special needs, please contact us at (222) 555-5555

What type of program would you like the library to have?

What type of tour would your group like?

Figure 4.7 Tour Request

CHECKLIST

- Determine if you want to charge printing fees.
- Include continuing education for you and your staff.
- Do you want to offer word processing capabilities?
- Check with the city/county attorney for laws pertaining to disposing of library furniture and equipment.
- How do you want to record volunteer hours and work?
- Will attendees receive an evaluation form at every program, or only for certain programs?
- Do you want to make exceptions to printing fees for economically disadvantaged patrons?
- If you do not allow patrons to use staff phones, will you make exceptions, such as a child calling a parent to pick them up from the library?

Part II: Administrative Forms and Policies

Chapter 5

MISSION STATEMENTS

OVERVIEW

The goal of the Mission Statement is to convey:

- Where the library fits within the community;
- Why the library is vital to the life of the community;
- How the library will meet community needs;
- Who the library will serve;
- What the library's objectives/goals/purposes are;
- How the library will meet those objectives/goals;
- What strategy the library will use;
- What services the library offers.

The mission statement is possibly the hardest policy for a library to write. In a few short paragraphs you must state your reasons for existing, your place in the local community, your place in society, and your place in the fabric of learning. You can accomplish this in one or many paragraphs, but the message must always be powerful. It is the foundation for everything the library does. It covers all aspects, from the scope and depth of the collection to the services you offer. Are you an information center that emphasizes electronic resources? Are you a resource center for local genealogists? Do you support more instructional and educational material or do you turn toward more leisure, popular, and recreational material? Many policies in this book include phrases such as, "this supports the library's objectives," or "in keeping with the library's mission." Each policy traces its origins back to the mission statement, whether it is general and philosophical or detailed and concrete; below are several examples. The wording and tone are intentionally similar. They are all excellent representations of what a library does for its community. Not all of the libraries offer the same services. For your own mission statement, pick those sentences, services, phrases, or complete policies that meet your individualized needs or even combine phrases to individualize it further. The Mission Statement is the shortest and most fundamental policy in the book, but also the most difficult to write. The examples will give you the information you need to craft just the right policy for your library. There are more samples on the CD-ROM for your convenience. Some of the samples are much shorter than represented here. The statement does not have to be long to be good. Short policies can be very effective and descriptive. Choose what best expresses your purpose and overall philosophy.

ADMINISTRATIVE POLICIES

Features of an Effective Policy

- Identifies community needs;
- Emphasizes types of material, such as genealogical, recreational, instructional, or electronic resources that are available;
- Defines the scope of the collection, such as research level, limited coverage, or general coverage;
- Sets goals, then defines strategies to reach the goals;
- Defines a community need and states how the library will meet that need.

Benefits of an Effective Policy

- Communicates your commitment to the community;
- Acts as an excellent public relations document;
- Highlights services and programs;
- Underscores your community involvement;
- Serves as a common document to be used in discussions;
- Justifies budget requests to reach stated goals, needs, and objectives identified by the community assessment.

Policies

Marshall Public Library   **Pocatello, Idaho**

The Marshall Public Library provides recreational reading and information about popular cultural and social trends; general information and answers to questions, supplementary curriculum support for K-12 students; support for personal growth and development through lifelong learning; and training and instruction in finding, evaluating, and using information effectively.

Service Response: Current Topics and Titles

A library that provides Current Topics and Titles helps to fulfill community residents' appetite for information about popular cultural and social trends, and their desire for satisfying recreational experiences.

Service Response: Formal Learning Support

A library that offers Formal Learning Support helps students who are enrolled in a formal program of education or who are pursuing their education through a program of home schooling to attain their educational goals. The Library concentrates on providing materials that supplement rather than duplicate the resources available in institutions of formal learning.

Service Response: General Information

A library that offers General Information helps meet the need for information and answers to questions on a broad array of topics related to work, school, and personal life.

Service Response: Information Literacy

A library that provides Information Literacy service helps address the need for skills related to finding, evaluating, and using information effectively.

Service Response: Lifelong Learning

A library that provides Lifelong Learning service helps address the desire for self-directed personal growth and development opportunities, and to help satisfy the desire of community residents to gain an understanding of their own cultural heritage and the cultural heritage of others through the exploration of literature, history, arts, and poetry.

Pikes Peak Library District   **Colorado Springs, Colorado**

The Pikes Peak Library District provides resources and service to inform, empower, inspire and encourage respect for individuals and ideas.

The five service responses selected are:

- Current topics and titles—The library offers current, high-demand, high-interest materials in a wide variety of formats.

- General information—The library provides information and answers to questions on a broad array of topics related to school, work and personal life.

- Lifelong learning—The library provides a collection of circulating materials on a wide variety of topics in which the general public has a sustained interest to address the desire for self-directed personal growth and development opportunities.

- Local History and Genealogy—The library provides a significant collection of materials and other resources that chronicles the history of the Pikes Peak Region and provides genealogy research tools.

- Cultural awareness—The library provides materials and resources to help residents to gain an understanding of their own cultural heritage and the cultural heritage of others.

Newark Public Library   **Newark, New Jersey**

Purpose Statement

The purpose of The Newark Public Library is to empower Newark residents, students and workers to enrich their own lives with knowledge, information, education and culture.

Mission Statement

The mission of The Newark Public Library is to provide for the people of Newark an easily available local collection of and global access to the universal record of human thought, wisdom, ideals, information, experiences, and artistic expressions.

The Library provides information useful for daily living, supports formal education and independent learning efforts and assists researchers and scholars.

Deriving its principal support from the City of Newark, the Library emphasizes services for Newark's residents and students. Affirming its belief in the power of education and in the potential of libraries to change lives, the Library strongly supports the children of Newark in their efforts to learn and grow and achieve.

As a major library resource for New Jersey, the Library strives also to serve those who work in the City, and libraries and people throughout the state.

In support of this mission, the Library: selects, collects, organizes and makes available for use a broad, deep and diverse collection of materials in a variety of formats; provides excellent personal information services and guidance in the use of library resources; and offers programs for personal enrichment.

In pursing this mission the Library strives to fulfill its unique responsibility to ensure free, open and equal access to information for all the people that the Library serves.

The Library actively seeks to serve and reflect the diverse Newark community in its collections, services, programs and staff. It affirms a commitment to preserve, promote and celebrate the multicultural heritage of the people of Newark.

The Newark Public Library contributes to the economic life of the City, the vitality of its neighborhoods and the quality of life of its citizens.

Morton Grove Public Library   Morton Grove, Illinois

Library Mission Statement

The Morton Grove Public Library's Mission Statement guides the selection of materials as it does the development of services and the allocation of resources. This statement articulates broad principles for library programs and services.

The mission of the Morton Grove Public Library is to serve informational, educational and recreational needs of the Morton Grove community through acquiring and maintaining quality materials, programs and services within comfortable facilities, with emphasis on information which is of immediate relevance and interest; and in a manner commensurate with responsible fiscal planning.

The Library's mission extends to providing access to the universe of information beyond the Library's own collections through interlibrary cooperation and efficient use of technology.

Mission of the Morton Grove Public Library

Morton Grove residents will have access to innovative library services, delivered in an efficient, effective, and professional manner within comfortable facilities and with responsible fiscal planning. These services will:

- Provide the materials, programs, and services needed to meet their recreational needs;

- Provide the information services needed to answer their personal and work-related questions

- Enable them to develop their ability to find and use information in a variety of formats

- Assist them to continue growing and learning throughout their lives.

Library Service Responses to the Community

With the Village of Morton Grove's Vision Statement as a starting point, the Community Planning Committee, made up of members representing the residents of Morton Grove, established four service priorities for library services, which they felt will best meet the needs of the community:

- Current Topics and Titles

  Adults in Morton Grove will have available materials and services to meet the residents' desire for information on current, high-interest topics and to provide satisfying recreational experiences; these materials and services will reflect an openness and awareness of the cultural diversity of the community.

  Children and teens in Morton Grove will have high-interest materials and services to stimulate their imaginations and to encourage them to read for pleasure; these materials and services will reflect an openness and awareness of the cultural diversity of the community.

- General Information

  All residents of Morton Grove will be able to get answers to their personal and work-related questions.

- Informational Literacy

  All residents of Morton Grove will have the skills they need to find, evaluate, and use information in a variety of formats.

- Lifelong Learning

  Residents of Morton Grove will have materials, programs, and services to support their personal growth and self-education; these materials, programs, and services will reflect an openness and awareness of the cultural diversity of the community.

Dayton and Montgomery County Public Library   **Dayton, Ohio**

The Mission of the Dayton Metro Library is to respond to the interests and needs of its community by providing recorded information and thought.

Goals

- Continue as the most comprehensive source of information for the community.

- Strengthen and provide community resources through cooperation with other libraries and community agencies.

- Ensure that the library is user oriented and meets the needs of all who require special assistance.

- Actively promote our programs, materials, services and role in fostering free communication within our democratic society.

- Structure our organization and manage our operations effectively.

- Preserve our rare and valuable materials for continuing use.

- Provide special programs to encourage use of the library.

- Provide training and development opportunities to library staff for occupational and professional growth.

- Provide a collection of materials and technological tools that accesses information that meets the interests and needs of the community and represents various points of view on controversial subjects.

- Develop sources of funding to supplement the Library and Local Government Support Fund.

- Monitor and respond to trends and developments in library practices.

- Provide assistance and training to the public through knowledgeable and customer oriented Staff.

Strategies

- Continue the Total Quality Management philosophy and attitude throughout the library.

- Employ appropriate technologies.

- Emphasize staff development and training.

- Increase the awareness of the library's role and its importance to its community.

- Provide physical facilities to meet the challenges of the 21st century.

- Develop and maintain sources of supplemental funding.

- Assist and train our customers in the use of new technology available at the library.

- Strengthen governmental relations.

Laramie County Library System   **Cheyenne, Wyoming**

The Laramie County Library System's mission is to serve all people in their quest for life-long learning and adventure.

Our commitment is to:

- Provide free and easy access to the printed word, information and cultural enhancement;

- Promote reading and literacy for children and adults;

- Offer a dynamic, current, pertinent and uncensored collection of materials in a variety of formats;

- Maintain high quality customer service through well-trained professional librarians, managers, staff and volunteers;

- Strengthen the library by developing, maintaining and sharing resources in a responsible manner;

- Be a focal point for access to information, self-improvement, social interaction, cultural exposure and leisure;

- Remain committed to continually utilizing and providing state of the art technology;

- Provide appropriate facilities to meet the needs of all people of Laramie County;

- Promote the services of the library.

CHECKLIST

- What are the characteristics of your community, such as is a tourist economy, a rural area with farming and ranching, or an urban area with a culturally diverse population?

- Determine what services and type of collection emphasis will best meet the area's unique needs, such as after school programs or a broad, deep, and diverse collection.

- Use active verbs in the statement, such as inform, empower, inspire, enrich.

- What type of information are you going to provide, such as high-interest, high demand, genealogical materials, or offer global access through electronic resources.

- What will you do for the community, such as contribute to the economic life, serve the informational, educational, and recreational needs.

- Follow the flow, structure, and length of the samples provided.

Chapter 6

Gifts, Memorials, and Donations

Overview

The goal of a gift policy is to give the library complete control over the donations, allow patrons to make informed decisions about giving to the library by making them aware of the criteria you use, and clearly explain the library's option of selling, using, or disposing of the gift as the library deems necessary before accepting a gift. Each policy serves the function of communicating to the patron the library's policy and is an internal framework that protects the collection and library from unwanted gifts. The library's objectives, mission, and selection guide your evaluation process. Policies for artwork and display items have a separate set of criteria and a distinct evaluation process.

Patrons genuinely believe that they give us what they think we need. Usually, we do not need the actual item. It can be a duplication of what we have; it may be out-of-date and in poor condition; or, it may fall outside the collection guidelines. Patrons need to understand the gift policy before making the donation.

This chapter covers policies and forms in the following areas:

- Support the Position of the American Library Association
- Monetary Donations
- Gift Books
- Memorials
- Art Work
- Major Gifts
- Special Collections
- Miscellaneous Gifts
- Endowments, Securities, and Properties
- Acknowledgements
- Criteria for Including Material in the Collection
- Material Needed and Not Needed
- Memorial and Gift Forms
- Notification Form
- Notification and Gift Form
- Gift Agreement Form
- Gift Waiver Form
- Simple Donation Form
- Gift Plates

Experienced librarians know that most donations are never added to the collection. While some gifts may make it to the sale table, others are simply thrown out, or donated to a community organization such as a nursing home. A cynical librarian might think patrons as a dumping ground or a place of last resort for unwanted books. An insulted patron is confused how and why this misunderstood process happens. Clearly written policies and forms will solve the problem. Clear explanations keep you from surprising the patron when they see their donation on the sale table, or worse yet, in the trash.

PUBLIC SERVICE POLICIES

Features of an Effective Policy

- Does not create special sections for donated material, all material is interfiled;
- Informs the donor that material not added to the collection will be disposed of as the library deems appropriate;
- Makes the gift policy consistent with the library's objectives and goals;
- Subjects artwork to the same type of criteria as books and other items;
- Measures historical material, landscaping objects, display material, and other gifts by a well-defined set of criteria;
- Works with the donor and board on how best to acknowledge gifts;
- Earmarks contributions for such things as equipment and furniture, but the library maintains control on such issues as the brand, color, make, and other purchasing decisions;
- Leaves the library in complete control over gifts, but allows rare exceptions to the rule under unusual circumstances.Benefits of Effective Policies
- Complies with American Library Association guidelines on contributions;
- Avoids a disjointed and confusing collection, by interfiling gifts into the collection instead of creating a special area;
- Encourages donors to give in a wide variety of ways, such as money, gift books, art work, and stocks and bonds;
- Provides a public service, by allowing individuals to give material in honor of someone or some event;
- Adds appropriate gift books to enhance the library's collection;
- Allows the library to obtain material it could not otherwise afford;
- Ensures that the library is not saddled with an expensive piece that is difficult to maintain and expensive to insure;
- Gives the library the power to say no to inappropriate gifts;
- Establishes endowments that are the gifts that keep giving and benefits the library for years to come;
- Generates money for the library when material is sold on the book sale table;
- Encourages patrons, who see bookplates placed in books or plaques honoring individuals, to donate material themselves.

Policies

Support for the Position of the American Library Association

Hibbing Public Library   **Hibbing, Minnesota**

The Board of Trustees of the XYZ Public Library subscribes to the policy stated below regarding gifts and bequests to libraries as adopted by the Council of the American Library Association. The Library has long been favored by public-spirited citizens as a beneficiary of gifts because it is a democratic, educational institution carrying on from generation to generation a great, free, humanitarian service to young and old, sick and well, rich and poor of every race, creed, and station of life. Changing social and economic conditions have produced a need for new ideas, for testing methods, and for departure from previous practices in this field of private beneficence.

Although the American Library Association believes and declares that the community served is primarily responsible for the financial support of its public library, it further believes that private philanthropy and private initiative still have important roles to play in the building of library resources in America, and in extending, enriching, and improving the service of the library.

The Association, therefore, believing that gifts and bequests to libraries, both tax-supported and privately endowed, and to libraries of colleges, universities, and other institutions, should be encouraged, invites the attention of library trustees, lawyers, trust officers, and other Friends of Libraries to the following considerations:

- The Association recommends that, in recognition of the economic situation, any program for gifts and bequests should be formulated carefully and with long-term objectives, which should be kept constantly in the public mind.

- The Association believes that memorials in the form of funds for library purposes have a strong appeal to many people because they present the opportunity to carry on the life interest of an individual or a group and can continue a beneficent service through the years. It recommends, therefore, the encouragement of such memorials.

- The Association believes that the development of trust funds presents a field for constructive work on the part of library boards and recommends to such boards, or to others responsible for the administration of libraries, that the possibilities and opportunities presented by such funds be called to the attention of their constituencies.

- The Association believes that one way to broaden the base of giving to libraries is to interest a large number of people in writing bequests into their wills, and it recommends that libraries let it be known that a modest bequest may be made with just as much sincerity and dignity as a large one and that it is just as acceptable to the library.

- The Association believes that insurance policies, including annuities, offer a form of gifts to libraries, the possibilities of which have as yet not been fully explored, and it recommends that libraries be suggested as the beneficiaries of such policies.

- The Association strongly urges that in considering any gift or bequest, the donor be asked to consult the library administration in order to make the benefaction of the greatest possible use both for the present and for the future and that he be asked to protect his gift legally in such a way that changed conditions in future years may be met without impairing the usefulness and general purpose of the gift.

Monetary Donations

Cook Memorial Public Library   **Libertyville, Illinois**

Projects.

The Library accepts monetary donations without conditions on their use or for projects previously approved by the Board. Such money is deposited in the Trust Account for future expenditure by the Board.

Library Materials.

The Library accepts monetary donations for the purpose of purchasing Library material consistent with the objectives of the Library collections. Money that is donated is deposited in the Trust Account for expenditure by the Library Director.

Public acknowledgment of monetary gifts is at the discretion of the Library Board.

Gift Books

Irving Public Library   **Irving, Texas**

The Library gladly accepts the donation of books and other items with the understanding that the Library may do with them as it sees fit.

Gift materials will be added to the collection if they are needed and if they meet the selection standards that are applied to all materials added to the collection. Gifts accepted for the collection become the property of the City of Irving. Gifts not added to the collection will be disposed of in a way that will be most advantageous to the Library.

Upon receipt of gift materials a receipt is given to the donor acknowledging the gift items. Due to Internal Revenue Service regulations, the Library is prohibited from providing an estimate of monetary value of the donation.

Memorials

Irving Public Library   **Irving, Texas**

The Library actively encourages donations as memorials and as tributes to living individuals on special occasions. Such acts provide the Library with an opportunity to add materials or equipment which it might not otherwise be able to afford. In addition, it is felt that such donations provide individuals with a rich opportunity to honor loved ones with a lasting statement of admiration and respect.

Except in rare circumstances, memorials and tributes are accepted in the form of monetary donations to a special fund administered by the Friends of the Irving Public Library. The Library will make every effort to honor the donor's wishes regarding the selection to be purchased. However, the final decision rests with the Library in accordance with its needs and selection criteria.

A bookplate will be placed in the item purchased with the memorial and tribute gift funds. The bookplate will record the honoree as well as the donor. The Library will send letters to notify all parties of this gift.

In those instances where an individual wishes to donate a memorial book from his personal library, the decision to accept the gift will be based on the principles described in Section IV of these policies. If accepted, the bookplate and notification will be handled in a normal manner. If it is not accepted, the book will be returned to the donor.

Artwork

Cook Memorial Library   **Libertyville, Illinois**

The Library has stated responsibility for providing facts, ideas, and creative expression. These responsibilities are reflected in the Library service, the materials collections, the architecture of the Library and the utilization of decorative and display objects within the Library. In keeping with these responsibilities, the Library will avoid the installation of permanent displays or artistic decorations, in favor of rotating displays and works of art that will serve to stimulate and renew interest. The following points must be considered by the Library before accepting a gift of this kind:

- Evaluation of the object itself will be based upon several considerations:

- Does it conform to the general architecture of the building?

- Will it fit comfortably into the space available?

- Does the object make optimum use of the space available?

- Is the object appropriate to Library objectives, or would it be better elsewhere?

- Will it cost more to accept the gift than it is worth to the District?

    a. Cost of insurance

    b. Cost of restoration

    c. Cost of display

    d. Cost of material and labor maintaining the gift

    e. Cost of disposing of it or storing it.

- Is it generally acceptable to the Board?

    a. No gift will be accepted by the Library unless it is freely given to the extent that the Library may:

113

b. Dispose of the gift as it sees fit (selling it, discarding it or giving it away, etc.)

- Store the gift or move it to various locations.

All gifts shall be acknowledged by a personal note from the librarian to the donor.

Major Gifts

Irving Public Library   **Irving, Texas**

Major gifts to the Library may be accepted by the City Council upon recommendation of the Library Board and the Library Director. Major gifts may include but are not limited to land, buildings, art objects, and substantial collections of books or other materials that have either a significant monetary, historical, or literary value.

Special Collections

Ely Public Library,   **Ely, Minnesota**

The library will put a bookplate into books purchased with donated monies when appropriate; however, the library will not agree to form separate collections of either donated materials or materials purchased with donated money.

Irving Public Library   **Irving, Texas**

Special collections of materials will be accepted if they meet the Library's selection criteria as outlined in Section IV. The Library reserves the right to determine such issues as classification, arrangement and shelving of gift materials. The Library will not accept special collections of materials with any donor's stipulations that these be kept together as a special collection or entity, or restricted as to use in any way. Collections will be accepted only with the understanding that they will be integrated into the general collection with the Library determining location and usage of the materials. The Library subscribes to the American Library Association's Restricted Access to Library Materials: An Interpretation of the Library Bill of Rights, (Appendix N), regarding gifts of special collections.

Miscellaneous Gifts—Furniture, Equipment, Landscaping, and Historical

North Castle Public Library   **Armonk, New York**

The decision as to the acceptance of furnishings and equipment shall be made by the Library Board of Trustees on the advice of the Library Director. Among the criteria on which the decision shall be based is need, space, impact on staff time, and expense and frequency of maintenance.

The decision as to the acceptance and location of gifts of landscaping items shall be made by the Library Director. The mayor criterion on which the decision shall be based is the appropriateness of the offered gifts to the landscaping plan for the building.

The decision as to the acceptance and location of gifts of exterior ornamentation, sculpture and signage shall be made by the Library Board of Trustees on the advice of the Library Director.

Villa Park Public Library   **Villa Park, Illinois**

The Library does not accept as a gift any printed or manuscript items or any objects if the condition of acceptance requires permanent exhibition since the Library believes all exhibits should be changed periodically to maintain interest. Such gifts will be referred to a museum or historical society.

Gifts of furniture and equipment will be accepted only when, in the opinion of the Library administration, the proposed gift is of a type that is compatible with the Library's existing furnishings. Generally, it is recommended that donors contribute money for the purchase of such articles.

Endowments, Securities, and Property

North Castle Public Library   **Armonk, New York**

Gifts of cash, securities, real property and bequest that support the mission of the Library will be handled by the Library Director, who, with the Library Board of Trustees, will work out terms of acceptance that are compatible with Library policies, the donor's intent, and applicable laws.

Oakville Public Library   **Oakville, Ontario**

Individuals, businesses or foundations, contribute to the Oakville Public Library's Endowment Fund through gifts of cash, publicly-traded securities or property. The gifts are held in perpetuity to provide capital that will generate an on-going and reliable source of future income for the Library. Funds that are established today provide an important stream of revenue to support Oakville's future library needs.

The Library's Endowment Fund is managed by the Community Foundation of Oakville (CFO). A number of Oakville community agencies pool their endowed funds with the CFO to benefit from reduced overhead costs and the return rate generated on larger investment portfolios. The funds are professionally managed to ensure the safety of capital and maintain a proper balance between meeting income requirements and preserving capital to meet future needs.

You can direct your donation toward general support for the Library by making a gift of any size to the Endowment Fund at any time. Alternatively, you can establish a named fund within the Library's Endowment Fund with a minimum contribution of $5,000. Income from the named endowment can be directed to provide interest income for general support or to any of the areas described below. A named fund for specific purposes may be established with a minimum contribution of $20,000.

An endowment is a very special and meaningful way to create a permanent remembrance or ensure that your own long-term philanthropic goals will be fulfilled. Once a fund has been created, it can be built up through additional future contributions.

If you would like to establish a named endowment, please contact our Development Office.

ADMINISTRATIVE POLICIES

Overall, patrons would like to donate material but they do not know what the library needs. A wish list solves this problem. Equally important is the "Material the Library Can Not Use" list. Sometimes patrons would like their material to be located in a special collection, but in all the policies below, all donated material is inter-filed in the collection. Creating special areas for each donation leaves the collection disjointed and confusing. Guiding this process are your important criteria for accepting or rejecting gifts. Below are policies you will use frequently.

Features of an Effective Policy

- Uses the same criteria for gifts as it uses in selecting new material;
- Allows the library to retain ultimate control over gifts;
- States that the library cannot appraise material for tax purposes (in the United States);
- Helps patrons understand what type of material the library needs with Wanted and Not Needed lists;

Benefits of Effective Policies

- Enhances the collection;
- Makes public acknowledgements, which is an excellent way to communicate with patrons and is a good public relations tool;
- Reserves for the library ultimate control over gifts, which gives the library many options in how it handles each gift;
- Allows some exceptions to the rule on control of gifts, if it does not compromise the library or the collection;
- Keeps inappropriate gifts, art work, and display items out of the library.

Policies

Acknowledgements

Charlevoix Public Library   **Charlevoix, Michigan**

Gift bookplates or nameplates will be affixed to those materials chosen or accepted by the librarian in order to satisfy a donor's request.

Cook Memorial Public Library District   **Libertyville, Illinois**

The names of people making donations to the Library will not be released without their consent. The details of any such release will be approved by the donors. Library materials, equipment or display objects will be displayed in a way appropriate to their use by the public as determined by the Library.

Norfolk Public Library   **Norfolk, Virginia**

The library will ensure that each sponsor receives acknowledgement and to the degree that the donor is willing, public recognition. The following guidelines will be used in providing acknowledgement to and recognition for sponsors:

- A letter of acknowledgement for gifts of money and in-kind support will be sent to all sponsors and a copy will be placed on file.

- Any special recognition agreements will be stipulated in the letter.

- Public acknowledgement of sponsorship in the library's promotional materials will normally be restricted to a statement of the sponsor's name and a display of logo. Standards controlling the size format and location of such acknowledgment will be developed by the public information specialist to ensure both consistency and quality of appearance. Such acknowledgement will not take precedence or have prominence over the library's own logo or promotional material.

- For gifts and/or sponsorships valued at over $500, the library may submit a press release to local newspapers and/or publish an article regarding the sponsorship in their own newsletter if the sponsor is willing.

- Acknowledgement of sponsorship may also take the following forms at the library's discretion:

  - Launch of a special program or media campaign to announce the gift.

  - Sponsor's name on promotional materials.

  - Small standardized plaques may be placed on donated furniture or equipment.

  - Library bookplates.

In all cases, the type and scope of donor recognition required by the donor will be weighed against the benefit to the library.

Criteria for Including Material in the Collection

Shawnee Library System   **Caterville, Illinois**

Donation of Books and AudioVisual Materials. In accepting a gift of materials the library reserves the privilege of deciding whether items donated should be added to the collection. Out of the many books and other materials which citizens so generously give, a considerable proportion can be used. Some cannot, because any library material, though of value in itself, may be:

(1) a duplicate of an item of which the library already has a sufficient number;

(2) outdated interesting but not of sufficient present reference or circulating value to the library; and/or

(3) in poor condition—which would not justify the expense of processing it, i.e., cataloging and preparing it for circulation.

The material will be judged by the same standards of selection as those applied to the purchase of new materials. The XYZ Public Library accepts gift books with the understanding that books, which are useful to the library collection, will be retained and other books disposed of in whatever manner the librarian deems best. The Library necessarily reserves the right to interfile gifts with other collections on the same subject, so that all collections are organized and classified according to library standards for the best public service.

Charlevoix Public Library   **Charlevoix, Michigan**

Donations of books or artifacts will be accepted provided that, in the opinion of the professional staff, they enhance the value of the library's collection. Materials, which do not meet the library's selection criteria, will be disposed of at the discretion of the library. Books not added to the library's collection may be sold at the Friends of the Library's ongoing book sale. All donations (money and materials) become the sole property of the library. The library may or may not put materials into the collection based on their physical condition and usefulness to library patrons. The library is not obligated to keep donated materials for any length of time.

Material Needed List

Charlevoix Public Library   **Charlevoix, Michigan**

The library is most interested in the following types of materials:

- Hard bound current novels for recreational reading.

- Information books.

- Broadway plays and musical materials.

- General college textbooks recently published.

- Children's books.

- Fine bindings.

- Anything published prior to 1900.

- Manuscripts and other hand written materials.

- Paperback books.

- Biographies and autobiographies.

- Books of local interest.

- Media material: books on tape, videos, DVDs, audio tapes, CD-ROM, etc.

Hibbing Public Library   **Hibbing, Minnesota**

The following are of particular interest to the library:

- Gifts of printed or manuscript materials on the history of the community and the region.

- Hardcover books that are current or classic adult novels or popular non-fiction titles published in the last two years.

- Children's books.

- Paperback books published within the last five years.

All books should be in good condition. We will not accept books with torn pages or covers that have notes or highlighting on the pages. We will not accept books that are damaged or mildewed.

Material Not Needed List

Charlevoix Public Library   **Charlevoix, Michigan**

Books and periodicals that we cannot use or even dispose of:

- Outdated informational books (e.g., technological, tax, investment medical, educational, legal, etc.)

- Books that have been kept in storage and have mildewed.

- Reader's Digest condensed books.

- 78 or LP records.

- Outdated textbooks.

Park Ridge Public Library   **Park Ridge, Illinois**

Donations of the following types of materials will not be accepted by the Library:

- Textbooks

- Non-current business and professional books

- Magazines and journals other than American Heritage, Horizon or publications of similar quality. The Library has a very complete collection of National Geographic and regrets that no further donations of that title can be accepted.

- Reader's Digest Condensed Books

- Encyclopedias

FORMS

Benefits of Written Forms

- Allows the donor to designate where they want the gift to go;

- Asks for all pertinent donor information;

- Ensures that the donor supplies the proper spelling of names and dates of events, which the library will only copy;

- Informs the patron of the selection process;

- Gives the donor the option of retrieving the gift if it is not added to the collection.

I/we would like to contribute $_____ for a book to be placed in the library.

As a memorial for _____

or in honor of _____

on the occasion of a birthday , wedding anniversary _____

graduation , or other (please specify)_____

The subject matter we prefer for this book is (please specify if you have a

preference:_____

Figure 6.1 Memorial and Gift Form

Oakville Public Library   **Oakville, Ontario**
Tribute and Memorial Gift:

Birthday

Mother's Day

Father's Day

Graduation

Retirement

Anniversary, please describe:

In Memory of_____

In Remembrance of_____

Other_____

Please send gift acknowledgement to:

Name_____

Address_____

City_____ State _____Zip _____

Telephone_____

I would like to designate my donation to: (Please check one)

Where it is needed most

Outreach & Literacy
New Technologies & Equipment
Special Needs
Services for visually impaired and homebound Library users
Local History Preservation
Adult Collections
Children's Collections
Endowment Fund
Other:_____
I wish to receive more information on:
XYZ Public Library's Endowment Fund
Gifts of publicly-traded securities.

Figure 6.2 Memorial and Gift Form

Park Ridge Public Library   **Park Ridge, Illinois**

Thank you for selecting a gift to the XYZ Public Library as a means of honoring or remembering a loved one. In order to proceed, we need some information. Please complete this form and return it to: XYZ Public Library,

Name of person giving gift (Donor):_____

Address: _____

                    _____

Telephone Number: (_____)_____

Kind of gift (Check one):

* Memorial
* Anniversary
* Birthday
* Birth of a child
* Other, please specify_____

Name of person(s) being remembered or honored as it should appear on the bookplate:

_____

Name of the donor(s) as you wish it to appear on book plate (optional)

_____

Name and address of person to notify of the gift:

_____

_____

Amount of gift:_____ (Please make checks payable to XYZ Public Library.)

The gift donation should be designated for one of the following two funds:

_____Restricted Gift Fund:

When you donate to the Restricted Gift Fund, the gifts and bequests will be placed in this special fund until their purposes shall be fulfilled.

Type of material you would like the library to purchase (check one):

* Book: (Children's_____ or Adult_____
* Recording
* Videocassette
* Other, please specify_____

Figure 6.3 Memorial and Gift Form

Suggested subjects or titles:

_____

_____

If you do not have a preference, our Library Department Heads will select an appropriate item.

A bookplate will be affixed to the item indicating the person being honored and the donor. A letter will be sent to the donor, as well as the recipient, indicating a gift has been given in his/her name. In the case of a deceased person who is being remembered, the letter will be sent to a family member when the name and address is noted.

_____ Endowment Fund:

When you donate to the XYZ Public Library Endowment Fund, gifts and bequests, unless otherwise designated, shall be placed in this permanent fund. Purchases from the interest accumulated by the Fund are made periodically. When an item is purchased, a commemorative plate is affixed to it stating that funds from the Endowment Fund were used to purchase the item.

Donors names will appear in the Endowment Fund Registry which is kept on display in the Adult Reference Room of the Library.

Figure 6.3 continued

Notification Form for Memorials or Donations Honoring an Individual

The Library will notify the following that this donation has been added to the Library's collection in memory of or honoring the above. In the space provided, please indicate the relationship between the honoree and the person to be notified of the donation.

Relationship:——————————————

Name of person to be notified:　　——————————————

Address of person to be notified:　　——————————————

Donor Information

Name of donor:　　——————————————

Address of donor:　　——————————————

Please make checks payable to the XYZ Public Library

Please return this form to:——————————————

Figure 6.4 Notification Form

Donor Information _____

Name   _____

Organization   _____

Address, City, State, Zip Code _____

Home Phone   _____

Work Phone   _____

Date   _____

Signature   _____

Gift/Memorial Information

Individual /Group Being Recognized/Memorialized_____

In Memory Of In Honor Of_____

Special Event_____

Program_____

Special Instructions_____

Item Donated and Estimated Cost_____

Donation Amount _____

Notification Information (Please notify the following person(s)/group(s) on my behalf)

Name _____

Relationship to Person/Group Being Recognized/Memorialized_____

Address, City, State, Zip Code _____

_____

Name_____

Relationship to Person/Group Being Recognized/Memorialized_____

Address, City, State, Zip Code _____

_____

Figure 6.5 Notification and Gift Form

Shawnee Library System   **Caterville, Illinois**

Gift Agreement Form

Date:_____

Donor_____

Address   _____

             _____

Description of material donated:

Information concerning the material or donor which would be helpful in organizing and cataloging this materia

This Gift Agreement transfers legal title of the gift to the XYZ Public Library.

              Unrestricted gift   Restrictions (please specify)

              _____

              _____

I have read the gift policy provisions of the XYZ Public Library and agree that they are acceptable.

Donor signature: Date_____

Accepted for the Library by: Date_____

Library director

Signature:_____

For restricted gifts only:

President of Library Board

Signature _____ Date_____

Secretary of Library Board

Signature:_____ Date_____

Date of Board Approval _____

Figure 6.6 Gift Agreement Form

Oskaloosa Public Library   **Oskaloosa, Iowa**

XYZ PUBLIC LIBRARY GIFT ITEM WAIVER

The following waiver is necessary for our records. It can be used as a receipt for the items and may be used as an attachment to your Income Tax Return.

I hereby agree that the items given are governed solely by the wishes of the Library Board of Trustees.

And as such these items may be utilized as needed; sold to raise funds for the Library, or given to another library if sufficient material is already in the holdings of the Oskaloosa Public Library, or disposed of in any other manner.

Further, I hereby relinquish all claims, now or in the future, to the items given.

Signature of Donor _____

Name of Donor (Please Print) _____

Street Address _____

City State Zip _____

Brief description of item(s):

Staff initials _____ Date _____

Figure 6.7 Gift Waiver Form

Donation Form

Name:_____

Address: _____

_____

Telephone:_____

List of Donated Items:

All Material will be given careful consideration by the library staff.

Items that do not fit within the Selection Guidelines may not be added to the collection. Would you like the material returned to you if it could not be added?

_____yes_____no

May the material be keep for sale purposes so money may be raised for the library?

_____yes_____no

Figure 6.8 Simple Donation Form

XYZ Public Library

Gift from:

_____

In Honor of:

_____

Figure 6.9 Gift Plate Honoring a Person or Event

In Memory of an Individual

XYZ Public Library

In Memoriam:

_____

Date:

_____

Figure 6.10 Gift Plate Memorial

CHECKLIST

- Coordinate adding gifts, gift books, and donations with selection criteria.
- Are you able to establish a library fund for major gifts, endowments, securities, and property?
- Who will manage the library fund?
- Can you include in the policy the option to refuse gifts that are too expensive to maintain, such as artwork?
- Do you need to include the library board in your decisions?
- Do you want to have a "Material We Need" list and a "Material We Can Not Use" list at the circulation and reference desk for patrons?
- How do you want to acknowledge large gifts?
- Do you want to include automatically Memorials gifts in the collection?
- Can you use gift plates as a way to advertise for gifts and donations?

Chapter 7

LIBRARY BOARDS

OVERVIEW

Many libraries have boards—some advisory, some governing. Advisory boards do that—they advise the library. The director is responsible for policy, administration, budget, and day-to-day operations. Governing boards usually hire the director and make policy and budget decisions turning day-to-day operations over to the director. The goal for working with any type of board is to consult them in decision-making; explain library operations; listen and implement suggestions and ideas; prepare reports; review policy; conduct meetings; and actively foster good will. Clear well-written bylaws defining each role within and in relationship to the board, as well as the various procedures of the board, keep duties and responsibilities straight and disagreements to a minimum.

This chapter covers policies and forms in the following areas:

- Advisory Board
    - Role of the Librarian
    - Board Duties
    - Bylaws

- Governing Boards
    - Role of the Librarian
    - Board Duties
    - Bylaws

- Board Appointments

- Committees

- Meetings

- Sample Agenda

- Sample Order of Business

- Sample Report

ADMINISTRATIVE POLICIES

Features of an Effective Policy

Whether you have a governing or an advisory board, the policies of any type of board share certain features in common. Clearly defined roles, duties, and responsibilities help decrease misunderstandings that can adversely impact you, trustees, and library operations. Use the examples below to see how other librarians word their policies and what elements they include, or you may choose to reprint a policy you find, as it is presented. Whether you start with a blank sheet of paper or simply want to rewrite your policy, begin with the elements outlined below in the different policies. If you have a governing board, you must revise your policy with the trustees, or they must do it. If you have an advisory board, then start by defining your duties, and proceed to the functional aspects of meeting information, board duties, officers on the board duties, committees, and procedures for making amendments.

Positions on the board may be elected by the library's constituency, or appointed by local governmental officials, for a specified time period and for limited reappointments. Duties vary from locale to locale, but there are many similarities. According to one survey, only about one third of librarians reported having either standing or special committees (Wade, 1991: 37). Board size often determines the appropriateness of committees. If you have five or fewer trustees, then work is better accomplished with all members present. Among the similarities between advisory and governing boards are regular reports on library activities, delivered in writing at each meeting or mailed to trustees before the meeting, and a regular day, time, and place for each meeting. Whether out of courtesy or as a requirement, boards post public notice informing the public of its meetings and their agenda.

Benefits of an Effective Policy

- Eliminates confusion over responsibilities and duties;
- Informs everyone about what is expected of them;
- Creates a smooth transition when directors and board members change, because the written document remains constant, even when people come and go;
- Outlines procedures;
- Establishes rules concerning the creation and composition of committees;
- Provides for both standing and ad hoc committees;
- Requires committees to issue regular reports to the director;
- Creates an organizational structure within which to work;
- Articulates what procedures need to be followed;
- States the rules and regulations;
- Serves as a common document for the board to utilize when problems or issues arise;
- Requires that meetings be at a regular time and place;
- Calls for a written agenda at meetings;
- Gives helpful hints on structuring meetings;
- Makes provision for special meetings;
- Establishes what constitutes a quorum and requires that there be one at each meeting.

Policies

Advisory Board

Role of the Librarian

Texas State Library and Archives Commission   **Austin, Texas**

The library director is responsible for the organization, planning, direction, and administration of library services and activities to provide quality library service. The director works with the advisory board, as well as with other groups, to promote the library.

The library director's duties and responsibilities include:

- Meeting with the library board at regularly scheduled meetings

- Helping prepare the meeting agenda with the board chair

- Keeping the board informed of the activities, acquisitions, and new personnel of the library

- Informing the board regarding budget and financing implications

- Guiding the board with professional expertise

- Directing the care and maintenance of the library building and equipment

- Supervising the selection, training, and performance of the library staff

- Preparing the annual budget proposal

- Overseeing the expenditures of the budget

- Assuming the responsibility for the monthly and annual reports of library services and activities

- Attending meetings, workshops, seminars, and conferences of organizations appropriate to the library and management fields

- Supervising the selection and processing of all library materials and equipment

- Keeping informed of library trends through professional reading

- Recognizing that the library director and others on the staff are professionals in the field of librarianship and respecting their expertise

- Remembering that advising is not deciding; the board's role is to make recommendations to the governing body

- Acquiring an awareness of public library standards and library trends

- Becoming informed about state and national library laws and actively supporting state and national library legislation which would improve and extend library service

- Supporting intellectual freedom and the right to access in the public library

Board Duties

Texas State Library and Archives Commission   **Austin, Texas**

The advisory board is appointed by the library's governing body to serve as a liaison between the library and its citizens. The board advises the library director and the governing body in matters related to the library and its services, and promotes the library and its programs.

The advisory board's duties and responsibilities include:

- Attending board meetings

- Acting in an advisory capacity to the governing body in matters that pertain to the library

- Receiving suggestions and recommendations from citizens relating to library service

- Referring complaints, compliments, and suggestions to the library director, who reports to an administrative official, who then reports to the governing body

- Knowing how the library is organized and functions

- Knowing the collection, the staff, and the activities of the library in order to communicate knowledgeably with citizens and with elected officials

Pasadena Public Library   **Pasadena, California**

To advise the City Council on matters relating to the public library system, in order that the library is well managed in a manner consistent with the law and policies, and to advise library administration on the development of library policies.

Members should have an interest in the development and improvement of cost efficiency and equality of community library services. Prior or current community service is desirable.

By laws

Texas State Library and Archives Commission   **Austin, Texas**

ARTICLE I

NAME

As authorized by the City Charter, City of _____, and City Ordinance No._____. This body shall be known as the _____ Public Library Board.

ARTICLE II

MEETINGS

Section 1.

The regular meeting of the Library Board shall be held at a time designated by the Board in the library or such other place the Board may determine.

Section 2.

Special meetings may be called by the Chair or at the call of any two members of the Board, provided that notice thereof be given to all Board members.

Section 3.

A majority of the members shall constitute a quorum at all meetings of the Board.

Section 4.

All questions presented for a vote of the Library Board shall be decided by a simple majority of the quorum, including the vote of the Chair.

Section 5.

Any member of the Board who misses three consecutive meetings without good cause shall be deemed to have resigned, and the Board will recommend to City Council that a replacement be appointed for the balance of the unexpired term.

Section 6.

Robert's Rules of Order, Newly Revised shall govern in the parliamentary procedure of the Board, in all cases to which they are applicable and in which they are not inconsistent with these by-laws.

ARTICLE III

OFFICERS

Section 1.

The officers of the Board shall be a Chairperson, a Vice-Chairperson, and a Secretary.

Section 2.

Officers shall be elected and take office at the first regular meeting after new Board members have been appointed and sworn in.

Section 3.

Vacancies in office shall be handled as follows:

(a) In the event of resignation of incapacity of the Chair, the Vice-Chair shall become the Chair for the unexpired portion of the term.

(b) Vacancies in officers other than the Chair shall be filled for the unexpired term by special election.

Section 4.

Duties of the officers shall be as follows:

(a) Chair:

(i) Preside at all meetings.

(ii) Represent the Library Board at public functions.

(iii) Appoint special committees.

(iv) Assist Library Director in establishing the agenda for each meeting. Agenda items requested by any Board member will be included.

(b) Vice-Chair:

(i) Assist the Chair in directing the affairs of the Board and act in the Chair's absence.

(c) Secretary:

(i) Be responsible for the accuracy of the minutes of the Board meeting and bring any corrections to the attention of the Board at its next meeting. The Secretary shall sign the approved minutes and file in Record Book.

ARTICLE IV

COMMITTEES

Section 1.

Committees may be appointed for special purposes by the Chair and with the consent of the majority of the Board. All committees will have at least one Library Board member serving on them. These committees are automatically dissolved upon completion of the assignment.

ARTICLE V

LIBRARIAN

Section 1.

The Library Director shall be an ex-officio member of the Board.

ARTICLE VI

POWERS AND DUTIES OF BOARD MEMBERS

Section 1.

Board members shall:

(a) Abide by applicable ordinances of the City of _____.

(b) Act in an advisory capacity of the City Council, City Manager, and Library Director.

(c) Recommend policies to govern the operation and program of the library.

(d) Assist in planning and give guidance for expansion of library facilities.

(e) Assist in interpreting the policies and functions of the Library Department to the public.

(f) Encourage in every possible way the development and advancement of the public library.

ARTICLE VII

AMENDMENTS

Section 1.

These by-laws may be amended by a majority vote at any regular meeting, provided all members have been notified of the proposed amendments at least ten days prior to such meeting. Such amendment would then be subject to approval by City Council.

ARTICLE VII

AMENDMENTS

Section 1.

These by-laws may be amended by a majority vote at any regular meeting, provided all members have been notified of the proposed amendments at least ten days prior to such meeting. Such amendment would then be subject to approval by City Council.

Governing Board

Role of the Librarian

Appleton Public Library   **Appleton, Wisconsin**

The Library Director is responsible for:

- Administering, interpreting, enforcing, and establishing procedures consistent with applicable laws, regulations, City ordinances, rules and the policies of the City and the Board

- Maintaining performance records of all Library employees

- Making reports and recommendations to the Board and City Officials

- Recruiting, selecting, and assigning Library employees

- Coordinating staff training

- Disseminating information regarding personnel policies, fringe benefits, conditions of employment, and all relevant policies to library employees

- Appointing or removing employees

- Conducting the appropriate steps in the Grievance Procedure

- Reviewing and making recommendations to the Board on modifications in the table of organization

- Administering discipline

- Delegating such authority to subordinates as is appropriate

- Recommending changes in policy as necessary

Neuschafer Community Library   **Fremont, Wisconsin**

- The Director shall be responsible to the Library Board in matters pertaining to and concerning the library. Be present at monthly meetings and prepare and present such reports as requested.

- The Director shall prepare a presentation of monthly bills in an efficient manner; prepare an annual budget to be presented to the Village Board by the President of the Library Board.

- The Director recruits, selects, hires, supervises, evaluates and terminates library staff in conformity with civil service regulations. Oversees the staff training program. Recommends improvements in staffing, organization, salaries and benefits to the library board.

- The Director shall have the responsibility for collection development for all materials in the library; this includes selection, ordering, processing, weeding, and inventory of the collections to the guidelines in the policy.

Board Duties

Appleton Public Library   **Appleton, Wisconsin**

The Library Board is responsible for:

- Employment of the Library Director

- Reviewing and approving Library policies

- Approving the annual salary schedule, including adjustments for excellence

- Reviewing grievances appealed from the ruling of the Personnel Committee

Wisconsin Department of Public Instruction, Public Library Development

- Legal responsibility for the operation of the Public Library is vested in the Board of Trustees. Subject to state and federal law, the Board has the power and duty to determine rules and regulations governing library operations and services.

- The Board shall select, appoint and supervise a properly certified and competent library director, and determine the duties and compensation of all library employees.

- The Board shall approve the budget and make sure that adequate funds are provided to finance the approved budget.

- The Board shall have exclusive control of the expenditure of all moneys collected, donated or appropriated for the library fund and shall audit and approve all library expenditures.

- The Board shall supervise and maintain buildings and grounds, as well as regularly review various physical and building needs to see that they meet the requirements of the total library program.

- The Board shall study and support legislation that will bring about the greatest good to the greatest number of library users.

- The Board shall cooperate with other public officials and boards and maintain vital public relations.

- The Board shall approve and submit the required annual report to the Division for Libraries, Technology, and Community Learning, and the [city council, village board, town board, county board, and/or any other governing body].

By laws

Nebraska Library Commission Library Development Services Lincoln, Nebraska

- Selection, appointment, terms, number and composition of board

- Place, time, and responsibility for regular meetings and date of annual meeting

- Procedures for calling special meetings

- Attendance requirements

- Definition and requirements of a quorum

- Parliamentary rules to be followed

- Duties of officers

- Appointments and duties of any standing committees

- Duties of individual library board members

- Provision for special committees

- Role, relationship with, and responsibilities of the library director

- Limitations on board members

- Required reports and yearly timetables

- Procedures for adopting or amending by-laws

Jackson County Public Library   Seymour, Indiana

ARTICLE I

NAME AND AUTHORITY

Section 1.1 Name.

The name of this board is the Board of Trustees of the Jackson County Public Library, hereinafter referred to as "The Board" and "The Library."

Section 1.2 Authority.

The Board exists and operates by virtue of the Indiana Public Library Law of 1947 and assumes its powers and responsibilities under Indiana Code ("I.C.") 20–14.

ARTICLE II

MEMBERSHIP

Section 2.1 Status.

The application, appointment, term, and removal of Members of The Board is in accordance with Indiana statute.

Section 2.2 Compensation.

Members of The Board serve without compensation in accordance with law and, with the exception of the Treasurer, may not be a paid employee of The Library.

Section 2.3 Term.

The term of a Member is four (4) years. However, a Member may continue to serve until his successor is qualified as provided by law. Members of The Board may not serve more than four consecutive terms of four years each for a total of sixteen (16) years.

ARTICLE III

MEETINGS

Section 3.1 Regular Meetings.

Regular meetings of The Board are scheduled on the third

Tuesday of each month at 5:00 p.m. in the Conference Room at the Seymour Library, with one meeting held each year at both the Crothersville and Medora branch libraries.

The date and time may be changed by the President in order to ensure a quorum or to meet special situations. Such regular meetings of The Board may be held without notice to members of The Board or upon such notice as may be fixed by the members. Public notice is given of every meeting of The Board.

Section 3.2 Special Meetings.

Special meetings of The Board may be called by the President of The Board or upon written request by two or more Members of The Board. Notice of the time and place of a special meeting shall be served upon, telephoned, mailed, telegraphed, or cabled to each Member at his or her usual place of business or residence at least forty-eight (48) hours prior to the time of the meeting. Members, in lieu of such notice, may sign a written waiver of notice either before the time of the meeting, at the meeting, or after the meeting. Attendance by a Member in person at any such special meeting shall constitute a waiver of notice.

Section 3.3 Open Meetings.

All meetings of The Board, except executive sessions, are subject to the Indiana Open Door Law (I.C. 5–14–1.5) and are open to the public.

Section 3.4 Executive Sessions.

Executive sessions of The Board are called by the President or by two or more Members of The Board and appear on the meeting's written agenda. Executive sessions are held under the limitation of I.C. 5–14–1.5–6.

Section 3.5 Quorum.

Four Members of The Board constitute a quorum at each Board meeting. When a quorum is present at any meeting, the vote of a plurality of the Members having voting power shall decide any question brought before such meeting.

Section 3.6 Dissent.

A Member, who is present at a meeting of The Board at which action on any matter is taken, shall be conclusively presumed to have assented to the action taken, unless (a) his dissent shall be affirmatively stated by him at and before the adjournment of such meeting (in which even the fact of such dissent shall be entered by the Secretary of the meeting in the minutes of the meeting), or (b) he shall forward such dissent by registered mail to the Secretary of The Board immediately after the adjournment of the meeting. The right of dissent provided for by either clause (a) or clause (b) of the immediately preceding sentence shall not be available, in respect of any matter acted upon at any meeting, to a Member who voted at the meeting in favor of such matter and did not change his vote prior to the time that the result of the vote on such matter was announced by the chairman of such meeting.

Section 3.7 Rules of Order.

The latest revision of Robert's Rules of Order governs the conduct of all Board meetings.

ARTICLE IV

OFFICERS

Section 4.1 Officers.

Officers of The Board are President, Vice-President, Secretary, and Treasurer.

Section 4.2 Election of Officers.

The Officers shall be chosen annually at the regular December meeting. Each such Officer shall hold office until his or her successor shall have been duly chosen and qualified, or until his or her death, or until such Officer shall resign, or shall have been removed in the manner provided by law.

Section 4.3 Assistant Officers.

The Board may have one or more Assistant Officers who shall have such powers and duties as the Officers whom they are elected to assist shall specify and delegate to them and such other powers and duties as The Board may prescribe. An Assistant Secretary may, in the event of the absence of the Secretary, attest the execution of all documents by The Board.

Section 4.4 Duties of President.

The President presides at all Board meetings and appoints committees of The Board.

Section 4.5 Duties of Vice-President.

The Vice-President presides over meetings in the absence of the President and shall become President should a vacancy occur in that office between elections.

Section 4.6 Duties of Secretary.

The Secretary signs all documents requiring the Secretary's signature. Board minutes are recorded by a Library staff member designated by the Members and are approved monthly by The Board.

Section 4.7 Duties of Treasurer.

The Treasurer, who is bonded, monitors the budget, financial records, reports, audits, and investments. The Treasurer and President sign warrants which are approved by The Board for payment of expenses lawfully incurred by The Library.

ARTICLE V

COMMITTEES

Section 5.1 Appointment of Committees.

Committees are appointed as needed by the President. Committees include, but are not limited to, the Budget Committee and Personnel Committee.

ARTICLE VI

FINANCE

Section 6.1 Board of Finance.

The full Board and its Officers constitutes The Board of Finance and meets annually in January to review finances and depositories.

Section 6.2 Financial Powers.

The Board has all financial powers and responsibilities as provided by statute, establishes funds for the safekeeping of The Library's finances, and invests The Library's funds in accordance with Indiana law and regulations.

ARTICLE VII

LIBRARY DIRECTOR

Section 7.1 Library Director.

The Director is appointed by, responsible to, and evaluated by The Board.

Section 7.2 Duties of Director.

The Director is responsible for the administration and management of The Library.

Section 7.3 Policy.

The Director implements all policies adopted by The Board, reports monthly to The Board, advises The Board, and recommends policies and procedures to The Board.

ARTICLE VIII

AMENDMENTS

Section 8.1 Amendments.

These by-laws may be amended by a plurality vote of the Members of the Board at any regular meeting, providing that notice of the amendment was given at the preceding regular meeting of The Board.

Board Appointments

Pasadena Public Library   Pasadena, California

Nine members, one appointed by each Council member and the Mayor. The Mayor will nominate one additional member from persons recommended by the seven Council members. Three years, limited to two consecutive terms.

Ohio County Public Library   Wheeling, West Virginia

Members of the Board of Trustees are appointed by the Clerk of Circuit Court of Ohio County for a term of five years each, except that any person appointed by the Board to fill a vacancy occurring before the expiration of the term vacated, shall serve only for the unexpired term. Members of the Board of Trustees shall be eligible for reappointment, shall serve without compensation, and shall hold no remunerative political office, either state, county, or municipal. No member of the Board of Trustees shall be eligible for appointment to any remunerative office or position under the jurisdiction of the Board of Trustees, and not more than three of the members shall belong to the same political party. At least two of the members of the Board of Trustees shall be women.

Neuschafer Community Library   Fremont, Wisconsin

- The officers shall be a President, a Secretary, and a Financial Record Keeper elected from among the appointed Trustees at the annual meeting of the Board. The duties of the Treasurer shall be shared by the Fremont Village Clerk and the Financial Record Keeper.

- The Library Board shall consist of five (5) members. One member shall be a Village Board Trustee appointed by the Village Board President, one member shall be a representative of the public school system (school district administrator or his representative) and the other three members shall be appointed by the Village President and approved by the Village Board on the 2nd Monday of April each year. Not more than one Village Board member shall serve at any one time.

- Trustees shall serve a three year term from the annual meeting at which they are appointed until their successors are duly appointed. Vacancies must be filled for unexpired terms in the same manner as regular appointments are made.

- Officers shall be elected annually at the May meeting.

145

Committees

Wisconsin Department of Public Instruction   **Madison, Wisconsin**

The following committees:_shall be appointed by the president promptly after the annual meeting and shall make recommendations to the Board as pertinent to Board meeting agenda items. [Examples of possible standing committees are Personnel, Budget, Building, and Policy.] Ad hoc committees for the study of special problems shall be appointed by the president, with the approval of the Board, to serve until the final report of the work for which they were appointed has been filed. These committees may also include staff and public representatives, as well as outside experts. [Examples of possible ad hoc committees are Planning and Automation.]No committee shall have other than advisory powers

New London Public Library   **New London, Wisconsin**

- The president shall appoint committees of one or more members for such specific purposes as the Board may require from time to time. The committee shall be considered to be discharged upon completion of the purpose for which it was appointed and after the final report is made to the Board.

- All committees shall make a periodic progress report to the Library/Museum Board.

- No committee will have other than advisory powers unless, by suitable action of the Board, it is granted specific power to act.

Meetings

Texas State Library and Archives Commission   **Austin, Texas**

The first part of any meeting plan is a written agenda. The agenda should be prepared jointly by the board chair and the library director. It lists the topics to be discussed and the order of discussion. If your library is required to follow the mandate of the Open Meetings Act, the agenda must be posted at least 72 hours in advance of the meeting in the legally designated posting places for your local government.

The agenda must contain the name of the board holding the meeting, the address of the meeting, and the date and time the meeting is to be held. Certification or verification that the meeting was posted on a specific date and at or by a specific time must appear at the conclusion of the agenda. The certification or verification must be followed by the signature of a legally chair.

An ideal meeting runs about one to two hours. Despite your best intentions, your meeting may run over the allotted time; therefore, put the least important topics at the end of the agenda and your most important topics at the beginning. Then, even if you do not finish your agenda, your most important work has been done.

A well-planned agenda will help you do first things first, focus on one item at a time, leave the least important items for last, and set a tone for the meeting. All of these will help you get work done and conclude the meeting on time so that people will want to come to the next meeting.

New London Public Library   **New London, Wisconsin**

The regular meetings shall be held each month, the date and hour to be set by the Board at its annual meeting.

Section 2. The election of officers shall be held at the time of the regular meeting in July of each year.

Section 3. The order of business for regular meetings shall include, but not be limited to, the following items, which shall be covered in sequence shown so far as circumstances will permit:

1. Roll call of members

2. Disposition of minutes of previous regular meeting and any intervening special meeting

3. Action on bills

4. Progress and service report of the Museum director

5. Progress and service report of the Library director

6. Action

7. Adjournment

Section 4. Special meetings may be called by the president, or at the request of four members for the transaction of business as stated in the call for the meeting.

Section 5. A quorum for the transaction of business at any meeting shall consist of four members of the Board present in person.

Section 6. Conduct of meetings: Robert's Rules of Order shall govern Proceedings of all meetings.

FORMS

Benefits of Written Forms

- Keeping board members informed about library activities
- Using information contained in reports to get cooperation for new ideas or solving problems that arise
- Creating a history for you to refer back to
- Informing the community about library activities when the agenda and reports are made available to the public
- Keeping you organized for meetings

- Call to order

- Reading and approval of the minutes

- Report of the library director

- Committee reports

- Old business

- New Business

- Adjournment

Figure 7.1 Sample Order of Business

DeSoto Public Library   **DeSoto, Texas**

The regularly scheduled meeting of the DeSoto Public Library Board will be held at 7:00 p.m. on Thursday, October 3, 2002. In the library administration conference room of the DeSoto Public Library, 211 East Pleasant Run Road, DeSoto, Texas 75115.

    I. Call to Order

    II. Approval of Minutes from September 5, 2002 Board Meeting

    III. Staff Reports

    IV. Old Business

        A. TIF Funding / legislative issues

        B. DeSoto Public Library Citizen Advocacy Team (DeSoto Public Library CATs)

        C. Citizen Survey

        D. Other

    V. New Business

        A. Election of Officers 02/2003

        B. Christmas Parade

        C. Board and Commission Banquet

        D. Other

    VI. Announcements

    VII. Adjournment

Figure 7.2 Sample Agenda

Texas State Library Archives and Commission   **Austin, Texas**

Notice of Meeting

———————————— Public Library Board

Address of Meeting Location

Date

Time

Agenda

Call To Order

Approval Of Minutes

Citizen Comments

Discussion Items:

   1. Library Reports
   2. Review suggestions for marketing library programs and services
   3. Review library goals and objectives

Action Item:

   1. Discuss and consider approval of Internet Acceptable Use Policy

Adjournment

ACCESSIBILITY STATEMENT:———————————— Public Library is wheelchair-accessible. For sign interpretive services, call the City Secretary's office at (Phone number), at least 72 hours prior to the meeting. Reasonable accommodation will be made to meet your needs.

CERTIFICATION: I certify that this notice was posted on (legally designated posting place) no later than (time) on (date).

Signature————————————

Figure 7.3 Sample Agenda

Rockaway Township Free Public Library   **Rockaway, New Jersey**

Monthly Statistical Report

- Total circulation for the month of January 2000 was 20,653.

- During the month of January there were 46 story time programs at the Main Library and 12 at the Hibernia Branch and 905 people attended.

- There was 1 trip to the Library by a scout troop with 7 children. There was 1 trip to the Hibernia Branch by the Sunset Nursery School with 15 children.

- There was 1 special program for children in grades 4–6 with 11 children.

- There were 11 Computer Basics classes in the new Computer Training Center with 68 people in attendance. There were 9 Internet Basics Classes with 54 people in attendance. There were 5 Library Web Catalog classes with 48 people in attendance. The total number of classes given in January was 25 with a total of 146 people in attendance.

- There were 2 in-house meetings and 27 people attended.

- There were 6 meetings by outside organizations and 73 people attended.

- There were a grand total of 94 programs and 1,184 people were in attendance.

Figure 7.4 Sample Report

CHECKLIST

- Clearly describe the relationship between the library staff and the board members.
- Clearly defined your duties and responsibilities.
- Clearly defined the board's duties and responsibilities.
- Work with the board on crafting a new policy in all areas of operations, whether you are required to in the instance of governing boards, or seek the board's advice before changing policies with an advisory board.
- All policies should cover meetings, agendas, officers' duties, committee procedures, and keep bylaws current.
- Include the requirement for continuing education for you and your staff. Stress the need to keep current with library trends by attending workshops, conferences, and meeting with other librarians.
- With boards consisting of five or fewer members, committees are not recommended.
- Give yourself as much latitude as possible.
- Use forms as a way to keep the board informed about library operations.
- Require that board members be an active library user or active in the community before being appointed to the board.

Chapter 8

Exhibits, Displays, and Bulletin Boards

OVERVIEW

The goal of the Exhibits, Displays, and Bulletin Boards policy is to allow groups and individuals to post and exhibit items that are of interest to the community. As an important information resource center and a forum for free expression, Libraries perform a community service by providing space for citizens to display material. These policies and guidelines help you to decide who can use the space and determine what people can post or exhibit. The guidelines can be narrow allowing library-related material, or broader allowing nonprofit and even for-profit displays, if they are connected to a library program. Below you will find the contrasting policies. They all set excellent criteria, establish priorities, have reasonable time limits, ensure fair access to public space, apply guidelines equally, and protect the library from theft and damage claims. Written guidelines in a formal policy give you consistent control over your space, while offering the flexibility to make exceptions as the need arises. All of these policies are consistent with the American Library Association's "Exhibit Spaces and Bulletin Boards" statement.

Written policies ensure equal access, because the same rules are applied the same way each time you receive a request for space. Inconsistency creeps in when tradition and unwritten rules determine who can display and what can be displayed. A policy that is consistent with the library's mission and supports your intellectual freedom policies provides the community with a diverse important avenue of expression. Many libraries post a disclaimer near the space saying the "library does not advocate or endorse the viewpoints of any exhibitor or exhibit."

This chapter covers policies and forms in the following areas:

- Exhibits and Displays
- General Policies
- Priorities
- Criteria
- Artwork
- Pamphlets, Browsing Shelves, and Bulletin Boards
- General Policies

- Pamphlets, Posters, and Flyers
- Browsing Shelves
- Bulletin Boards
- Who Controls Policy
- Release Form
- Exhibit Proposal Form
- Exhibit Application Forms

Public Service Policies

Features of an Effective Policy

Display space will always be in demand. Local groups and individuals, as well as individuals outside the community, will want to display a variety of paintings, collections, photographs, notices, opportunities, crafts, or other material. This is a forum for individual free expression. The policies in this section include guidelines, criteria, procedures, and priorities that enable you to manage your space more effectively and equitability.

Their primary features include the following:

- Complies with American Library Association guidelines on exhibit spaces;
- Gives type of space, time limits, and limits on the number of times space can be used;
- Defines what type of material is allowed;
- Explains the permission process;
- Establishes and lists priorities;
- Ensures equal access to space;
- Explains what organizations, individuals, and groups can use the space;
- Clearly lists procedures for reserving space;
- Protects the library from damage and theft claims;
- States who controls the policy;
- Is flexible enough to make exceptions to the rule when the situation demands it;
- Has separate but interrelated criteria for artwork;
- Posts a disclaimer stating that the library does not endorse or sponsor any displays;
- Establishes criteria for exhibits;

Benefits of an Effective Policy

- Decreases misunderstandings about dates, times, and items allowed;
- Releases the library from liability for any damage to the exhibit;
- Minimizes confusion for exhibitors when procedures and rules are in writing and consistent from request to request;
- Communicates to the community your commitment to equal access;
- Ensures every group and individual has equal access because the same rules and procedures apply to every request.

Policies

Exhibits and Displays

General Policies

David and Joyce Milne Public Library   **Augusta, Maine**

The Mission of the David and Joyce Milne Public Library is to provide a welcoming and inspiring community center for lifelong learning. Facilities for the display of books and other materials on issues of interest to members of the community served by the Library can enhance this role in significant ways, adding an important educational tool to its many other cultural services.

General Guidelines

Use of the exhibit space is available at no charge only to individuals and non-profit groups engaged in educational, cultural, intellectual or charitable activities.

Allocation of exhibition space follows the principles of intellectual freedom as described in the Library Bill of Rights specifically Article VI states: "Libraries which make exhibit space available to the public should make such facilities available on an equitable basis, regardless of the beliefs or affiliations of individuals or groups requesting their use." The Library allows for a broad spectrum of opinion and a variety of viewpoints; however, authority over the particular design and use of the display facilities rests with the Library Director and the Board of Trustees.

An application, written proposal, and preview must be submitted to the Library Director for consideration. The proposal should state clearly the theme of the exhibition, its content, and the design of the display materials including physical dimensions.

The mounting, design and scheduling of exhibitions will take place at the discretion of the Director and designated staff. Exhibitions must be mounted by the individual or outside group in consultation with the Director. Time apportionment will be based upon demand for the space and the staffing needs of the Library. A suggested standard length of time for a given display is four weeks, but that time may vary. Priority is determined on a first come, first served basis.

The Library will not censor or remove an exhibition because some members of the community may disagree with its content. Those who object to the content of any exhibition should submit their own proposal for a countering exhibition. If an issue is particularly controversial, the Library Director may wish to divide the exhibition space in an impartial manner and in such a way to present all viewpoints.

A notice may be placed near the exhibition space stating that the Library does not advocate or endorse the viewpoints of the exhibition or exhibitor.

Anchorage Municipal Libraries   **Anchorage, Alaska**

The primary use of Anchorage Municipal Libraries Public Library is that of public library. When designated exhibit spaces within the library and/or branch libraries are not in use for library exhibits, space may be made available for exhibits, dependent upon the availability of staff resources to preview and coordinate exhibits and library programming needs.

General Terms and Conditions of Use

- Permission to use exhibit space is at the discretion of the Municipal Librarian and may be made available to organizations engaged in educational, cultural, intellectual or charitable activities on an equitable basis, regardless of the beliefs or affiliations of individuals or groups requesting their use.

- Permission may be denied to, or revoked for any exhibit whose purpose is personal, commercial and/or has the potential to cause, or causes, substantial disruptions or material interference with the functions of the library or is not in compliance with the Library Exhibit Policy.

- Permission to exhibit materials does not imply Library sponsorship, endorsement of content or responsibility for representation of all points of view. All proposed exhibits must be consistent with the requirements. The exhibitor accepts full responsibility for his/her/their exhibit including but not limited to content and/or accuracy of any statements or representations made in such materials.

- Permission to use exhibit space is conditional upon user agreement to save, hold harmless, and indemnify the Municipality of Anchorage from any claims, law suits, or judgments arising from loss, damage to property, injury to persons from or during their exhibit, and/or their exhibit material(s) or any part thereof. A signed "release" form is required.

- A completed and signed "Exhibit Request" form is required for consideration of a request to exhibit. The "Exhibit Request" must include the exhibit title, location requested, begin and end dates name, address and telephone numbers and signature of the contact person in charge of the proposed exhibit. (must be consistent with application form)

- All measures necessary to insure installation and removal of exhibits are the physical and financial responsibility of the exhibitor including but not limited to, shipping, packaging, storage, signage, labels, framing, installation and removal and equipment /supplies needed for same.

- Exhibitors agree to be responsible for and to pay for any and all damages to library property including exhibits, display/exhibit spaces, walls, floors, grounds and furniture resulting from the installation or removal of an exhibit and that any damage or loss thereto occasioned by fire, theft, or in any manner, to the exhibit, shall be sustained by the exhibitor.

- Installation and removal of exhibits must be accomplished during library open hours and in such a manner that causes the least possible disruption or material interference with library business. Exhibit items may not be unpacked or repackaged within the library proper. Hanging order and/or arrangement is to be arranged prior to installation by the exhibitor. Items for hanging may be leaned against elevator core walls in preparation for hanging, but may not be spread out on the floor, leaned against book shelves, service desks or be placed in such a way so as to interfere with normal traffic flow. Any children accompanying individuals involved in installation/removal of an exhibit must be directly supervised by an adult not involved with the installation/removal of the exhibit.

- Exhibit photos, artworks etc., must be framed, mounted or packaged and displayed in a safe and attractive manner. No heavy items may be placed over entrance, exit or elevator doors. Any electrical connections are to be hidden from public view as far as possible and may not be placed so as to cause or create a safety hazard.

- Labels, posters and or signs, used to identify items or the exhibit, must be clear and legible, preferably accomplished by computer or neat calligraphy. Each exhibit must contain an informative explanation to assist the general public in discerning subject material or purpose of the exhibit. This information may be provided by explanatory labels on individual items, in poster or sign form or be contained within the exhibit itself. Exhibitors are encouraged to provide a contact phone number as part of the exhibit on label, posters or signage for members of the general public who may wish more information about the exhibit. Events associated with the exhibit or items in the exhibit that may be for sale may not be advertised with the exhibit. Exhibits that include informational brochures pertaining to the exhibit are acceptable. In addition the Library encourages the use of bibliographies and books relating to the subject matter of the exhibit as part of the exhibit.

- When space allows the Library will include the exhibit title and description information from the "Exhibit Request" form in the "Activities Calendar" as a means of notifying the public of the exhibit.

- Video taping, cameras setup on tripods, television filming or interviewing arranged or accomplished by the exhibitor is not allowed within the library proper without the express advance written permission of the Municipal Librarian.

- Arrangement must be made in advance, with the library display coordinator, for exhibit(s) and/or items that are too large to be hand carried into the library, to be brought into the library through shipping and receiving during normal shipping and receiving hours. No exhibit item or packaging may be stored in any area of the library pre, post or during an exhibit. No exhibit, items or material used in installation may be shipped directly to the library.

Priorities

Gates Public Library   **Rochester, New York**

Where space limitations pose a problem, the Director is free to assign the following priorities for display of posters and free literature:

- Official town publications

- School District publications and posters

- Official Monroe County publications

- Official state or U.S. government publications

- Community-based non-profit, non-partisan, non-Sectarian organizations

- Other area public library literature and posters

- Other area non-profit organizations of a cultural nature

- Other area non-profit organizations of a non-partisan, non-Sectarian nature

- All other organizations and individuals

Criteria

Des Plaines Public Library   **Des Plaines, Illinois**

Criteria for Exhibits

1. Exhibits shall relate to the mission of the library. The mission of the Des Plaines Public Library is to provide free an open access to information in a welcoming environment and topromote literacy, lifelong learning, and the love of reading for all residents of Des Plaines.

2. The exhibit case may be used by not-for-profit community groups serving Des Plaines.

3. The exhibit case may be used for one month.

4. Exhibits should be aesthetically pleasing.

5. Exhibits shall display materials relevant to the organization.

6. Exhibits may not promote individual business or commercial ventures.

Artwork

Chelmsford Public Library   **Chelmsford, Massachusetts**

Art Exhibit Policy

The Chelmsford Public Library welcomes the opportunity to allow groups, organizations, or individuals to use the library picture rail on the main level for art exhibits. Space is provided for educational, cultural, civic, or recreational exhibits. Space is not available for strictly commercial purposes.

The purpose of the exhibit policy is to provide guidance in the selection of exhibits; to inform the public about the principles upon which exhibits are arranged; and to encourage equitable utilization of exhibit areas by artists in the Chelmsford area.

Goals of the Exhibits:

- To broaden horizons by presenting a wide range of art, collections, or displays;

- To support community cultural and artistic activities;

- To nourish intellectual, aesthetic and creative growth;

- To encourage individuals who may be contributing to the increase of knowledge or extension of the arts;

- To reach non-traditional library patrons.

Criteria for Selection

All exhibits, whether generated by library staff or the public, will be considered in terms of the standards listed below. Not all exhibits will meet all standards. Responsibility for the selection of exhibits rests with the Library Director, Assistant Director and Head of Community Services. The following will be considered when selecting or approving exhibits:

- subject, technique and style are suitable for intended audience;

- artistic expression;

- appropriateness to special events, anniversaries, holidays, etc.;

- historical or regional relevance;

- relation to other events or exhibits in the community;

- ease of installation;

- representation of an influential movement, genre, trend or national culture;

- significance of the contributor;

- attention of viewers and the public.

The Board of Library Trustees has the final authority for approving exhibits and reserves the right to prohibit any person or group from displaying artwork.

To Apply for Exhibit Space:

Exhibits are scheduled by the Head of Community Services. Reservations may be made up to one year in advance. Individual exhibitors or groups are limited to a single one-month exhibit annually. Educational groups may schedule exhibits more than once a year, provided there is space available.

Each artist/group is responsible for hanging his/her own works and taking down the same when the exhibit has ended. Library Staff assistance is not available.

Artists must sign an exhibit agreement and a waiver form that releases the Library from any responsibility for loss or damage to works on display.

Exhibits must conform to the space restrictions of the exhibit areas provided.

Nothing should be attached to walls. Do not use tape, labels, thumbtacks, or adhesives for signage on any of the walls in the library.

The Chelmsford Public Library does not allow solicitation or selling of items in the library. Artistic works for sale may be purchased directly from the artist, but only outside the library.

No price tags may be affixed to the works exhibited or pricing lists distributed in the library.

Artist/groups who fail to remove paintings on or before the specified date will not be allowed use of the library space in the future.

The Library will not provide storage for the property of exhibitors.

A library representative only can transfer an exhibit reservation to another artist.

The Library's need for exhibit space takes precedence over the public's request to use such areas.

Procedures for Reserving Space

Anchorage Municipal Libraries   **Anchorage, Alaska**

When a request is made for an exhibit, the library will provide The Anchorage Municipal Libraries Exhibit Policy, "Exhibit Request" form and "Release" form.

A completed "Exhibit Request" form is required for acceptance of a request to exhibit. The request must be consistent with the requirements and procedures stated in #5 of the General Terms and Conditions stated above.

Exhibit requests are processed in the order received and with regard to other exhibits scheduled and/or planned. The Municipal Librarian or his/her designee reviews the request and proposed exhibit materials according to the Library Exhibit Policy criteria. The librarian may accept or reject a proposed exhibit if inconsistent with the library's Exhibit Policy. The Municipal Librarian may suggest alternate dates, appropriate locations and/or modifications. The requester is notified of the decision. An "Exhibit Request" is considered accepted when it has been signed by the librarian or his/her designee and the "Release" form has been signed by the exhibitor and received by the Library display coordinator.

If an exhibit request is denied and/or permission revoked or modifications suggested after acceptance, the requester may appeal that decision to the Library Advisory Board, which will provide advice to the municipal Administration. The Director of Cultural and Recreational Services will make the final decision concerning the exhibit.

Pamphlets, Browsing Shelves, and Bulletin Boards

General Policies

Joplin Pubic Library   **Joplin, Missouri**

- As part of its public service and information mission, the Joplin Public Library makes available a browsing shelf for handouts, display and exhibit areas, and bulletin boards. The use of these areas is intended to increase public awareness of the range of information available in the library collection and to make available information created by and of interest to the local community. When space is limited, preference is given to Joplin organizations.

- Displays, exhibits, handouts, and materials posted on bulletin boards are covered by the intellectual freedom policies of the Library. Materials displayed or distributed in public forum areas may advocate a position, but the display and distribution do not constitute endorsement of the materials' content by the Library or the city of Joplin.

- All handouts or materials for public forum areas must be evaluated for compliance with these guidelines and approved by the Library Director, in consultation with the Adult Services Librarian when necessary, for distribution or posting. Unauthorized material may be discarded.

- Materials approved for the public forum areas will be stamped with the date of posting.

- A disclaimer will be displayed in all public forum areas stating that the availability of handouts does not imply endorsement of the organization or its views by the Library or the city of Joplin.

- Political campaign materials will not be accepted for display or distribution.

- The Library reserves the right to establish and amend further policies for public forum areas.

Indian Valley Public Library   Telford, Pennsylvania

- It is part of the library's function to provide access to intellectual and cultural resources to the community. Thus, the Indian Valley Public Library welcomes community groups, organizations and individuals to use the various display areas and the public bulletin board of the library. Space is provided for items of an educational, cultural, civic, or recreational nature, rather than for commercial or political purposes.

- The bulletin board is a community service to publicize local groups, meetings, cultural events, non-partisan political events, fund-raising events for non-profit organizations, educational opportunities, or other services that are of a non-profit, non-self-promoting nature.

- Educational or instructional opportunities may be posted, regardless of whether they are of a for-profit or non-profit nature.

- Personal ads, campaign literature, baby-sitting, and garage sales are not posted.

- Items may be rejected for lack of space.

- Space on the bulletin board is also reserved for Area School District information.

- The date items are received will be stamped "Posted" (by the Reference Librarian)and the items will be removed after one month or when timeliness has ceased.

- Exhibits in the library are seen by anyone who walks into the building—both children and adults who may have various degrees of sophistication. Exhibits must therefore meet what is generally known as "a standard acceptable to the community".

Pamphlets, Posters, and Flyers

Cumberland Pubic Library   Fayetteville, North Carolina

The distribution of leaflets, cards or other printed materials, whether political, religious or business, is not allowed in public library facilities unless it is to supplement a program being presented. Distribution of printed materials in the public library to library users and staff is disruptive to the operations of the library and its use by the public.

The library is a public forum for ideas and information. Access to ideas and information is fundamental to our social, political and cultural heritage. In order to carry out this purpose, the library adopted the following policy concerning the display of information on posters, pamphlets and flyers:

- Public posters, pamphlets and flyers will be displayed as space permits on a first-come, first-served basis on library bulletin boards or spaces set aside for this purpose.

- Materials submitted cannot exceed 16" by 20" except by special permission of the community relations coordinator.

- Only one item will be posted per event or function.

- Any materials submitted that (a) would tend to incite or produce imminent lawless action, (b) are obscene, (c) are obviously false or contain misleading information, (d) are defamatory, (e) or are purely commercial advertising will not be posted.

- Any questions regarding this policy should be referred to the community relations coordinator. Final authority rests with the director.

Browsing Shelves

Joplin Public Library   **Joplin, Missouri**

The Library reserves the right to limit quantities of materials accepted for handout. Items may be refused because of their size if at the time there is no available space for them.

All materials on the browsing shelf are the responsibility of the organization or group providing the material.

Handouts of for-profit groups, companies or organizations and handouts of an individual are generally not accepted. Possible exceptions might include community newspapers produced by for-profit organizations but distributed free of charge.

Materials that have been on the browsing shelf for more than four weeks may be removed to make room for newly submitted materials.

Bulletin Boards

Gates Public Library   **Rochester, New York**

The bulletin boards and display areas were designed and intended to directly aid and supplement the primary activities of the library, and as such all library activities will have first call for the use of these areas.

One bulletin board in the lobby next to the entrance corridor is designated as the bulletin board continuously available to the public as space and reasonable time display permit.

All other boards and display areas are reserved for library use. Library use can include occasional displays from Gates educational institutions or groups.

Middletown Thrall Public Library   **Middletown, New York**

The Library bulletin board is to be used for the posting of notices of

- library business or activities and

- public service items of educational or cultural interest to the community.

Members of the public are not permitted to post notices. Only authorized library personnel may post notices on the Library bulletin board. Any notice to be considered for posting must be submitted to Library management for approval.

Notices posted without authorization will be removed.

The bulletin board is not to be used for advertising or for commercial notices.

All notices intended for posting on the Library bulletin board must contain the following:

- name of sponsoring agency, and

- address and telephone number of sponsoring agency or authorized representative.

Notice size (physical dimensions) can be restricted if deemed necessary to maximize available space.

Notices may be removed after two weeks, when they are no longer timely or when space is required for more current items.

The Library does not necessarily advocate or endorse the viewpoints of organizations permitted to post notices on the Library bulletin board. The Library accepts no responsibility for loss or damage to any item accepted for posting.

Failure to comply with these rules may result in denial of future posting privileges.

This policy is determined by the Library Board of Trustees and is subject to periodic review and/or revision at the discretion of the Board. Appeals may be submitted to the Board in writing.

Who Controls Policy

Gates Public Library   **Rochester, New York**

The bulletin boards and all potential display areas in the library portion of the Gates Community Center are under the sole control of the Library Board of Trustees, with the Library Director administering the policy as established by the Library Board. All questions arising from this policy are to be brought to the attention of the Library Board, if not resolvable by the Director.

163

FORMS

Benefits of Written Forms

- Retains a history of what was and was not a successful exhibit;
- Knows which individual or group exhibited their material and why;
- Limits use of the space per year to ensure that no one monopolizes the area;
- Keeps a record of material that was rejected and why;
- Helps plan the year's exhibit calendar;
- Gives background information on groups who apply for space again;
- Provides contact names and telephone numbers for exhibitors;
- Keeps you organized giving you one less thing to think about.

Indian Valley Public Library   **Telford, Pennsylvania**

Public Library Exhibit Release

I/we the undersigned, hereby lend the following works of art or other material to the Indian Valley Public Library for exhibit purposes only. In consideration for the privilege of exhibiting them in the library, I/we hereby release said library from responsibility for damage to or the loss and/or destruction of these materials or any part thereof while they are in the possession of the library.

Exhibition to be held in the _____

During _____

Description of materials loaned

Signature _____

Date _____

Permanent address   _____

                       _____

Telephone number   _____

Figure 8.1 Release Form

Joplin Public Library   **Joplin, Missouri**

Exhibits must be scheduled through the Library Director or his or her designee. Exhibits may be shown subject to the time, place, and manner determined by the Library. Library sponsored exhibits shall receive first priority. Exhibits shall be shown on a space available basis. Commercial exhibits are not accepted and no exhibit may advertise materials for sale. Price information may not be displayed or be provided by staff. Displays may be exhibited for no longer than four weeks. No exhibit shall interfere with the operation of the Library or pose a physical hazard to Library patrons or staff.

Name of Organization: _____

Address of Organization: _____

_____

Phone Number of Organization: _____

Fax Number: _____

Name of Contact Person: _____

Daytime Phone No: _____

Position of Contact Person (with Organization): _____

Address of Contact Person: _____(If different than organization)

_____

Nature of Organization:_____

Nature of Meeting: _____

Number of persons expected: _____

Large Room Small Room (Must be completed) (Circle one)

Library Preference: Please indicate options for location, date, and/or hours of use. While every effort will be made to schedule your meeting site, we cannot guarantee availability. (Attach additional sheet, if necessary.) LIBRARY LOCATION:_____

DAY/DATE:_____ START TIME:_____ END TIME:_____

(One meeting per month per organization) * On Friday and Saturday, meeting rooms are not available after 4:30 PM. Group must be in the library at least one half hour (1/2 hr) prior to closing time. Those meeting rooms with Sunday hours will only be scheduled for use between (DATE):_____. It is understood by the users that County assumes no responsibility whatever for any property placed in any county building or facility in connection with a meeting;

Figure 8.2 Exhibit Proposal Form

and that the county is hereby expressly released and discharged from any and all liability for any loss, injury, or damage to persons or property which may be sustained by reason of a meeting. In signing this application, the organization and/or its representative agrees to the stipulations, rules, and regulations on the attached sheet. (Please read these before signing).

_____ Date: _____

Signature of Authorized Representative Method of Payment: Check / Credit Card (Visa/MC)

_____

Number: _____ exp. _____

For office use only Approved Rental #_____

By: _____ Date:_____

Comments:

8.2 *continued*

Lithgow Public Library   **Augusta, Maine**

EXHIBIT APPLICATION

Please print this form to fill it out. You may mail it to us, submit it in person, or fax it to us. Alternatively, you may copy, paste, edit and e-mail it to us adult reference desk.

EXHIBITOR: Name:_____

Contact person, if group:_____

Address: _____

_____

Telephone:_____ day _____ evening

May we give this info. to public, if asked:

Y or N (circle one)

EXHIBIT:

Title:_____

Medium: _____

Space Requirements: _____

Number of pieces: _____

OTHER INFORMATION:

Dates you would like exhibit to run: _____ to _____

Do you have information for publicity or ready-made publicity?

Y or N

If yes, please attach.

Do you need to schedule the conference room for an event coinciding

with your exhibit?

Y or N

If yes, please see our librarian and schedule that separately.

WAIVER OF INSURANCE:

I have read and agree to abide by the Exhibit Policy of XYZ Public Library.

Figure 8.3 Exhibit Application

I hereby do not hold XYZ Public Library liable for any damages, injuries,

theft, etc. while said artist is displaying his/her works at the Library.

Signature of Artist/Exhibitor————————————— Date:————————

Signature of Librarian————————————— Date:————————

Figure 8.3 *continued*

David and Joyce Milne Public Library   Williamstown, Massachusetts
Exhibition Rules and Application Form

Regulations

1. Exhibits or displays will be scheduled in conjunction with the Library exhibit calendar. Library exhibits have precedence over all outside exhibits.

2. A written proposal for an exhibition, accompanied by this completed application form, must be submitted to the Library Director for consideration. The proposal must state clearly the theme of the exhibit, its content, the design of the display including physical dimensions, and how the display can be placed specifically in the space available.

3. Arrangements for an exhibition must be made from one month to one year in advance. Priority is determined on a first come, first served basis.

4. The Library does not insure articles or materials exhibited, and is not responsible for theft or damage. Exhibitors must make their own arrangements for insurance.

5. Displays may not advertise the sale of exhibit items.

6. It is the exhibitor's responsibility to set up and dismantle the exhibit and provide the Library with a sample press release subject to editorial review by the Library Director if applicable.

APPLICATION

Date: _____ Month of Exhibit: _____

Name: _____

Organizational Affiliation: _____

Address: _____

_____

Phone Home: _____ Work: _____

Description of Exhibit:

Is exhibition insured? Yes No (Please circle)

I have read the above regulations, understand the library's exhibition policy and comply with both.

Signature of Applicant_____ Date_____

Figure 8.4 Exhibit Application

CHECKLIST

- Determine if you want to establish a priority list, such as deciding whether local government or library functions come first.
- Ensure equal access to the space.
- Determine with your library's attorney if you need an insurance requirement.
- Include that meetings or functions cannot interfere with library operations.
- Determine if you want for-profit or only educational, cultural, or library notcies to be posted on flyers.
- Set size limits and physical specifications on postings and handouts.
- Include a provision that allows you to reject material based on space limitations.
- Require all postings to have prior approval from staff.
- Stipulate who is responsible for removing the posted item, when it must be removed, and the library's recourse if the item is not removed by that date.

Chapter 9

Meeting Rooms

OVERVIEW

The goal of the meeting room policy is to provide an appropriate gathering place for events, book talks, meetings, lectures, presentations, programs, and other activities that enhance your ability to provide service. Meeting space is a tremendous asset in the community. Libraries vary on what type of individuals and groups may use the facility. You must determine insurance requirements, equipment costs, amount of effort to set up, conduct rules, liability issues, safety regulations, and priorities,. Impromptu management of the physical space leads to confusion for the staff and those using the room. With these policies you can streamline operations.

All these policies conform to the American Library Association's **"Meeting Rooms: An Interpretation of the Library Bill of Rights,"** with one exception. Most public libraries do not provide space for religious services or partisan political campaign meetings.

This chapter covers policies and forms in the following areas:

- General Policies
- Rules of Conduct
- Priorities
- Reservations
- Fees and No Fees
- Insurance Requirements

- Equipment and Set-up
- Damage Clauses
- Disclaimers
- Reservation, Insurance, and Liability Form
- Meeting Room Application

PUBLIC SERVICE POLICIES

Features of an Effective Policy

Unwritten rules and procedures are your worst enemy. Written policies are your best friend. To treat all community members fairly, it is essential to handle each request the same way. Establishing guidelines pertaining to a fee or no-fee policy, damages fees, rules of conduct, insurance requirements, and other meeting room details, makes the process relatively easy. Everything is predetermined—your criteria, your reservation system, and your priorities, make for smooth operations.

The following list delineates the features of an effective meeting room policy:

- Describes meeting space priorities, such as assigning the highest priority to the library and governmental agencies, and relegating for-profit workshops and classes to the lowest priority;

- Sets minimum age requirement for who can reserve space and who must be in charge of the room at all times;

- Prohibits admission fees unless cleared by the director;

- Requires a room-check by staff before the organizer leaves to make sure there is no damage or material left in the area;

- Stipulates that meetings must be opened to the public;

- Forbids individuals and organizations from storing equipment, supplies, and personal effects in the room;

- Requires those who use meeting rooms to observe safety rules, such as not blocking exits;

- Does not allow a care giver to attend an activity in a meeting room, while leaving a child or children unattended in the library;

- Retains the right to revoke meeting room privileges for groups who violate the rules;

- Excludes social gatherings such as wedding showers but allows library related events such as dedicating a new wing;

- Operates on a first come, first served basis ensuring equal access;

- Complies with American Library Association's policy on meeting rooms;

Benefits of a Written Policy

- Ensures that a participant can be removed if she or he becomes unruly;

- Gives library programs priority;

- Protects the library's property with damage fees;

- Prohibits admission fees, thereby ensuring no one will excluded because of financial reasons;

- Protects and cares for children, by providing they can be not be left alone in the library;

- Requires those in attendance to observe safety rules, which protects the public;

- Makes the process fair for all applicants, by equally applying the rules to everyone.

Policies

General Policies

Jasper County Public Library   **Rensselae, Indiana**

The Jasper County Public Libraries have meeting areas available for the purpose of promoting the library's mission to:

> Inform, enrich and empower those in our community by creating and promoting easy access to ideas and information, and by supporting an informed citizenry, lifelong learning and love of reading.

The meeting rooms are available for use by area clubs, organizations, committees, individuals and businesses with restrictions on use noted below. The library's programs and meetings shall have first priority for use.

The meeting rooms will be available to groups in the community regardless of the beliefs and affiliations of their individual members.

Meetings may not be used for

- Sale or promotion of products or services, except in conjunction with a library program. Names of participants cannot be collected by program presenters for later financial gain.

- Partisan political activities, except for events such as candidates' nights, when all candidates are invited by the library or independent civic organizations

- Purely social or fund-raising functions unless sponsored by the library or a library group

No admission charge may be made for any function held in the library.

Membership dues and/or registration fees covering the cost of materials or speakers are acceptable. Tickets may not be sold nor donations or free will offerings taken.

The individual reserving and assuming responsibility for the room must be a resident of the Jasper County Public Library district. Exceptions to this requirement will be made for representatives of U.S. or Indiana governmental agencies. Elected officials may use the meeting room for "office hours" to meet with constituents, but such meetings may not be used for re-election purposes.

The Board of Trustees reserves the right to make a final decision if questions arise concerning use of the libraries.

Fayette County Public Library   Fayetteville, Georgia

The Fayette County Public Library has meeting rooms for library programs (the Distance Learning Center and the Public Meeting Room), and makes these facilities available to nonprofit organizations within Fayette County (Maximum of four (4) meetings per year). The Distance Learning Center is available for small meetings and has a capacity of up to 15 people and the Public Meeting Room is available for large meetings and has a capacity of up to 150 people.

Permission to use the rooms does not constitute endorsement or sponsorship of any program or event by the library. The library's name may be used only in reference to location, not sponsorship. Applications for use of the rooms must be submitted at least 10 days in advance of the proposed meeting. The library may cancel any reservation in the event of a conflict with a library program. Notice of such cancellation will be given as soon as possible. Organizations must notify the library of any cancellation on their part as soon as possible. The library cannot be responsible for items left in the rooms.

- A $50.00 refundable deposit shall accompany the application. The deposit must be a check or money order payable to the Fayette County Public Library with the name of the person or organization requesting the room imprinted on the check. Deposits will be returned if the reservation cannot be confirmed or after the meeting upon inspection of the room.

- The organization conducting the meeting shall be financially responsible for damage to walls, floor covering, tables, chairs, kitchen equipment and/or fixtures and any other contents of the rooms.

- The organization in whose name the reservation has been confirmed shall be the same organization conducting the meeting for which the application is made. Applicants must be at least 21 years of age and must be residents of Fayette County. No admission fee may be charged.

- Use of the library meeting rooms shall be limited to the dissemination of information. Library meeting rooms may not be used for personal or private profit.

- Library meeting rooms may not be used for social gatherings.

- Library meeting rooms may only be scheduled for use during regular library operating hours. All meetings must concluded by 8:30 p.m. Monday through Thursday, and 5:30 p.m. Friday and Saturday.

- After the meeting, a representative of the organization must meet with a library staff member to check the room, return the key and record the number of participants at the meeting.

- Programs or meetings may not disturb the use of the library by other patrons.

- Smoking and/or alcoholic beverages are not permitted.

- Groups using the kitchen must furnish their own supplies such as cooking and eating utensils, cloths, cleaning supplies, paper goods, et cetera, and must leave the kitchen in an orderly fashion.

- The room must be vacuumed and the garbage must be taken out. A vacuum cleaner and broom are available at the circulation desk and must be returned after use.

- Nothing may be attached to any surface of the room other than the bulletin board. Bulletin boards and dry erase boards must be cleaned at the close of the meeting.

- Use of the room by the library or the county governing authorities for any purposes shall be permitted.

- All meetings must be open to the public should anyone wish to attend.

Rules of Conduct

Austin Public Library   **Austin, Texas**

- Please leave meeting rooms as they are found. If the furniture is rearranged, it should be returned to the original arrangement at the end of the meeting.

- Furniture and/or equipment from the main area of the Library may not be brought into meeting rooms.

- Personal furniture or equipment may be provided by a group with prior approval. Arrangements for the use of any personal furniture or equipment should be made at scheduling time. In order to ensure easy removal of equipment after the meeting, the appropriate staff member (either Library Security or the Branch Librarian) should be notified when the equipment is brought into the building.

- Equipment, supplies, or personal effects cannot be stored or left in Library meeting rooms before or after use.

- Keep all exits unlocked at all times. Open aisles must be maintained within the seating arrangement to provide clear access to exits.

- Public entrances are to be used for entrance to and exit from the building, and for all deliveries.

- Any announcements or notices to publicize an activity should not be posted or distributed without prior approval from the librarian in charge.

- Attendance at meetings will be limited to the capacity of the individual meeting rooms as listed at the end of this policy. Seating and/or supplementary furniture are not allowed in corridors outside the meeting rooms.

- Simple refreshments including coffee, doughnuts, box or sack lunches, may be served, but kitchen facilities or equipment will not be provided by the Library. (Minimal kitchen facilities are available at Carver Branch and the Austin History Center with permission from the librarian in charge.)

- All trash resulting from the serving of refreshments must be removed by the organization.

- The individual making the reservation, as well as the membership of the group as a whole, will be held responsible for any and all damages that may occur as a result of the use of the facilities.

- Permission to use Library meeting rooms may be withheld from groups failing to comply with the Meeting Room Policy and from any group that damages the room, carpet, equipment, or furniture, or causes a disturbance.

The City of Austin is committed to compliance with the Americans With Disabilities Act. Reasonable modifications and equal access to communications will be provided upon request.

Bernardsville Public Library   Bernardsville, New Jersey

No admission fee, registration fee, donation or monetary solicitation may be sought from meeting attendees, unless the Library co-sponsors the program.

- Smoking is not permitted in the Community Room or anywhere in the Library.

- Food and beverages may be served provided that all evidence of food is removed from the premises before leaving, the pantry is cleaned, and all trash is properly bagged and discarded in the Library dumpster. A refundable deposit of $50 is required for groups wishing to serve refreshments of any kind. This deposit will be returned within 24 hours, once it has been determined that the meeting room has been left in good condition. No food or beverages may be stored at the Library.

- The serving of alcoholic beverages is strictly prohibited.

- Preparation of the room for the meeting and clean-up following the meeting are the responsibilities of the group requesting use of the room. The group will also be responsible for any damage to Library property.

- After each meeting, all furniture must returned to its original arrangement and the room left in the condition in which it was found. Failure to do so will result in revocation of room rental privileges.

- The library staff is not responsible for the supervision of children while adults are attending meetings. A copy of the Library's Policy on Unattended Children may be obtained from the Library. (See Circulation Chapter for policies on Unattended Children)

- The Library is not responsible for lost or stolen items.

- Groups holding regular meetings at Library must complete a Room Rental Form at the beginning of each year at which time the rental fee will be determined. However, either party has the right to terminate this agreement upon 30 days of written intent to do so.

Priorities

Hershey Public Library   **Hershey, Pennsylvania**

Governmental or non-profit groups, and for-profit groups or businesses located in Derry Township are invited to use the library's meeting rooms. The library reserves the right to schedule and make room assignments according to the library's needs. Additionally, the library reserves the right to alter the meeting room schedules according to the library's needs. In general, the library allows groups to reserve meeting rooms on a first-come, first-served basis, or (in case of conflict) according to the following order of priority:

- Library Programs and Meetings—which involve efforts of library staff, Library Board, Friends of the Hershey Public Library or Hershey Public Library Endowment Trust.

- Local Government Meetings/Programs—official meetings or programs of Derry Township, Dauphin County, or Commonwealth of Pennsylvania agencies/departments.

- Meetings or Programs of Nonprofit Educational, Cultural, Civic or Social Organizations—open to the public. Priority will be given to Derry Township organizations. A Derry Township organization has 60% or greater of its members residing in the township.

- Activities of For-Profit Organizations/Businesses—classes, workshops, and meetings, excluding activities that result in direct profit, promotion, sales solicitations, or requiring a fee to attend. Only businesses located in Derry Township may use the rooms. Any advertisement for the meeting or program must include the following disclaimer: "The Hershey Public Library is not sponsoring or endorsing this program or any goods or services offered."

Reservations

Washoe County Library System   **Reno, Nevada**

- County related meetings: County Departments will reserve meeting facilities by contacting the facility to be reserved.

- Non-County related meetings: Facilities will be reserved by contacting the Library facility to be reserved. Facilities may be reserved no more than 60 days in advance.

- All reservations are accepted on a first-come, first-served basis. The Library retains the right to cancel a reservation for cause it deems sufficient. In addition, the Library may cancel the use of a facility for Library purposes, but will do so with no less than twenty-four (24) hour notice.

Lucius Beebe Memorial Library   **Wakefield, Massachusetts**

Requirements for Room Reservations

All groups using any meeting room shall complete, submit and, at the request of the library staff, update an application on a form approved by the Board of Library Trustees. Such a form shall incorporate by reference this policy and shall recite that the applicant group has received a copy of this policy and agrees to abide by the terms and conditions of this policy.

Reservations shall be made through the office of the Library Director, or its designee. No group may reserve or use any meeting room unless it complies in all respects with the provisions of this policy and submits, in fully executed form, the application and indemnification agreement called for in this policy, and any insurance certificate requested pursuant hereto. No meeting room reservation shall be deemed complete until the library staff receives a complete, signed original form (together, if applicable, with an original insurance certificate).

Any false, misleading or incomplete statement on the application form shall be grounds to forbid the use of meeting rooms by the applicant group.

The Board of Library Trustees and the library staff reserve the right to reject a reservation request if the anticipated meeting is likely to be unreasonably disruptive to regular library functions, too large for the applicable room capacity, disorderly, dangerous to persons or property, or in any other way inconsistent with or in contravention of any of the terms and conditions of this policy. In determining whether such a likelihood exists, the Board of Library Trustees and/or the library staff may take into consideration the contents of the application form, the history of the group's meeting room use in the library, the history of the group's use of meeting facilities elsewhere, and such other information as they may deem appropriate.

The Board of Library Trustees reserves the right to determine, in its reasonable discretion, whether any proposed use of a meeting room will require a police detail or other extraordinary police protection, and if so the anticipated cost thereof. In making this determination, the Board of Library Trustees may take into consideration the contents of the application form, the history of the group's meeting room use in the library, the history of the group's use of meeting facilities elsewhere, and such other information as such Board may deem appropriate, and may consult with the Chief of Police or his designee. If the Board of Library Trustees determines that such police protection will be reasonably necessary, the group seeking to reserve the use of a meeting room shall be required, as a condition of such reservation, to pay to the Board of Library Trustees by such date in advance of the meeting as the Board of Library Trustees reasonably sets, the anticipated cost of such police protection, and such sum shall be applied thereto, with any surplus being returned to the group after the meeting. The group shall be liable to the Board of Library Trustees and/or the Town of Wakefield for any deficiency.

Reservations may be made up to one year in advance for up to twelve (12) meetings annually. Reservations shall be accepted, subject to the provisions of this policy, in the order received.

Failure to notify the library of cancellations may result in forfeiture of future bookings.

Minors may not reserve a meeting room, nor can they serve as sponsors.

Administrative Policies

Features of an Effective Policy

- Requires a disclaimer stating that the library does not endorse or sponsor the meeting;
- Requires proper insurance to protect the library against lawsuits;
- Requires a damage clause and sets fees to protect library property;

Benefits of Effective Policies

- Protects the city/county from lawsuits ranging from injury to unequal treatment;
- Ensures consistent fees, deposits, charges, and insurance requirements for all groups giving each group equal treatment.

Policies

Rental Fees and No Fees

Jasper County Public Library   Rensselaer, Indiana

There is no charge for single or monthly meetings or programs. Groups wishing to hold regular weekly meetings must obtain permission from the Board of Trustees and may be charged a fee. All meetings must be cleared with the Director or Agency Librarian.

Donations to the library's gift fund are accepted with pleasure.

Bernardsville Public Library   Bernardsville, New Jersey

Local non-profit organizations One meeting per year is free

> $25 half-room $50 whole room

Non-local non-profit organizations

> $50 half room $75 whole room

For-profit organizations

> $175 half room $225 whole room

Hershey Public Library   Hershey, Pennsylvania

Meeting Room Fees: The use of meeting rooms is free of charge to non-profit civic, social, cultural, educational, and government organizations, as long as the meetings or programs they hold are open to the public, are free of charge, and are not held with the intention of generating revenue. The fee assessed for for-profit groups or businesses located in Derry Township using or reserving the meeting room is $75.00 per hour for the full multi-purpose room. The use of one part of the divided multi-purpose room is $40.00 per hour.

For-profits presenting educational seminars are subject to meeting room rental fees unless the program is being presented at the direct invitation of the township, Library, its boards and committees.

Payment or a billing arrangement must be made at the time of reservation. The library will bill organizations or agencies that wish to be billed. Any group that fails to pay their bill within thirty calendar days of being billed will be denied meeting room use privileges until its account is cleared, and will be required to pay in advance for any future use of the meeting room.

Insurance Requirements

Lucille Beebe Public Library   Wakefield, Massachusetts

All groups using any of the meeting rooms shall execute and deliver a written undertaking in a form to be prescribed by the Board of Library Trustees by which such groups shall agree to hold the Board of Library Trustees, and the XYZ city/county and all library staff, harmless from and to indemnify them against all costs, damages, losses, claims, and expenses incurred, directly or indirectly, as a result of such group's use of a meeting room.

Such costs, damages, losses, claims, and expenses shall include, without limitation, any damage to the meeting room or any other part of the library building, grounds or collection; the cost of employee overtime, if occasioned by the use of the meeting room; the cost of police protection, if deemed necessary by the Board of Library Trustees; and any claim asserted by any third person against the Board of Library Trustees, the XYZ city/county, and/or any library staff on account of any alleged injury causally related to the meeting, together with defense costs including reasonable attorneys' fees.

The said written undertaking shall also constitute a release by the group and each and all of its members of any claim against the Board of Library Trustees, the XYZ City/County and the library staff for any injury to persons or damage to property suffered by such group or any of its members during or as a result of the use of the meeting room, except insofar as such injury or damage is directly and solely caused by the negligence or intentional misconduct of any person belonging to or acting on behalf of the Board of Library Trustees, the town government of the Town of Wakefield or the library staff.

The Board of Library Trustees reserves the right to require any applicant group to supply a certificate of insurance, from an insurer licensed to do business in Massachusetts, in such amount and in such form as the Board of Library Trustees may reasonably deem appropriate, such amount not to exceed $1 million, naming the Board of Library Trustees as an additional insured, and covering damage to the library building, grounds and collection and injury to persons occasioned by the meeting. Such certificate shall evidence that the insurance it represents is not cancelable except on at least ten (10) days' written notice to the Board of Library Trustees. In the event of such cancellation, the meeting reservation shall be canceled unless the group forthwith substitutes a new insurance certificate meeting the aforesaid requirements.

Bernardsville Public Library   Bernardsville, New Jersey

Certificate of Insurance: Please note that the Borough requires that this "Certificate of Insurance shall be written with a company maintaining a rating of at least "A-", according to A.M. Best's. Said policy shall be in the amount of not less than one million dollars ($1,000,000) per occurrence." The Borough of Bernardsville must be listed as an additional insured on the Certificate of Insurance

Equipment and Set-up

Lawrence Public Library   Lawrence, Kansas

- Set-up and special arrangements are the responsibility of the user. No special room set-ups will be provided by the Library.

- No tacks, nails or adhesive tape are to be placed in or on doors, walls, or furniture.

- Lighted candles or flames, because of fire hazard, are not to be used within the meeting rooms. All paper and decorations used in decorating the meeting rooms must be flame proof.

- A variety of audiovisual equipment is available for use in the meeting rooms.

Available equipment includes a TV/VCR, overhead projector, and an AV cart. The equipment should be used by someone experienced in its operation. The TV/VCR must be checked out and back in by the person responsible for reserving the room. Any damage due to misuse of audiovisual equipment is the responsibility of the organization or group reserving the room. Audiovisual equipment must be checked back in by 8:45 p.m. Monday through Friday, and 5:45 p.m. on Saturday and Sunday.

Equipment—various types of audiovisual equipment are available for loan, such as 16mm projectors, 8mm projector, slide projector, cassette tape recorder/player, and Polaroid land cameras.

Damage Clauses

Bernardsville Public Library   **Bernardsville, New Jersey**

Certificate of Insurance: Please note that the Borough requires that this "Certificate of Insurance shall be written with a company maintaining a rating of at least "A-", according to A.M. Best's. Said policy shall be in the amount of not less than one million dollars ($1,000,000) per occurrence." The Borough of Bernardsville must be listed as an additional insured on the Certificate of Insurance.

Hershey Public Library   **Hershey, Pennsylvania**

Clean Up and Damage: The sponsoring group or individual making application for use of facilities assumes all responsibility for damage to library property and for leaving the premises in the condition in which it was found, including the arrangement of furnishings and the cleanup of trash. A minimum fee of $25.00 will be assessed for excessive cleanup. Damage to the facility will be billed to the group or individual responsible for the room and could result in restriction from further use. A $20.00 charge will be assessed if a room is not vacated by the scheduled time.

Disclaimers

Jasper County Public Library   **Rensselaer, Indiana**

The fact that a group is permitted to meet at the Library does not imply Library approval of the group or of the ideas presented at the meeting. Publicity for meetings or programs must make it clear that the Library is not a sponsor of the event.

Lucius Beebe Memorial Library   **Wakefield, Massachusetts**

In allowing a group to use a meeting room, the Board of Library Trustees and library staff do not imply any endorsement of the group's beliefs, policies or program. No group shall in any of its publicity state or suggest that the XYZ Library, the Board of Library Trustees, the XYZ city/county or the library staff sponsors or endorses the meeting, the group or any particular set of ideas.

Groups may identify the library and provide its address in their publicity for the meeting, but may not give out the library's telephone numer or invite potential attendees to contact the library.

FORMS

Benefits of Written Forms

- Makes contact names and addresses readily available;
- Maintains a history of use (what group used each room, when and how often);
- Publicizes the library's rules and regulations to inform potential users of its usage guidelines;
- Protects the library, by requiring organizers to sign the forms stating that they are aware of the rules governing use of the space;
- Informs the library about what equipment and facilities are needed;
- Prevents post facto disagreements, by having in writing what facility, equipment, and services each applicant requested.

Bernardsville Public Library   **Bernardsville, New Jersey**

COMMUNITY ROOM

Please read the Meeting Room Policy before completing this form.

COMMUNITY ROOM RENTAL FORM

Date of Application: _____

Name of Organization _____

Non-Profit /For-Profit

Name of Contact Person_____

Position in Organization   _____

_____

Address   _____

_____

Phone _____(Day) _____(Eve)

Program Information:

Date(s): _____

Hours:_____

Type of Activity: _____

Expected Attendance: Adults_____ Children_____

Will refreshments be served? _____

Requested: _____Side A (pantry) _____Side B_____Whole Room

Room Rent: $_____

Note: Attendance is limited to 35 persons for half the room and 85 for the whole room.

We have read and agree to abide by the XYZ Public Library's policies and procedures governing the use of the Library's Community Room. We also agree to defend and hold harmless and indemnify the city/county and any of its employees or agents from any claims, suits, or other actions arising from, caused by, or which are the result of any alleged act or omission of any organization, corporation, guest, invitee, licensee, visitor or other person present on the Library premises for the purpose of participating in, organizing, assisting, enjoying, supervising or in any other way furthering the activity to be held (as described above) on the date(s) listed above.

Figure 9.1 Reservation, Insurance, and Liability Form

The undersigned is authorized to execute this agreement on behalf of this organization.

Signature of Applicant_____

Date_____

Title_____

Please return this completed form to the Library, no less than 30 days before your scheduled use of the room, along with:

_____Certificate of Insurance, $1,000,000 or more

_____Check payable to the XYZ Public Library

If you have questions, please call the director at 555–5555

Approved: _____Date:_____

A copy of this application will be mailed to you as confirmation if requested.

Figure 9.1 continued

Fayette County Library   **Fayetteville, Georgia**

Date:_____

Name of Applicant:_____

Home Address:_____

City:_____ State:_____ Zip Code:_____

Home Telephone:_____ Business Telephone:_____

Name of Non-Profit Organization:_____

Organization classification under the Internal Revenue Code:_____

Meeting room requested: Distance Learning Center (15 persons):_____

                    Public Meeting Room: (150 persons)_____

Date needed:_____ (Must be at least 10 days in advance)

Time needed: Start:_____ Finish:_____

Purpose of meeting:

Number of participants expected:_____

Equipment needed: TV/VCR Slide Projector Overhead Projector

Filmstrip Projector

I have read the attached XYZ Public Library Meeting Room Policy and agree that my organization will abide by these rules. I further agree that the organization will be responsible for any damages to library property which may occur as a result of my organization's use. I certify that I am authorized to make these representations on behalf of my organization.

Signature:_____ Date:_____

For Library Staff Use Only:

Tentative reservation by:_____Date:_____

$50.00 deposit attached and received by:_____

Confirmed reservation by:_____ Date:_____

Walk-through after meeting:

Staff_____ Participant_____

Figure 9.2 Meeting Room Application

CHECKLIST

- Discuss with the city/county attorney the liability release to protect you against lawsuits.
- Have you checked with the city/county attorney about liability, damage and insurance requirements in your city/county?
- Have you clearly articulated steps for enforcing the rules, such as if participants get too loud?
- What steps will you take if children are left in the library, while the caregiver is in the meeting?
- Determine what types of groups can utilize the space and for what purposes, such as political meetings, religious services, birthday parties, or only non-profit groups.
- Establish whether and how much of a rental fee to charge.

Chapter 10

FOUNDATIONS

OVERVIEW

Tax money alone never all the needs and wants of a library. A vibrant thriving library depends on donations, as well; they are essential. One of the best avenues for raising, coordinating, maintaining, and expending money is to create a foundation separate from the library. Federal tax law gives foundations the freedom to collect and support such programs. All donors need to be aware that their gifts are tax deductible. Federal law does not allow you to appraise gifts for tax purposes in the United States. Use the same guidelines presented in Chapter 6, "Gifts, Memorials, and Donations," to limit donors from attaching stipulations on donations. Bylaws define roles, responsibilities, and relationships vital to the health of the foundation. To avoid business and financial scandals, it is imperative to have a clear investment strategy and business plan. Smooth operations and diligent decision making will increase donations and further the library's mission in the community.

PUBLIC SERVICE POLICIES

A mission statement for your foundation serves the same purpose as the library's mission statement. It speaks to the community as a whole and serves to tell potential donors why the gifts are needed, and how they will enhance the library and further the library's commitment to your citizens. Potential donors need to know all the avenues of support you can accept.

Features of an Effective Policy

- Employs the same guidelines as those that govern how the library handles gifts, memorials, and donations (see Chapter 6);
- Outlines clearly guidelines on the programs the foundation will support;
- Publicizes the many ways to donate;
- Stresses that tax dollars alone are not sufficient to furthering the library's mission;
- Affirms the library's commitment to utilize all its resources wisely.

Benefits of an Effective Policy

- Creates a good rapport with potential donors;

- Makes donors feel involved in the life of the library;
- Allows many avenues to raise money;
- Clarifies the role of the foundation, for the community;
- Makes known to the community what programs the foundation supports;
- Severely limits stipulations being placed on donations;
- Gives the foundation flexibility in how it supports the library.

Mission Statements

Jacksonville Public Library Foundation   **Jacksonville, Florida**

It's been said that at the heart of every great city is a great library. To ensure this, the Jacksonville Public Library Foundation is committed to developing resources—above and beyond taxpayer support—for a public-private partnership to help keep our library vital for all customers.

The Jacksonville Public Library Foundation has three key functions:

1. To raise funds over and above taxpayer support and free of political influence by generating private sector philanthropy to support the Jacksonville Public Library.

2. To manage endowment funds to maximize long-term support for Library programs, services and collections.

3. To grant funds to the Jacksonville Public Library in four essential areas:

   - Lifelong Learning, including lectures, children's programs, senior programs and the Center for Adult Learning

   - Library Collections, including but not limited to our growing Florida, genealogy, African American and map collections

   - Infrastructure Investments to fund future initiatives in the areas of technology and building enhancements to library branches

   - Capacity Building to ensure the Library's continued growth through resources including grant writing and development

River Falls Library Foundation   **River Falls, Wisconsin**

The Mission of the River Falls Library Foundation is to enhance the quality of River Falls Public Library services to the community by securing resources to support library programs and projects not normally met by public funding.

It is the intent and function of the River Falls Library Foundation through its Board to implement its Mission by means of these Guidelines:

To maintain at all times a core of community and individual memberships in a River Falls Library Foundation, whose purpose is the greater welfare of the River Falls Public Library;

To serve as a liaison between the River Falls Public Library and those of the larger communities and the various individuals which it serves, for the purpose of providing and maintaining a support group with vested and various interests in the financial well-being of the River Falls Public Library;

To assist the library, its staff, and its board in relationships with the larger communities, various individuals, and the local government of River Falls, with special reference to the seeking out and the acquiring of larger scale donor support for the greater development and improvement of the informational systems of the River Falls Public Library;

To raise, manage, and distribute large donations and other sums for the long-range benefit of the River Falls Public Library;

To solicit, manage, and distribute annual membership subscriptions and related smaller monies for the purpose of supporting the discretionary necessities of the River Falls Public Library;

To invest wisely the various acquired monies, both major capital and annual donor, for the production of incomes related to both capital expenses and discretionary funds needed for the development and improvement of the informational systems of the River Falls Public Library.

Kirkwood Public Library   Kirkwood, Missouri

The Kirkwood Public Library Foundation was established in 1996 to support the Library in fulfilling the growing needs of the community. It is governed by a board of directors comprised of volunteers dedicated to helping the community through improvements to the Library.

An independent, charitable organization, the Foundation solicits, receives and administers gifts for the Library's benefit. Gifts are used to fund projects, enhancements and improvements to the collections and services.

Private contributions from generous individuals, families, businesses, foundations, and organizations throughout the community help create funding. The income generated is used to fund projects the Library could not otherwise afford through its annual operating budget. Contributors may choose to give to the Library in a number of ways:

- Gifts of cash

- Gifts of stocks or bonds

- Assets with low cost basis

- Gifts of real property

- Gifts of life insurance policies

- Bequests in wills

- Matching gifts from corporations

- Charitable remainder trusts and estate arrangements

Oakland Public Library Foundation   **Oakland, California**

The mission of the Oakland Public Library Foundation is to enhance the Oakland Public Library as a community resource by funding special projects and building an endowment for the support of the Library.

The Foundation's current emphasis is on sustaining and expanding the literacy programs sponsored by the Oakland Public Library and to develop financial support for the new African American Museum and Library at Oakland (AAMLO).

Types of Gifts

Chapel Hill Public Library Foundation   **Chapel Hill, North Carolina**

Methods of Giving

There are several options for giving to the Foundation. If you would like to speak with someone from the Foundation concerning the options listed below, please contact us.

Cash

Cash gifts are the simplest, most direct means of support for the Foundation. The giver is entitled to an income tax deduction for the entire amount of the gift, providing the deductions are itemized and do not exceed certain limits. Checks should be made payable to the Chapel Hill Public Library Foundation and mailed to: Treasurer, Chapel Hill Public Library Foundation Chapel Hill, NC

For your convenience, you may print the Gifts and Bequests form to include with your donation.

Securities

Appreciated securities continue to be an excellent and popular method of making gifts. Depending on the particular situation, gifts of securities which qualify for long term capital gains treatment may be deductible at full fair market value on the date of the gift, and there may be no capital gains taxes on the appreciation.

Real Estate

Gifts of debt-free real estate, depending on the situation, may be deductible at the full fair market value on the date of the gift, and there may be no capital gains tax on the appreciation. Although an appraisal is needed to support the income tax deduction, it is possible to avoid the typical costs and delays associated with selling real estate.

Life insurance

Over time, a person's life insurance coverage needs may change, as assets increase and the needs of dependents become less pressing. Life insurance policies, which have a cash value, may be donated to the Foundation. The owner receives an income tax deduction for the value of the policy on the date of the gift.

Methods of Making Planned Gifts

Bequests

The Foundation encourages you to include a bequest to the Foundation in your will and, if needed, can provide a sample statement to include in your will to do so. If a will has already been signed, a simple codicil can be added, making a bequest to the Chapel Hill Public Library Foundation.

A will functions as the basic instrument of any estate plan by establishing how assets are going to be distributed. If a person dies with no will, the state provides for the division of the property following a rigid set of laws, and the beneficiaries may not be the same ones that the deceased would have chosen. With a will, you choose how your property is to be distributed.

Gifts with a Retained Income

An individual may want to make a meaningful gift to the Foundation but not wish to relinquish the income from the gift property. If this is the case, several types of gifts in trust can be considered. These are methods of making a current gift to the Foundation while retaining the income for your life, and if desired, for additional life of a spouse or other beneficiary. An attorney can help to design an estate plan that provides income and also benefits the Chapel Hill Public Library Foundation.

Contact the Foundation

If you would like to discuss a gift in trust or any other method of contributing to the Chapel Hill Public Library Foundation, please contact the foundation. We will be glad to explore options which best fit your needs and desires.

Friends of the Chapel Hill Public Library

In addition to making a gift to the Foundation, you can also support the Chapel Hill Public Library by join Friends of Chapel Hill Public Library and enjoying the many activities they sponsor, including Meet the Author Teas and book sales. Membership in the Friends is very affordable and helps to meet the day to day needs of the Library, while building community support for reading-related activities.

Salem Public Library Foundation   Salem, Oregon

Giving Through Gift Annuities

Another common way of making a planned gift is with a charitable gift annuity. A charitable gift annuity is a simple contract. Between you and the recipient. In exchange for an irrevocable gift to the SPLF, the SPLF agrees to pay you or another annuitant a fixed dollar amount for life.

The gift can be funded with cash or appreciated property. You receive a tax deduction based on your age, the size of the annuity and other factors. It you use appreciated property, tax on capital gains is spread over the time of the annuity. Estate tax will be avoided.

A deferred charitable gift annuity is similar, but the annuity payments are agreed to begin at a later date, more favorable to your financial situation.

Giving Through Stocks and Securities

Charitable gifts of appreciated stocks and securities can provide even greater tax benefits than a cash gift of equal value. You can take a charitable deduction for the full fair market value of the property, avoiding capital gains taxes. The IRS has limits on these deductions that must be considered.

Giving Through Real Estate

The advantages in giving property are very similar to those of giving stocks and securities. The fair market value can be a charitable deduction on income taxes and no capital gains taxes are paid by you or by the SPLF.

Giving Through Charitable Remainder Trusts

A charitable remainder trust is a way to make a gift to the SPLF that allows you to retain income from your property for life or for another period of time that you specify. When the trust ends, at the death of the income recipient or the expiration of the time period, whatever remains in the trust is passed on to the SPLF. A tax deduction is allowed at the time of the creation of the trust. There are several types of charitable trusts. A professional advisor can assist in selecting one suitable.

Giving Through Retirement Plans

Retirement plans may provide a way to make a very meaningful gift to the SPLF. If you have an individual retirement account (IRA), a tax sheltered annuity, a Keogh plan or a comprehensive retirement or profit sharing plan, you have another option for making a gift to the SPLF. Should you or your other beneficiaries no longer need these funds, you can name the SPLF to receive all or part of what remains and at the same time you may receive a tax deduction and other benefits for your generosity.

Giving Through Life Insurance

A gift of life insurance can be a unique way to make a significant contribution to Salem Public Library. There are several ways to do this. You can name SPL Foundation as a primary, secondary, final or remainder beneficiary in a current policy. You can donate a paid up policy you no longer need or purchase new policy naming SPLF. Such gifts entitle you to a charitable tax deduction.

ADMINISTRATIVE POLICIES

Everyone must be on the same page and work toward common goals for the foundation to be effective and meet its mission. Clearly defined roles and responsibilities create a working relationship between the library director, the foundation, the library board, and the Friends group. Donors must have confidence in how money is invested and allocated, or the foundation will suffer and not be effective.

Features of an Effective Policy

- Clearly defines the roles of the board of directors;
- Clearly defines the relationship between the foundation and the library;
- Clearly defines the role between the foundation and the Friends group;
- Clearly defines the functions of committees;
- Develops a sound investment policy;
- Avoids any conflicts of interest;
- Requires the foundation to hold regular meetings;
- Develops a sound investment policy and guidelines for short- and long-term investment strategy.
- Examines financial records regularly through independent audits;
- Presents a business plan;
- Outlines an allocation plan for money raised.

Benefits of Effective Policies

- Holds the foundation accountable to the library and its constituency;
- Plans for the wise investment and spending of foundation resources;
- Precludes any conflicts of interest on the part of board and committee members, which might effect the reputation of the foundation;
- Improves working relationships by clearly defining roles;
- Gives unambiguous direction to the foundation through a clearly defined business plan;
- Ensures that the Friends group and the foundation work toward the same goals;
- Clarifies for library board members the relationship between the foundation and the board;
- Assists the foundation in maintaining required governmental documents and in abiding by all applicable laws.

Bylaws

River Falls Library Foundation   **River Falls, Wisconsin**

MEMBERSHIP:

Qualifications and Conditions

    Any natural person, corporation, association, or organization shall be eligible for membership in the Foundation. An applicant shall be admitted to membership on payment of membership dues as determined from time to time by the Board of

Directors. Honorary lifetime membership shall be conferred by action of the Board of Directors.

Memberships shall not be transferable but may be surrendered.

Classification of Members

Membership shall consist of two types as follows: Annual and Honorary. All members shall be entitled to vote. No person may hold more than one type of membership.

The Board of Directors shall have the authority to set forth the requirements for each type of membership.

General Voting Rights

An Annual Meeting of the membership of the Foundation shall be called in September of each year, specifically to elect a requisite number of Directors and to hear a report of the affairs of the Foundation.

At any regular or special meeting of the members of the Foundation, each voting member in good standing shall be entitled to one vote on any question or issue voted on by the membership, except that in the election of Directors each such member shall have as many votes as there are directorships to be filled at the election.

Except as otherwise provided by law, or these By-Laws, all matters voted on by the members at any meeting shall be decided by vote of the majority of the members present, provided however that in any election of Directors, the number of directorships to be filled shall be filled by those candidates who receive the highest number of votes cast, without regard to the presence or absence of an absolute majority in any case.

Power and Rights of Members

Members in good standing shall have the power:

1. To elect the Directors of the Foundation at the Annual Meeting of members.

2. To remove from office any Director or Officer for good and sufficient cause, at a regular or special meeting.

3. To hear, consider, and approve or disapprove reports of the Board of Directors, Officers, and Committees of the Foundation.

4. To hear and act as final arbiter in any dispute between or concerning the Directors, the Officers, or individual members.

5. To amend these By-Laws by majority of all the voting members in good standing; and to waive or suspend any By-Laws by resolution adopted by a two-thirds majority of the whole active membership.

Members may adopt resolutions for the guidance and direction of the Foundation at any Annual or special meeting, and such resolutions shall be binding on the Board of Directors and continue in effect until the next Annual Meeting of members.

Each voting member shall have the right at reasonable times to inspect the books of accounts and membership records of the Foundation, on written request to the Secretary.

Termination or Suspension of Membership

Membership in the Foundation, and all rights incident thereto, shall be terminated by one of the following:

> 1. Written resignation of the member submitted to the Secretary.
>
> 2. Failure to pay the required dues.
>
> 3. The death of a member.

4. The expulsion, following a hearing before the Board of Directors, of a member for a willful violation of or failure to comply with the Articles of Incorporation, By-Laws, or the duly promulgated rules and regulations of the Foundation.

DIRECTORS:

Directors—Term of Office

Original and Successor Directors

> Those persons named in the Articles of Incorporation as Directors shall hold office and comprise the Board of Directors until the first meeting of members, at which meeting an election of seven Directors shall be held and the successors to the original Directors chosen by the members. The Directors so elected shall serve until the next Annual Meeting of members and until their respective successors are elected and have qualified.
>
> No person may be a Director who is not a member of the Foundation.

Directors—Term of Office

Staggered Terms

> The Directors shall hold office for a term of two years, with half the number elected in alternate years. Directors shall hold office until their successors have been elected and have qualified.

Resignation of Director or Officer

> Any Director or other Officer may resign at any time. Such resignation shall be made in writing, shall be submitted to the Secretary, and shall take effect at such time as is specified in the instrument. Acceptance of the resignation shall not be required to make it effective.

Appointment of Officers

The Board of Directors shall appoint the Officers of the Foundation at the Annual Meeting of the Board for the ensuing year.

In case of the temporary absence of any Foundation Officer or the inability for any reason to perform the duties of the office for longer than thirty (30) days, the Board shall delegate the powers and duties of such Officer to another Officer or Director or Member in good standing of the Foundation during the period of the absence or disability.

The Board of Directors shall exercise general supervision and control over the corporate Officers and shall require such information and reports from the Officers, both formal and informal, as may in the judgment of the Board be necessary or advisable. The Board may require the attendance of any Officer at any Board meeting. The President, Secretary, and Treasurer of the Foundation shall customarily attend each Board meeting.

No person may be an Officer who is not a member of the Board of Directors.

Removal of Director by Members

Any Director may be removed from the Board of Directors by affirmative vote of a majority of the members with voting power. Such action may be taken at any regular meeting or any special meeting at which due notice of the proposed removal shall have been duly given to the members with or as a part of the notice of the meeting.

Such removal may be accomplished with or without cause, but the Director involved shall be given an opportunity to be present and to be heard at the meeting at which the removal is considered.

Officers—Filling Vacancies

When any Foundation office shall become vacant by reason of the death, resignation, incapacity, or removal of the incumbent, or for any other cause, the Board of Directors, by majority vote of the whole Board, shall appoint a successor who shall hold office for the unexpired portion of the term of his/her predecessor.

Board of Directors—Filling Vacancies

A vacancy in the Board of Directors may be filled by a majority vote of the remaining Directors, even though less than a quorum is present, or by a sole remaining Director. Each Director, so elected, shall hold office until his/her successor is elected at an Annual, regular, or special meeting of the members.

Board of Directors—General Powers and Duties

Subject to the limitation contained in the Articles of Incorporation and to the provisions of the law requiring corporate action to be exercised, authorized, or approved by the members of the Foundation, and except as otherwise expressly provided in these By-Laws, all the lawful powers of the Foundation shall be vested in and exercised by or under the authority of the Board of Directors, and the affairs of the Foundation shall be conducted and controlled by such Board. The foregoing general grant of power to the Board of Directors shall not be deemed to be curtailed or restricted by other provisions of these By-Laws that declare or impose the duty of the Board of Directors in any specific matter.

Board of Directors—Delegation of Authority

The Board of Directors may delegate, to the extent that it considers necessary, any portion of its authority to manage, control, and conduct the current business of the Foundation, to any standing or special committee of the Foundation or to any Officer or agent thereof. Notwithstanding any delegation of authority that the Board may make hereunder, it shall exercise general supervision over the Officers and agents of the Foundation and shall be responsible to the members for the proper performance of their respective duties.

Board of Directors—Acquisition and Encumbering of Property

The Board of Directors shall have the power to acquire by gift, or any lawful manner, any property, both real and personal, rights, or privileges that the Foundation may lawfully acquire, on such terms and conditions as the Board shall deem proper and which comply with the stated purposes of the Foundation.

Board of Directors—Determination of Duties and Salaries of Foundation Officers

The Board of Directors shall have full authority, subject to other provisions of these By-Laws, to prescribe and assign the duties of all Officers of this Foundation, and to determine the entitlements, if any, of such Officers. No person shall be entitled to any compensation for any service performed or allegedly performed unless such salary, expense, or other compensation shall have been previously approved by the Board of Directors and is in the conformity with the expressed Foundation purpose.

OFFICERS: OFFICERS—POWERS AND DUTIES OF PRESIDENT

The President of the Foundation shall be the Foundation's principal executive Officer and shall exercise general supervision and control over all business and affairs of the Foundation.

Officers—Powers and Duties of Vice President

The Vice President shall exercise the powers and perform the functions that are from time to time assigned by the President or the Board of Directors. The Vice President shall have the powers and shall exercise the duties of the President whenever the President, by reason of illness or other disability, or absence, is unable to act, and at other times when specifically so directed by the Board of Directors.

Officers—Powers and Duties of Secretary

The Secretary of the Foundation shall be the custodian of and shall maintain the Foundation's books and records and shall be the recorder of the Foundation's formal actions and transactions. The Secretary shall also be responsible that an accurate and up-to-date list of memberships is maintained for the Foundation.

Officers—Powers and Duties of Treasurer

The Treasurer of the Foundation shall be its chief fiscal Officer and the custodian of its funds, security, and property. The Treasurer shall have the following specific powers and duties:

1. To keep and maintain, open to inspection by any member at all reasonable times, adequate and correct accounts of the properties and business transactions of the Foundation, which shall include all matters required by law and which shall be in form as required by law.

2. To have the care and custody of the funds and valuables of the Foundation and deposit the same in the name and to the credit of the Foundation with such depositories as the Board of Directors may designate.

3. To maintain accurate lists and descriptions of all assets of the Foundation.

4. To see to the proper drafting of all checks, drafts, notes, and orders for the payment of money as required to the business of the Foundation, and to sign all such instruments with the President.

5. To disburse the funds of the Foundation for proper expenses as may be ordered by the Board of Directors, and to take proper vouchers for such disbursements.

6. To render to the President and Secretary or to the Board of Directors, whenever they may require it, an account of all his/her transactions as Treasurer.

7. No disbursement shall be made, however, which is not in conformity with the purposes of the Foundation as stated in its Articles of Incorporation.

Librarian as Advisory Member of Board of Directors

In addition to the elected Board of Directors as provided for in these By-Laws, the Chief Librarian of the River Falls Library system shall also be a member of the Board of Directors, acting in an advisory and consulting capacity, but without voting powers. Nothing herein, however, shall be construed as barring the Librarian from being elected as a voting member of the Board of Directors should the membership wish to do so.

MEETINGS:

Regular Meetings

Immediately following the adjournment of and at the same place as, the Annual Meeting of the members, the regular Annual Meeting of the Board of Directors shall be held. At such meeting the Board of Directors, including Directors newly elected, shall organize itself for the coming year, shall elect the Officers of the Foundation for the year, and shall transact such further business as many be necessary or appropriate.

The Board shall further hold regular meetings, at such date and times as may be set by the Board. At such regular meetings the Board shall transact all business properly brought before the Board.

These meetings of the Board of Directors shall be held at the principal office of the Foundation or such other place within the State of Wisconsin as the Directors may unanimously agree on.

The order of business at any meeting of the Board of Directors shall be as determined by the Board.

Special Meetings

Special meetings of the Board of Directors may be held from time to time, in addition to the regular meetings scheduled in these By-Laws, on notice and call as herein provided. A special meeting may be called by the President, Vice President, or not less than two of the duly elected, qualified, and acting Directors.

Any special meetings shall be held at the principal office of the Foundation or at such place as shall be designated from time to time by formal resolution duly adopted by the Board of Directors or at such place as shall be consented to in writing by all members of the Board.

Special Meetings—Conference by Telephone

Special meetings of the Board of Directors may be held by means of telephone conferences or equipment of similar communications by means of which all Directors participating in the meeting can hear each other. Participating in the meeting by telephone or similar communications equipment shall constitute presence in person at the special meeting, except where a Director participates in a meeting for the sole purpose of objecting to the transaction of any business on the ground that the special meeting is not lawfully convened or called.

Notices

Notice of any special meeting of the Board of Directors shall be given in writing by personal service on each Director or by mailing to the Director's address registered with the Foundation, by first class mail, at least twenty-four (24) days before the date of the meeting, if applicable: the date and hour of the meeting; the place of the meeting, except that if no place is designated then the meeting shall be held at the principal office of the Foundation; and the business to be brought before the meeting. No business other than that so specified shall be transacted at any special meeting except by unanimous consent of all the Directors of the Foundation.

Waivers and Consents

Special meetings of the Board of Directors may be called informally by the Officer or Officers authorized to call such meetings by telephone or like method, and if all Directors of the Foundation meet at the time and place specified and execute written consents to the holding of the meeting and waivers of all notice requirements in regard thereto, then such meeting may be held with like effect as if formal written notice of the same had been given, and any Foundation business may lawfully be transacted at such meeting to which the Directors consent.

Indemnification of Directors and Officers

Each Director and Officer of the Foundation now or hereafter serving as such, shall be indemnified by the Foundation against any and all claims and liabilities to which he/she has or shall become subject by reason of serving or having served as such Director or Officer, or omitted, or neglected by him/her as such Director or Officer; and the Foundation shall reimburse each person for all legal expenses reasonably incurred in connection with such claim or liability, provided, however, that no such person shall be indemnified against, or be reimbursed for any expense incurred in connection with, any claim or liability arising out of the willful misconduct or gross negligence of any Director or Officer.

The amount paid to any Officer or Director by way of indemnification shall not exceed his/her actual, reasonable, and necessary expenses incurred in connection with the matter involved.

Annual Report—Presentation to Members

The Board of Directors shall present at each Annual Meeting, and when called for by vote of the members, at any special meeting of the members, a full, true, and clear report on the business of the Foundation for the period reported on, and its condition as of the date of the report. Each such report shall disclose in detail the financial condition of the Foundation and the income and expenses of the Foundation for the period of the report.

ADOPTION AND AMENDMENT OF BY-LAWS:

Amendment of By-Laws—By Members

Any of these By-Laws may be amended, rescinded, repealed, or altered, or additional By-Laws may be adopted, by affirmative vote of a majority of the members.

Amendment of By-Laws—By Directors With Approval of Members

The Board of Directors, at any regular or special meeting, is authorized and shall have the power and authority to make, amend, supplement, or repeal By-Laws of this Foundation, or to adopt new By-Laws, by affirmative vote of the majority of all the members of the Board; provided, however, that any such amendments or additions shall be submitted to the members at their next regular meeting for approval or disapproval, and any amendment or addition that is not approved shall thenceforth cease to be of any force or effect.

Amendment of By-Laws—Restrictions

No amendment of these By-Laws may be made which would conflict in any way with the stated purposes of the Foundation as set forth in the Articles of Incorporation.

Invalidity of Actions

> Any action of the Board of Directors, Officers, or of the membership at any Annual or special meeting which conflicts with the stated purposes of the Foundation as set forth in the Articles of Incorporation shall be void ab initio.

Certificate of Adoption of By-Laws By Directors

> We, the undersigned, being all of the members of the Board of Directors of River Falls Library Foundation, Inc., do hereby certify that the foregoing By-Laws were unanimously adopted at a meeting of the members of the Foundation.

By-Laws—Adopted and Approval Clauses

> Passed and adopted by unanimous vote as the By-Laws of River Falls Library Foundation, Inc., at the meeting of the Board of Directors of the Foundation on May 15, 1989.

Witness my hand and the Seal of the Foundation this 15th day of May, 1989.

Kirkwood Public Library Foundation   Kirkwood, Missouri
ARTICLE I

Offices

> The principal office of the Corporation shall be located in Kirkwood, Missouri, at such address as the Board of Directors may from time to time designate The Corporation may have such other offices, either within or without Kirkwood, Missouri, as the business of the Corporation may require from time to time. The principal office of the Corporation may be changed from time to time by the Board of Directors to any other city either within or outside Kirkwood, Missouri. The registered office of the Corporation, required by the Revised Statutes of Missouri to be maintained in the State o f Missouri, may be, but need not be, identical with the principal office in the State of Missouri, and the address of the registered office may be changed from time to time by the Board of Directors

ARTICLE II

Membership

> The Corporation shall not have members.

ARTICLE III

Directors

> Section 3a: General Powers. The property, business and affairs of the Corporation shall be controlled and managed by its Board of Directors.

> Section 3b: Number of Directors. The number of directors to constitute the first Board of Directors of the Corporation shall be nine (9), as set forth in the Articles of Incorporation. The initial Board of Directors shall consist of seven (7) elected directors and two (2) designated directors, as described in this Article

The number of directors of the Corporation shall remain nine (9) until such number is changed in the manner hereafter provided. The Board of Directors may at any time, and from time to (line, change the number of elected or designated directors to constitute the Board of Directors by adopting a resolution fixing the new number of directors to constitute the Board of Directors of the Corporation from and after the effective date of such resolution.

Section 3c: Election of Elected Directors. There shall be seven (7) individuals elected to the first Board of Directors whose terms of office shall be established so that the initial terms of office of three (3) of the Directors expire after one (1) year, the initial terms of office of two (2) of the Directors expire after two (2) years, and the initial terms of office of two (2) of the Directors expire after three (3) years At each annual meeting of the Board of Directors, a number of directors equal to the number of directors whose terms have expired shall be elected by the remaining director The Board of Directors may elect a director at any meeting of the Board upon a two-thirds vote of the Board.

Section 3d: Tenure of Elected Directors. After the election of the first Board of Directors for the terms of office described in Section 3c, each elected director of the Corporation shall be elected to serve for a term of three (3) years No elected director shall serve as a director for more than two (2) full consecutive terms unless the director (s elected to a subsequent term by a two-thirds vote of the Board of Directors An elected director shall serve as a director for the term for which the individual was elected or until the individual's death, resignation or removal.

Section 3f: Designated Directors. The initial and each subsequent Board of Directors shall include the persons serving in (he following positions, who shall serve as Designated Directors; (1) the Director of the Kirkwood Public Library, and (2) the Chairman of the Board of the Kirkwood Public Library A Designated Director shall serve as a director until the earlier of (i) the date he or she no longer serves in one of the positions described in this Section, or (ii) the individual's resignation or removal from the Board of Direct ors. A Designated Director may be removed from the Board and the vacancy may be filled as provided in this Article.

Section 3g: Advisory Council. The Board of Directors may, from time to time, appoint any number of individuals to serve as members of an Advisory Council which shall advise the Board of Direct ors of the Corporation Any such appointment shall be for the term and based on the criteria as the Board of Directors from time to time deems appropriate Members of the Advisory Council may attend Board meetings and participate in Board functions, however, members of the Advisory Council shall have no voting rights with respect to matters voted upon by the Board of Directors.

Section 3h: Removal of Directors. Any Director may be removed without cause by a two-thirds vote of the Board only at a special meeting called for the purpose of removing the direct or and the meeting notice mast stale that the purpose, or one of the purposes, of the meeting is removal of the director.

Section 3i: Vacancy. Any vacancy occurring in the Board of Directors may be filled by the affirmative vote of a majority of the remaining directors though less than a quorum of the Board of Directors. A director elected to fill a vacancy shall be elected for the unexpired term of his predecessor in office.

ARTICLE IV

Meetings of the Board of Directors

Section 4a: Annual Meeting. The annual meeting of the Board of Directors shall be held each year at the time and place, within or without Kirkwood, Missouri as may be designated from time to time by the Board of Directors If the Board of Directors does not fix a different time or place, such meeting shall be held at 1:00 p.m. Central Standard Time, on the second Thursday in March at the principal office of the Corporation in Kirkwood. Missouri The presence of a majority of directors shall constitute a quorum.

Section 4b: Other Regular Meetings. Other regular meeting so f the Board of Directors may be established by the Board of Directors Such meetings may be held without notice at the principal office of the Corporation or at such other place or places as the Board of Directors may from time to time designate.

Section 4c: Special Meetings. Special meetings of the Board of Directors may be called at any time by the Chairman, the President, or upon the written request of twenty percent (20%) or more of the directors A written request shall be made to the Secretary to call the meeting, and the Secretary shall give notice of the meeting, setting forth the time, place and purpose thereof, to be held between five (5) and sixty (60) days after receiving the request. If the Secretary fails to give notice of the meeting within seven (7) days from the day on which the request was made, the person or persons who requested the meeting may fix the time and place of the meeting and give notice in the manner hereinafter provided.

Section 4d: Notice of Meetings. Written notice of each annual meeting of the Board of Directors staling the time and place thereof shall be mailed, postage prepaid, not less than five (5) days nor more than sixty (60) days before the meeting, excluding the day of the meeting, to each director at his or her address according to the last available records of the Corporation Written notice of each special meeting of the Board of Directors slating the time, place and principal purpose thereof shall be mailed, postage prepaid not less than five (5) nor more than sixty (60) days before the meeting, to each director at his or her address according to the last available records of the Corporation. Any director may make written waiver of notice before, at or after a meeting The waiver shall be filed with the person who has been designated to act as Secretary of the meeting, who shall enter it upon the records of the meeting. Appearance at a meeting is deemed a waiver unless it is solely for the purpose of asserting the illegality of the meeting.

Section 4e: Quorum. A majority of the full Board of Directors from time to time constituted shall constitute a quorum for the transaction of business at any meeting of the Board of Directors, provided that if less than a majority of the directors are present at said meeting, a majority of the directors present may adjourn the meeting from time to time to a specified date not longer than thirty (30) days from the last adjournment without farther notice.

Section 4f: Board Decisions Manner of Acting. The act of the majority of the directors present at a meeting oft he directors at which a quorum is present shall be the act of the Board of Directors, unless a greater number shall be required by these By-Laws or by the Articles of Incorporation. Members of the Board of Directors, or of any committee designated by the Board of Directors, may participate in a meeting of the Board or committee by means of conference telephone or similar communications equipment whereby all persons participating in the meeting can hear each other, and participation in a meeting in this manner shall constitute presence in person at such meeting.

Section 4g: Actions of Board of Directors Without a Meeting. Any action required by the Revised Statutes of Missouri, with respect to nonprofit corporations, to be taken at a meeting of the Board of Direct ors of the Corporation, or any action which may be taken at a meeting of the Board o f Direct ors, may be taken without a meeting if consents in writing, setting forth the action so taken, shall be signed by all the directors Such consents shall have the same force and effect as a unanimous vote oft he Board of Direct ors at a meeting duly held and may be stated as such in any certificate or document filed under the Revised Statutes of Missouri. The Secretary shall file such consents with the minutes of the meetings of the Board of Directors.

ARTICLE V

Officers

Section 5a: Officers. The officers of the Corporation shall be a President, a Secretary and such other officers as may be elected in accordance with the provisions of this Article. The Board of Directors, by resolution, may create the offices of Treasurer and one or more Vice Presidents, Assistant Treasurers and Assistant Secretaries, all of whom shall be elected by the Board of Directors. Any two or more offices may be held by the same person, except the offices of President and Secretary. The officers need not be directors of the Corporation.

The Board of Directors may also, in its discretion, elect and designate one of its members to the office of Chairman of the Board of Direct ors In such event, the Chairman of the Board of Directors shall be the Chief Executive Officer of the Corporation and shall have general supervisory control over all of the executive officers of the Corporation and its administrative and financial affairs.

All officers and agents of the Corporation, as between themselves and the Corporation, shall have such authority and perform such duties in the management of the property and affairs of the Corporation as may be provided in the by-laws, or, in the absence of such provision, as may be determined by resolution of the Board of Directors.

Section 5b: Election and Term of Office. The officers of the Corporation shall be elected annually by the Board of Direct ors Vacancies may be filled or new offices created and filled at any meeting of the Board of Directors. Each officer shall hold office until his successor shall have been duly elected and shall have qualified or until his death or until he shall resign or shall have been removed in the manner hereinafter provided.

Section 5c: Removal. Any officer or agent elected or appointed by the Board of Directors may be removed at the discretion of the Board of Directors whenever in its judgment the best interests of the Corporation would be served thereby.

Section 5d: Vacancies. A vacancy in any office because of death, resignation, removal, disqualification or otherwise, may be filled by the Board of Directors for the unexpired portion of the term.

Section 5e: President. The President shall be the principal executive officer of the Corporation and shall in general supervise and control all of the business and affairs of the Corporation (unless there shall be in office a person serving as Chairman of the Board of Directors, in which case the President shall be subordinate only to the Chairman of the Board of Directors and shall be the Chief Operating Officer of the Corporation and shall be in charge of, and exercise general supervisory control over, all operating phases and departments of I he Corporation). The President shall preside at all meetings (if there be no Chairman of the Board, or if there be one, then in his absence or with his consent) of the Board of Direct ors He may sign, with the Secretary or Treasurer or any other proper officer thereunto authorized by the Board of Direct ors, any deeds, mortgages, bonds, contracts, or other instruments which the Board of Direct ors has authorized to be executed, except in cases where the signing and execution thereof shall be expressly delegated by the Board of Directors, or by these by-laws, to some other officer or agent of the Corporation, or shall be required by law to be otherwise signed or executed, and in general shall perform all duties as may be prescribed by the Board of Directors from time to time or by the Executive Committee, as established pursuant to Article VI.

Section 5f: Vice President. If a Vice President is designated by the Board as Executive Vice President, such executive Vice President, in the absence of the President, or in the event of his inability or refusal to act, shall perform the duties of the President, and when so acting, shall have all the powers of, and be subject to all the restrictions upon, the President. If there shall be no Executive Vice President or if there shall be an Executive Vice President, and he shall be absent, then the Vice President who shall have been first elected by the Board of Directors at the last annual meeting of the Board (and the order of the names of such Vice Presidents, as they appear in the minutes of such Annual Meeting of the Board, shall be conclusive as to which Vice President shall have been first elected), shall perform the duties of the President in the event of the latter's absence, inability or refusal to act Any Vice President shall perform such other duties as from time to time may be assigned to him by the President or by the Board of Directors or by the Executive Committee.

Section 5g: The Treasurer. If a Treasurer is designated by the Board, and if required by the Board of Directors, the Treasurer shall give a bond for the faithful discharge of his duties in such sum and with such surety or sureties as the Board of Directors shall determine. He shall: (a) have charge and custody of and be responsible for all funds and securities of the Corporation, receive and give receipts for money s due and payable to the Corporation from any source whatsoever, and deposit all such money s in the name of the Corporation in such banks, trust companies or other depositories as shall be selected in accordance with the provisions of Article VI I I of these by-laws, (b) in general perform all the duties incident to the office of Treasurer and such other duties us from time to time may be assigned to him by the President or the Board of Directors or the Executive Committee

Section 5h: The Secretary. The Secretary shall (a) keep the minutes of the meetings of the Board of Directors in one or more books provided for that purpose, (b) see that all notices are duly given in accordance with the provisions of these by-laws or as required by law, (c) be custodian of the corporate records and of the seal of the Corporation and see that the seal of the Corporation is affixed to ail documents, the execution of which on behalf of the Corporation under its seal is duly authorized in accordance with the provisions of these by-laws, and (d) in general perform all duties incident to the office of Secretary and such other duties as from time to time may be assigned to him by the President or by the Board of Directors, or by the Executive Committee

Section 5i: Assistant Treasures and Assistant Secretaries. The Assistant Treasurers shall respectively, if required by the Board of Directors, give bonds for the faithful discharge of their duties in such sums and with such sureties as the Board of Directors shall determine. The Assistant Treasurers and Assistant Secretaries, in general, shall perform such duties as shall be assigned to them by the Treasurer or the Secretary, respectively, or by the President or the Board of Directors, or the Executive Committee.

Section 5j: Executive Director. The Board of Directors may hire an Executive Director of the Corporation If the Board hires an Executive Director, such individual shall be employed by the Corporation to execute plans and programs as developed by the Board of Directors. The Board of Directors may designate the Executive Director to serve as the Chief Executive Officer of the Corporation and to execute on behalf of the Corporation all contracts, deeds, conveyances and other instruments in writing which may be required or authorized by the Board of Directors for the proper and necessary transaction of the Corporation's business The Executive Director may be responsible for the contracts, loans, checks and deposits, and day-to-day business of the Corporation and shall report on such activities to the Board of Directors as requested or directed by the Board.

Section 5k: Additional Powers. Any officer of the Corporation, in addition to the powers conferred upon these individuals by these Bylaws, shall have such powers and perform such additional duties as may be prescribed from time to time by said Board.

ARTICLE VI

Committees

Section 6a: Authority. The Board of Directors may act by and through such committees as may be specified in resolutions adopted by the Board of Directors. Each such committee shall have such duties and responsibilities as are granted to it from time to time by the Board of Directors. Each such committee shall at all times be subject to the control and direction of the Board of Directors.

Section 6b: Executive Committee. The Board of Directors may designate an Executive Committee composed of two or more directors which shall be authorized by the Board of Directors to manage the business of the Corporation During the interval between meetings of the Board of Directors, the Executive Committee shall at all times be subject to the control and direction of the Board of Directors. Additional members may be added to the Executive Committee as determined by the Board of Directors.

Section 6c: Nominating Committee. The Board of Direct ors may designate a Nominating Committee composed of any number of individuals as the Board may determine The Nominating Committee shall consider and recommend to the Board candidates for election as directors. The Board shall designate one individual as Chairman of the Committee, and may designate one or more individuals as alternate members of the Committee, who may replace any absent or disqualified member at any meeting of the Committee.

Section 6d: Finance Committee. The Board of Directors may designate a Finance Committee composed of three or more directors. The Committee shall advise the Board regarding financial management of the Corporal ion and determine and recommend investment policies and procedures for investment of the principal of the Corporation The Board shall designate one director as Chairman of the Committee, and may designate one or more directors as alternate members of the Committee, who may replace any absent or disqualified member at any meeting of the Committee. The Finance Committee shall at all times be subject to the control and direction oft he Board of Directors Additional members may be added to the Finance Committee as determined by the Board of Directors

Section 6e: Meetings and Voting. Each committee of the Corporation may establish the time for its regular meetings and may change that time as it deems advisable Special meetings of any committee of the Corporation may be called by the Chairman of that committee or by the Chairman of the Board of Directors. Two days notice of any special meeting of a Committee shall be given by mail, telephone, telegraph, or telecopy Such notice may be waived in writing or by attendance at the committee meeting. At all committee meetings of the Corporation, each committee member shall be entitled to cast one vote on any question coming before such meeting. The presence of a majority of the membership of any committee of the Corporation shall constitute a quorum at any meeting thereof, but the members of a committee present at any such meeting, although less than a quorum, may adjourn the meeting from time to time a majority vote of the members of a committee of the Corporation present at any meeting thereof, if there be a quorum, shall be sufficient for the transaction of the business of such committee.

ARTICLE VII

Endowment

Section 7a: Gifts. It is intended that the Corporation establish and maintain a permanent Endowment fund. Therefore, all contributions and gifts of the corporation shall, unless such contribution or gift shall be designated for a specific purpose, be placed in the permanent endowment funds for the Corporation. Said endowment fund shall be considered as principal and shall be retained and invested by the Corporation in debt and equity securities and in such manner as the board of directors shall from time to time determine, in order to provide a permanent fund the income of which will be used for the benefit of the Kirkwood Public Library. Specially designated gifts, when accepted by the Board, shall be used and expended in the manner specified by the Donor.

Section 7b: Income and Principal. The Corporation shall annually expend the income generated by its endowment fund (or such greater sums as may be required to be paid by law for private foundations) to benefit the Kirk wood Public Library all as determined by the Board of Directors in consultation with the Board and management of the Kirkwood Public Library. In addition, the Corporation may use a portion of its income for its ordinary and necessary expenses incurred in operating the Corporation.

ARTICLE VIII

Contracts, Loans, Checks and Deposits

Section 8a. Contracts. The Board of Directors may authorize any officer or officers, agent or agents, to enter into any contract or execute and deliver any instrument in the name of and on behalf of the Corporation, and such authority may be general or confined to specific instances.

Section 8b: Authority to Borrow, Encumber Assets. No officer, director, agent or employee of the Corporation shall have any power or authority to borrow money on behalf of the Corporation, to pledge its credit or to mortgage or pledge its real or personal property except within the scope and to the extant of the authority delegated by resolutions adopted from time to lime by the Board of Directors.

Section 8c: Checks. Drafts, etc. All checks, drafts, or other orders for the payment of money, notes or other evidences of indebted ness issued in the name of the Corporation, shall be signed by such officer or officers, agent or agents of the Corporation and in such manner as shall from time to time be determined by resolution of the Board of Directors.

Section 8d: Deposit of Funds. All funds of the Corporation not otherwise employed shall be deposited from time to time to the credit of the Corporation in such banks, trust companies or other depositories as the Board of Directors may approve or designate, and all such funds shall be withdrawn only in the manner or manners authorized by the Board of Directors from time to time.

ARTICLE IX

Indemnification

Section 9a. Action, Etc. Other Than By or In The Right of The Corporation. The Corporation shall indemnify any person who was or is a party or is threatened to be made a party to any threatened, pending or completed action, suit, or proceeding, whether civil, criminal, administrative or investigative, other than an action by or in the right of the Corporation, by reason of the fact that he is or was a director, officer, employee or agent of the Corporation, or is or was serving at the request of the Corporation as a director, officer, employee or agent of another corporation, partnership, joint venture, trust or other enterprise, against expenses, including attorneys' fees, judgments, fines and amounts paid in settlement actually and reasonably incurred by him in connection with such action, suit, or process if he acted in good faith and in a manner he reasonably believed to be m or not opposed to the best interests of the Corporation, and, with respect to any criminal action or proceeding, had no reasonable cause to believe his conduct was unlawful The termination of any action, suit, or proceeding by judgment, order, settlement, conviction, or upon a plea of nolo contendere or its equivalent, shall not, of it self, create a presumption that the person did not act in good faith and in a manner which he reasonably believed to be in or not opposed to the best interests of the Corporation, and, with respect to any criminal action or proceeding, had reasonable cause to believe that his conduct was unlawful.

Section 9b: Actions, Etc., By or In The Right of The Corporation. The Corporation shall indemnify any person who was or is a party or is threatened to be made a party to any threatened, pending or completed action or suit by or in the right of the Corporation to procure a judgment in its favor by reason of the fact that he is or was a director, officer, employee or agent of the Corporation, or is or was serving at the request of the Corporation as a director, officer, employee or agent of another corporation, partnership, joint venture, trust or other enterprise against expenses, including attorneys' fees, and amounts paid in settlement actually and reasonably incurred by him in connection with the defense or settlement of the action or suit if he acted in good faith and in a manner he reasonably believed to be in or not opposed to the best interest of the Corporation; except that no indemnification shall be made in respect of any claim, issue or mailer as to which such person shall have been adjudged to be liable for negligence or misconduct in the performance of his duty to the Corporation unless and only to the extent that the court in which the action or suit was brought determines upon application that, despite the adjudication of liability and in view of all the circumstances of the case, the person is fairly and reasonably entitled to indemnity for such expenses which the court shall deem proper.

Section 9c: Determination of Right of Indemnification. Any indemnification under subsections 9a and 9b of this Article, unless ordered by a court, shall be made by the Corporation only as authorized in the specific case upon a determination that indemnification of the director, officer, employee or agent is proper in the circumstances because he has met the applicable standard of conduct set forth in this Article IX. The determination shall be made by the Board of Directors by a majority vote consisting of directors who were not parties to the action, suit, or proceeding, or if such a quorum is not obtainable, or even if obtainable a quorum of disinterested directors so directs, by independent legal counsel in a written opinion.

Section 9d: Other Enterprises, Fines, and Serving at Corporation's Request. Notwithstanding any other provision of this Article, to the extent that a director, officer, employee or agent of the Corporation has been successful on the merits or otherwise in defense of any action, suit, or proceeding referred to in subsections 9a and 9b of this Article, or in defense of any claim, issue or matter therein, he shall be indemnified against expenses, including attorneys' fees, actually and reasonably incurred by him in connection with the action, suit, or proceeding.

Section 9e: Prepaid Expenses. Expenses incurred in defending a civil or criminal action, suit or proceeding may be paid by the Corporation in advance of the final disposition of the action, suit, or proceeding as authorized by the Board of Directors in the specific case upon receipt of an undertaking by or on behalf of the director, officer, employee or agent to repay such amount unless it shall ultimately be determined that he is entitled to be indemnified by the Corporation as authorized in this section.

Section 9f: Other Rights and Remedies. The indemnification provided by this Article shall not be deemed exclusive of any other rights to which those seeking indemnification may be entitled under sections 351.355, 355.471, 355.476 or 537.117 RSMo, any other provision of law, the articles of incorporation or bylaws or any agreement, a vote of disinterested directors or otherwise, both as to action in his official capacity and as to action in another capacity while holding such office, and shall continue as to a person who has ceased to be a director, officer, employee or agent and shall inure to the benefit of the heirs, executors and administrators of such a person.

Section 9g: Insurance. The Corporation may purchase and maintain insurance on behalf of any person who is or was a director, officer, employee or agent of the Corporation or is or was serving at the request oft he Corporation as a director, officer, employee or agent of another corporation, partnership, joint venture, trust or other enterprise against any liability asserted against him and incurred by him in any such capacity, or arising out of his status as such, whether or not the Corporation would have the power to indemnify him against such liability under the provisions of this Article.

Section 9h: Constituent Corporations. For the purpose of this Article IX, references to "the Corporation" include all constituent corporations absorbed in a consolidation or merger as well as the resulting or surviving corporation so that any person who is or was a director, officer, employee or agent of such a constituent corporation or is or was serving at the request of such constituent corporation as a director, officer, employee or agent of another corporation, partnership, joint venture, trust or other enterprise shall stand in the same position under the provisions of this Article with respect to the resulting or surviving corporation as he would if he had served the resulting or surviving corporation in the same capacity.

Section 9i: Definitions. For purposes of this Article IX, the term "other enterprise" shall include employee benefit plans; the term "fines" shall include any excise taxes assessed on a person—with respect to an employee benefit plan, and the term "serving at the request of the Corporation" shall include any service as a director, officer, employee or agent of the Corporation which imposes duties on, or involves services by, such director, officer, employee, or agent with respect to an employee benefit plan, its participants, or beneficiaries, and a person who acted In good faith and in a manner he reasonably believed to be in the interest of the participants and beneficiaries of an employee benefit plan shall be deemed to have acted in a manner "not opposed to the best interest of the Corporation" as referred to in this Article IX.

ARTICLE X

Miscellaneous

Section 10a: Fiscal Year. Unless otherwise fixed by the Board of directors, the fiscal year of the Corporation shall begin on January 1 and end on the succeeding December 31.

Section 10b: Corporate Seal. The Board of Directors shall provide a corporate seal which shall be in the form of a circle and shall have inscribed thereon the name of the Corporation and the words "Corporate Seal, Missouri" The seal shall be stamped or affixed to such documents as may be prescribed by law or custom or as directed by the Board of Directors.

Section 10c: Debts and Obligations of Corporation. The directors and officers of the Corporation shall not be personally liable for the debts or obligations of the Corporation of any nature whatsoever, nor shall any of the property of the directors or officers be subject to the payment of the debts or obligations of the Corporation to any extent whatsoever.

Section 10d: Amendments. These Bylaws may be altered, amended or repealed from time to time by a majority vote of the Board of Directors, provided that. Article VII may be altered, amended or repealed from time to lime only by a two-thirds vote of the entire Board of Directors.

Certificate

Upon motion duly made, seconded and unanimously adopted, the undersigned, constituting the Board of Directors of KIRKWOOD PUBLIC LIBRARY FOUNDATION do as of this _____ day of_____, 1996 adopt the foregoing bylaws of the Corporation and said bylaws are hereby ratified and adopted by the undersigned.

BEING ALL OF THE DIRECTORS

Investment Policy

Kirkwood Public Library Foundation   **Kirkwood, Missouri**

INVESTMENT POLICY STATEMENT

I. Purpose

> The purpose of this statement is to provide a clear understanding between the Kirkwood Public Library Foundation (KPLF) and investment managers, donors, and other interested parties concerning the investment policies and objectives of the Foundation assets. This statement outlines an overall philosophy that is specific, but flexible enough to allow for changes in the economy and securities market.

II. Delineation of Responsibilities

> All parties are subject to the Prudent Man Rule which states:

> Assets shall be invested with the care, skill, prudence, and diligence under the circumstances prevailing from time to time that a prudent man acting in a like capacity and familiar with such matters would use in the investment of a fund of like character and aims.

> A. KPLF Board of Directors

> > The KPLF Board of Directors is charged with the authority m this Policy Statement to hire and fire investment managers with the advice and upon the recommendation of the Finance Committee. The Board is responsible for all investments made by the Foundation, but as a practical matter, will do leg ate day-to-day management of the assets to the Finance Committee or to investment managers and consultants hired for that purpose.

> B. Finance Committee

> > The Finance Committee is charged with the direct oversight of investment managers when hired, asset allocation of the KPLF funds and oversight of outside consultants hired to assist the above. As a practical matter, the Committee may assign day-to-day management to a designated consultant.

> C. Consultants

> > The Board may designate an investment broker or financial planner to act as consultant to the KPLF Board of Directors regarding the investment of the KPLF's funds. Their dudes are, but not limited to, advice on asset allocation, screening and day-to-day monitoring of investment managers, independent reporting of investment results, custodianship of the KPLF assets, and any other duties the Board or the Committee deems appropriate.

III. Objectives

> The KPLF seeks to maximize income, growth of income, and long-term appreciation of capital while seeking to minimize principal fluctuations. The assets must be

invested with care and diligence with the overriding prudent man rule as a guide to investment management. The KPLF will, as a general guideline, make occasional disbursements, and care should be taken to ensure available funds.

A. Equity Fund Objectives

1. Long-Term Objectives

The KPLF seeks as a total return (income and growth) over a market cycle, or at a minimum of three years, a compounded return that should equal or surpass the Standard & Poor's 500. If appropriate, the Finance Committee may use, in addition to the Standard & Poor's 500, other recognized Equity Indices that may more closely parallel the style of the equity manager. If another index besides the Standard & Poor's 500 is used to judge any equity manager, then the manager will be notified in writing by the Finance Committee.

2. Short-Term Objectives

The assets should be managed in such a fashion so as not to exceed any loss of the Equity Index that is being used as a benchmark. Further, the assets should be managed so as not to have two consecutive quarterly losses.

B. Fixed Income Objectives

1. Long-Term Objectives

The KPLF seeks as a total return (income and growth) over a market cycle, or at a minimum of three years, a compounded return that should equal or surpass the Lehman Brothers Corporate/ Government Intermediate Bond Index. If appropriate, the Finance Committee may use, in addition to the Lehman Brothers Corporation/Government Intermediate Bond Index, other recognized fixed income indices that may more closely parallel the style of the fixed income manager.

If another index besides the Lehman Brothers Corporate/Government Bond Index is used, then that manager will be notified in writing by the Finance Committee.

2. Short-Term Objectives

The assets should be managed in such a fashion so as not to exceed any loss of the Fixed Income Index that is being used as a benchmark. Further, the assets should be managed so as not to have two consecutive quarterly losses.

C. Cash and Equivalent Objectives

There are not specific benchmark returns for cash. It is expected that equity and fixed income managers will be generally fully invested. Cash that is allocated by the Finance Committee will be subject to the rules described herein.

IV. Asset Allocation

The Finance Committee will make the overall allocation of equities, fixed income and cash investments as they deem appropriate.

The investment managers will have discretion, within the guidelines and prohibitions below to make individual security and industry decisions within their own discipline. The prudent man rule will apply to both individual securities and industry/sector weightings.

A. Equity Securities

Equity securities must have a minimum market capitalization of $300 million and must be traded on die New York, American Stock Exchanges or the United States domestic over-the-counter markets. The investment manager should invest only in corporations traded on the American Domestic Markets.

The Board does not permit any type of investment in specific foreign stocks.

B. Fixed Income Securities

Fixed income securities may be either U.S. Government and its Agencies, municipal debt, corporate debt and preferred securities as well as convertible issues issued only in U.S. dollars. The minimum quality credit rating for non-convertible debt is "A" rated.

In addition, a maximum of 20% of the portfolio may be in Mortgage Backed Securities that either implicitly or explicitly have the backing of the U.S. Government.

Asset Backed Securities may be a maximum of 10% of the portfolio, but must constitute Senior Debt with a minimum "AA" rating.

The maturities and duration are left to the discretion of the manager in accordance with the objectives in Section III.

C. Cash and Equivalents

Cash and Cash Equivalents may be invested directly in the money markets in Commercial Paper, Bankers Acceptance, Bank CD's, and Corporate Notes with a minimum rating of A-1 by Standard & Poor's or P-1 by Moody's Investment Services. Maturities may not exceed 90 days.

In place of, or in addition, cash may be invested in money market mutual funds which have the same general investment restrictions. All investments must be in U.S. dollars.

D. Prohibitions

The investment manager is prohibited from investing in letter stock, private placements, options, short sales, margin transactions, financial futures, commodities, or other specialized activities. No fund assets should be invested in speculative securities.

Additionally, specific Collateralized Mortgages that are Interest & Principal Only Strips (I/O's, P/O's). Inverse Floaters. Z-Bonds, and Accruals are strictly prohibited. In addition, investments in tobacco companies are strictly forbidden.

Investments not specifically addressed by this statement are forbidden without the KPLF's written consent.

V. Communications

Meetings between the KPLF and the investment manager will be held on BJO annual basis at a location selected by the KPLF. The performance of investments will be evaluated quarterly. Investment reviews will be sent quarterly to designated foundation board members, and the manager must be available for phone consultation on an as needed basis.

VI. Amendments

Amendments to this policy statement are allowed, as needed, by a majority vote of the Finance Committee, and any such amendment will be forwarded in writing to the investment manager.

Avoiding Conflicts of Interest

Kirkwood Public Library Foundation   **Kirkwood, Missouri**

Although it is impossible to list every circumstance giving rise to a possible conflict of interest, the following will serve as a guide to the possible types of activities that might cause conflicts of interest and that should be fully reported to the Kirkwood Public Library Foundation (KPLF) Board. Full disclosure of any situation in doubt should be made so as to permit an impartial and objective determination.

1. Outside Interests

a. To hold, directly or indirectly, a position or a financial interest in any outside concern from which the individual has reason to believe KPLF secures goods or services.

b. To hold directly or indirectly, a position or a financial interest in any outside concern that competes, directly or indirectly, with KPLF.

2. Outside Activities

To render managerial or consultative services to any outside concern that does business with, or directly competes with KPLF.

3. Gifts, Gratuities and Entertainment

To accept excessive gifts, entertainment, or other excessive favors from any outside concern that does, or is seeking to do, business with, or is a competitor of KPLF.

4. Inside Information

To disclose or use information relating to KPLF for personal profit or advantage of an individual or his/her immediate family.

Conflict of Interest Questionnaire

Kirkwood Public Library Foundation   **Kirkwood, Missouri**

Pursuant to the purposes and intent of the Kirkwood Public Library Foundation (KPLF) Board requiring disclosure of certain interests, a copy of which has been furnished to me, I hereby state that I or members of my immediate family have the following affiliations of interest and have taken part in the following transactions that, when considered in conjunction with my position, might possibly constitute a conflict of interest. (Check NONE where applicable).

1. Outside Interests. Identify the interests of yourself or your immediate family, as described in Item 1 of the attached Guidelines.

( ) NONE

2. Investments. List and describe, with respect to yourself or your immediate family, all investments that might be within the category described in Item 1 of the attached Guidelines.

( ) NONE

3. Outside Activities. Identify any outside activities, of yourself, or your immediate family, as de scribed in Item 2 of the Guidelines.

( ) NONE

4. Gifts, Gratuities and Entertainment. By signature below, I certify that neither I nor, to that best of my knowledge, any member of my immediate family have accepted gifts, gratuities or entertainment; that might influence my judgment or actions concerning business of KPLF.

( ) NONE

5. Inside information. By signature below, I certify that neither I nor, to the best of my knowledge, any members of my immediate family have disclosed or used information

relating to KPLF's business for the personal profit or advantage of myself or any members of my immediate family. I hereby agree to report to the KPLF Board any change in the responses to each of the foregoing questions which may result from changes in circumstances before completion of my next questionnaire.

( ) NONE

DATE _____

Name _____

Position _____

Internal Revenue Service Guidelines

Wyoming State Library   Cheyenne, Wyoming

What does 501(c)3 mean?

Any organization that holds and raises monies to advance the purpose of that group is subject to federal taxes. This means that annually the organization has to file a federal income tax form and could be obliged to pay taxes on the interest earned in its accounts and pay taxes on contributions given for defined activities. In order to move into a non-taxable status, an organization submits the IRS form 1023, Application for Recognition of Exemption Under Section 501(c)3 of the Internal Revenue Code to the IRS. The information provided on this form allows that agency to determine the appropriateness of exemption. Generally churches, schools, hospitals and medical research organizations; supporting organizations [e.g., library foundations]; homes for the aged or handicapped; child care businesses; scholarship benefits; and organizations that have, or will, take over for a for-profit institution are 501(c)3 entities. Private foundations fall under different IRS rules.

How does this affect state taxes? Any library foundation purchasing goods and services in Wyoming is exempt from state sales taxes per W.S. 39–15–105(a)(iv)(B). This includes such items as office supplies, furniture and food purchased in the conduct of its regular charitable functions. The foundation may need to request a charitable organization tax exempt certificate from the Wyoming Department of Revenue at 307/777–5287.

Any library foundation conducting occasional fund-raising activities is exempt from collecting sales taxes per W.S. 39–15–105(a)(iv)(C).

FORMS

Benefits of Written Forms

- Written Allows you to track donations by maintaining current records; are vital in tracking donations

- Federal Enables you to comply with federal and state law, which requires foundations to maintain written records;

- Ensures accountability;

- Increases the confidence for potential donors to see the permanent records of the organization.

Kirkwood Public Library Foundation   **Kirkwood, Missouri**

All Contributions are Tax Deductible. The Internal Revenue Service has determined that the Kirkwood Public Library Foundation is exempt from federal income tax under section 501(c)3 of the Internal Revenue Code. Bequests, legacies, devises, transfers, or gifts to the Foundation are deductible for income tax purposes. Consult your tax advisor for more information, or contact at

There are a number of levels of giving you may want to consider. One of them may be just right for you.

- Up to $500 Book Lover
- $501–$1000 Author
- $1001–$1500 Literary Agent
- $1501–$2500 Critic
- $2501–$5000 Editor
- $5001 and up Publisher
- Any gift to Endowment Fund—Bibliophile

Each donation, regardless of amount, is greatly appreciated!

The Foundation's current project is to help the Library with its most pressing need of tables & chairs. These are not ordinary tables & chairs, but those made specifically for libraries. A single table cost is $600, and a chair $400. Total cost for those needed is $26,000. Rather than dressing up and go to a fund raising event sponsored by the Foundation, the Foundation is asking you to stay home and read, and send the Foundation whatever you think you would spend to go to such an event. We can, and will, put your money to much better use.

Should you wish to purchase a chair or table, the Library will place a small plaque with your name on that item. Perhaps you might want to buy in honor or memory of a friend or loved one!

Please cut out this portion and send to Kirkwood Public Library Foundation

Yes, I want to affect the day!

Here's my check for $ _____. (Payable to the Kirkwood Public Library Foundation).

Bill to my credit card: _____ MasterCard _____ Visa

Credit Card Number: _____ Expiration Date: _____

Signature: _____

My gift is to be used for (Check appropriate item):

Figure 10.1 Foundation Contribution Form

_____ Unrestricted gift for the Kirkwood Public Library

_____ Foundation Endowment Fund

_____ A donation to help purchase tables & chairs.

_____ I wish to purchase a chair @ $400 or a table @ $600.

A "named" plaque will be placed on the table or chair.

(if applicable) My gift is in memory of _____ or in honor of

_____ .

Name (print): _____

Street (print): _____

City, State, Zip (print): _____

Phone (print): _____

The Kirkwood Public Library Foundation thanks you for your generosity!

Your company may match your contribution.

Figure 10.1 continued

Queens Borough Public Library   **Jamaica, New York**

BUY A BOOK

YOUR BOOK on Queens Library's shelves.

When you contribute $25* or more to QUEENS LIBRARY, your name, or the name of a person you choose to honor or memorialize, will be printed on a bookplate and placed in a new book that will circulate throughout the Queens Library system. It will be available for generations in your community to use and appreciate, and strengthens your public library.

Please print this page and return it with your payment to Queens Library Foundation, 89–11 Merrick Boulevard, Jamaica NY, 11432.

I want to buy a book for my community.

I understand that the new book I donate will become a resource for everyone in Queens for years to come. Bookplates will be placed in new books in my name or the name of a person I choose to honor or memorialize. A plaque will identify donors of shelves and stacks of books.

Name: _____

Address: _____

Please Print Clearly

Apt:_____ City:_____ State:_____ Zip_____

Telephone: _____

Enclosed is my gift of $_____

I Pledge for gifts of $100 or more $ _____to be paid in installments of $ _____

Starting Date:_____

Please bill me Quarterly_____ Monthly_____

Signature:_____

Please sign if pledging or charging to a credit card

Please charge my Visa or MasterCard Acct#_____

Expiration Date:_____

This gift is made: Anonymously_____ In my name_____

For the birth of: _____

For anniversary of:_____

In memory of:_____

For birthday of:_____

Figure 10.2 Foundation Contribution Form

In honor of:_____

Please notify (gift amount not to be disclosed)

Name:_____

Address:_____

City:_____ State:_____ Zip:_____

Thank you. Your donation to the Queen's Library is tax-deductible.

Matching gift?_____

*Check your company's policy

Figure 10.2 continued

River Falls Library		River Falls, Wisconsin	

Statement of Activities

For The Eight Months Ended July 31, 2003

		Temporarily		
	Unrestricted	Restricted	Total	

SUPPORT, GAINS AND OTHER REVENUE:

Individuals$9,991.44		$114,750.00	$124,741.44	
Memberships		70.00	0.00	70.00
Dividends 536.54		0.00	536.54	
Interest 8,492.61		0.00	8,492.61	
Unrealized Gains		5,563.59	0.00	5,563.59
Income Released from Restrictions		0.00	0.00	0.00
Total Support, Gains and Revenue		24,654.18	114,750.00	139,404.18

EXPENSES AND LOSSES :

Books Program		4,059.84	0.00	4,059.84
Equipment Program		0.00	0.00	0.00
Summer Reading Program		1,377.87	0.00	1,377.87
Library Building Program		0.00	20,032.00	20,032.00
Librarian's Fund		607.44	0.00	607.44
Software Program		0.00	0.00	0.00
Management & General		213.17	0.00	213.17
Fund-raising		0.00	0.00	0.00
Unrealized Losses		0.00	0.00	0.00
Total Expenses and Losses		6,258.32	20,032.00	26,290.32

Figure 10.3 Foundation Statement of Activities Worksheet

225

CHANGE IN NET ASSETS	18,395.86	94,718.00	113,113.86
Net Assets at Beginning of Period	473,765.68	62,215.41	535,981.09
Net Assets at End of Period	492,161.54	156,933.41	649,094.95

Updated on August 18, 2003

River Falls Public Library

10.3 continued

CHECKLIST

- State the relationship between the Friends group and the foundation.
- Delimit the relationship between the foundation and the director.
- Employ the same guidelines in the foundation's bylaws that apply to gifts, memorials, and donations made to the library (see Chapter 6), to limit restrictions on gifts;
- Determine what programs and activities you will support.
- Have an investment plan.
- File the proper paperwork with the Internal Revenue Service.
- Comply with state and federal laws governing foundations.
- Determine powers and duties for board members.
- Determine the length of time a board member will serve.
- Determine what happens to surplus funds.

Part III:
Collection Forms and Policies

Chapter 11

COLLECTION MAINTENANCE AND EVALUATION

OVERVIEW

Collection maintenance and evaluation policies are essential, virtually indispensable tools in creating a healthy library collection the community finds useful, entertaining and responsive to their needs. These policies are formal guidelines, standards, procedures, and criteria you use to make weeding, mending, bindery, and evaluation decisions. Written policies provide a framework that leads to consistent decision making and takes the guesswork out of the process. Guesswork costs you time, money, staff, and material, and leaves you with an ad hoc collection that is unbalanced, cluttered, ragged, and out-of-step with community needs. Weeding and evaluation are closely associated with the collection development process covered in Chapter 7.

Another vital part of maintaining the collection is using formal record keeping forms. Forms keep track of all the details like newspaper and periodical receiving (Figures 11.4, 11.6, and 11.8), mending (Figure 11.2), bindery (Figure 11.3), and disposal slips (Figure 11.1). You can keep track of in-house use data and the number of times your staff shelves and reshelves newspapers and periodicals with the Newspaper Statistics Sheet. (Figure 11.7) For periodicals and newspapers kept outside of the public area, keep track of usage with the Request Slip for Periodicals and Newspapers (Figure 3.5). Add these statistics to your Monthly Circulation Report (Figure 1.6 in Chapter 1). Many times these duties and usage do not get counted, yet it represents a great deal of staff time and collection usage. These forms easily keep track of important details and staff productivity and give you more time to spend in other areas.

On the CD-ROM you will find more policies on weeding, mending, binding, and evaluating the collection. Morton Grove Public Library has an excellent evaluation method. Although it was too long to be included in the book, it appears on the CD-ROM and is well worth your time to read. The record keeping forms in the Forms section of this chapter have data on the form for illustration purposes. The forms on the CD-ROM do not contain any data. They are ready for you to download "as is" and fill in your information or to edit part of it to meet your individual needs.

This chapter covers policies and forms for the following areas:

- Weeding
- Disposal Slip
- Mending and Bindery
- Mending Slip

- Bindery Slip
- Collection Evaluation
- Forms (for Record Keeping)
- Monthly Periodical Check-in
- Request Slip for Periodicals and Newspapers

- Daily Newspaper Check-in
- Newspaper Statistics Sheet
- Weekly Periodical and Newspaper Check-in Sheet

ADMINISTRATIVE POLICIES—WEEDING

These policies contain essential features of weeding a collection. In this process, librarians utilize standard measurements and pay attention to community needs. These are workable guidelines that are flexible enough to be used in any public library setting.

Features of an Effective Policy

- Compares material to standard lists;
- Uses circulation statistics to measure usage;
- Includes the place of primary works in the collection;
- Considers a book's unique coverage and information before weeding;
- Weighs the reputation of a book's author and publisher, as well as its literary merit;
- Retains works by local authors;
- Includes guidelines for materials of local importance;
- Assesses cost and availability when replacing titles;
- Employs retention guidelines;
- Requires the library to look proactively for material to weed, such as material that is damaged, obsolete, outdated, or past its prime;
- Discusses when replacement is unnecessary;
- Describes weeding as an ongoing process.

Benefits of an Effective Policy

Informal unwritten weeding policies lead to inconsistency and over time results in a haphazard collection. The written guidelines, standards, procedures, and criteria contained in the policies ensure that the collection is weeded the same way using the same standards, every time. Some of the benefits of following a policy are listed below. You probably will notice others not on this list as you work with these guidelines.

- Alerts you to out-of-date material;
- Removes worn, ragged, or stained material making the shelves more attractive;
- Makes space for new material;
- Increases circulation because items are easier to find and the shelves are more inviting;
- Replaces material that does not circulate with material that will circulate;
- Aids in collection development efforts;

- Saves staff time when locating and shelving books, because the shelves are not crowded;
- Sends a message to citizens that you are good stewards of their tax money, because their library is bright, clean, and attractive;
- Notifies staff about lost or stolen material, which they discover when they systematically work through the collection.

Policies

Reasons for Weeding

Memorial Hall Library   **Andover, Massachusetts**

- To identify and withdraw incorrect or outdated materials—Users are dependent on us to provide up-to-date information. Outdated medical, legal, travel, tax and educational information especially can cause serious problems for our users.

- To remove from the collection those materials that are no longer being used—if we kept every item we bought we would probably need to build a new library every ten years. If the collection is full of materials that are not being used, our users cannot find the materials that they do want. Since we add approximately 8,000 books each year, we should be withdrawing somewhat less than that (taking into account attrition from other sources). Optimally, shelves should not be more than 3/4 full.

- To remove worn or damaged materials—Attractive, clean materials are preferred by all users and give the message that the library is a modern, up-to-date source of information. A well-maintained collection sends the message that we expect users to treat our materials with respect and return them in the good condition in which they were borrowed. Users appreciate a well-maintained collection and are more likely to support it with their tax dollars than they would support a library collection that looks like someone's old attic. Popular worn titles should be withdrawn and replaced with attractive newer editions. Classics will circulate heavily if they are clean and inviting.

- To increase circulation—Paradoxically, decreasing the size of the collection often results in increasing circulation. Users find it difficult to find useful materials when the collection is overcrowded with outdated, unattractive, irrelevant materials. Weeding makes the "good stuff" more accessible. Death from overcrowding is a common result of collections that are not properly and regularly weeded

Discarding, Retention, and Replacement

Discarding

Tippecanoe County Public Library   **Lafayette, Indiana**

A. In order to maintain a vital, current collection that meets the needs of our community, examination of materials is an ongoing process. An item is considered for discard when it is:

- Obsolete or outdated.

- Worn beyond use.

- Damaged.

- No longer circulating and/or used for reference purposes.

- One of many copies of a formerly popular title.

B. A work chosen for discard may be replaced with another copy of the same title or another work on the same subject.

C. Aides used in discarding:

Books in Print, Public Library Catalog, Fiction Catalog, Children's Catalog, Junior and Senior High School Catalogs, Evaluating and Weeding Collections in Small and Medium-sized Public Libraries by Joseph P. Segal

Neill Public Library   **Pullman, Washington**

Discard:

- Materials with obsolete content

- Materials, which are infrequently used

- Materials that have no anticipated use

- Materials in poor or irreparable physical condition

- Older editions of encyclopedias, almanacs, directories, yearbooks and standard texts (Encyclopedias should be no older than 5 years in the reference collection)

- Materials which are incomplete sets in which items missing seriously impair their usefulness

- Works containing information that has been superseded or presented in newer, more comprehensive or more accessible formats

Retention and Replacement

Neill Public Library   **Pullman, Washington**

Retain:

- Materials with regular and on-going use

- Works containing useful local information

- Primary works in particular disciplines or topics

- Works representative of an era, trend or movement which provide unique coverage

- Works listed in standard or authoritative up to date bibliographies regularly used by staff and public

- Replacement of desired item

Pasadena Public Library   **Pasadena, California**

The last copy of a work in the Pasadena system is evaluated in terms of its value to the community, with consideration to the following:

- Local interest

- Reputation of author, publisher, producer, illustrator

- Significance as identified in standard bibliographies

- Quality of graphics

- Uniqueness of information for research

Replacement of materials withdrawn is not automatic. The decision to replace is influenced by:

- Availability of copies in the system

- Popular interest

- Adequacy of coverage in the subject area

- Significance in subject area

- Cost and availability

Weeding in Conjunction with the CREW Method

Eugene Public Library   **Eugene, Oregon**

The professional staff will evaluate the materials collection for replacement and/or discard on an ongoing basis, using the CREW method of evaluation developed by Joseph P. Segal. This process (Continuous Review, Evaluation and Weeding), uses the following criteria to evaluate a title's current usefulness to the materials collection:

- M = Misleading (and/or factually inaccurate)

- U = Ugly (worn and beyond mending or rebinding)

- S = Superseded by a truly new edition or by a much better book on the subject

- T = Trivial (of no discernible literary or scientific merit)

- Y = Your collection has no use for this book (i.e., irrelevant to the needs and interests of the community)

Date of publication, last date circulated and average number of circulations per year are useful indicators of the above factors.

Disposal Slip

( ) Bindery   ( ) Discard   ( ) Mend   ( ) Book Sale

( ) Make Display Item   ( ) Recycle Shelf

( ) Donate to:_____

( ) Other libraries in the area have this item

( ) Replace with this title:_____

( ) Has new edition:_____

Name of person weeding:_____

Approved by:_____

Figure 11.1 Disposal Slip

ADMINISTRATIVE POLICIES—MENDING AND BINDERY

These policies are both functional and easy to follow. Each contains specific criteria to use when working in your collection. As you weed and evaluate the collection, you will find material that can be repaired or bound instead of disposing of it.

Features of an Effective Policy

- Includes nonbook formats, such as CDs and Books-on-Tape;
- Sets a standard for the number of times a book must circulate if it is to be repaired;
- Does not spend the staff time and material on mending such items as spiral bindings;
- Articulates excellent replacement criteria;
- Distinguishes between when material should be mended and when it should be weeded;
- Establishes criteria for making bindery decisions;
- Uses the same criteria for making mending, binding, and weeding decisions that apply to selecting material.

Benefits of an Effective Policy

Following written policies is the only method that ensures consistent decision making. When faced with the question, "Should I throw this out or can it be repaired?" turn to the guidelines and standards in this policy. It makes collection maintenance and evaluation so much easier.

- Extends the life of materials;
- Saves money by catching damage early, when it can be repaired, and not waiting to the point when it needs to be replaced;
- Increases circulation when the collection is clean, neat, and material is not cluttered with ragged, worn books;
- Raises patron respect when they see an attractive well-maintained library;
- Saves important irreplaceable material by binding it;
- Keeps sets of material together, such as periodicals and newsletters by binding them.

Policies

Mending

Kitsap Regional Library   **Bremerton, Washington**

A limited number of items can be mended by the Library annually. Items are selected for mending following the same guidelines in the Collection Development Policy as they are selected for discard or addition to the collection. Before an item is mended, it is considered for discard. As a rule, items that are selected for mending must:

- Require a minimum of staff time to return to attractive, usable physical shape
- Be capable of sustaining a minimum of another ten uses after repair

- Be expected to be used at least three to five times a year for the next two years or have significant reference value

The following are generally not mended and are replaced with new copies if they are essential to the collection and in print:

- Items that have missing or cut pages and that are only copies
- Items with spiral bindings
- Items that have ink or other indelible markings
- Mass market paperback books with separated covers
- Dirty, stained, gummed, or water-damaged items

Items that would not normally be mended but that have active holds on them may be quickly and minimally mended to fill the holds.

Memorial Hall Library   **Andover, Massachusetts**

BOOKS

Mend if:

Book still is in demand

Book is in decent shape and is mendable

Replace missing pages if book is not replaceable and still in demand

Discard if:

Book is no longer in demand

We have adequate copies of title

We have sufficient information in other titles

Book has out-of-date-information

Book is in poor shape—yellowed pages, dried out binding, damaged cover, missing pages.

Repurchase if:

Book still in demand and is in print and we do not have adequate copies of the title or sufficient information in other books

Try hard to replace "classic" titles

BOOKS ON TAPE

Mend if:

Tape is mendable and entire set is in decent shape

Repackage as necessary

Replace if:

> Three tapes in set have been mended

> Two cassette abridgements are not mended

Repurchase if:

> Title is still in demand. Repurchase single cassettes where appropriate. Repurchase entire title, either from same vendor or another vendor if entire set is past its useful life.

VIDEOS

Mend if:

> Video is still in demand.

> Send out for repair.

Discard if:

> Video has had many circulations and is worn beyond repair (streaks, fuzzy, several breaks)

Repurchase if:

> Video is still in demand.

RECORDED MUSIC

Mend if:

> Audiocassettes are sometimes repaired, often discarded.

Discard if:

> CDS are durable, but if checking in CD player indicates problem, CD is discarded.

Replace if:

> Title is still in demand

Bindery

Pasadena Public Library   **Pasadena, California**

The decision to bind materials is made with consideration to the same factors involved in replacement. In addition, the following should influence the decision to bind:

- Adverse impact on circulation because of appearance

- Feasibility of binding

- Cost of binding vs. cost of replacement

Kitsap Regional Library   **Bremerton, Washington**

A small number of books that have significant reference value or that are expected to continue to be frequently used for the next five years are sent to a professional bindery annually. Books selected for binding are considered for discard and internal mending first. They most generally are not in print, have sufficient margins to allow them to open easily after binding, and, if in print, can be bound for less than they can be replaced. Books with significant reference potential for some time to come.

FORMS

Mending Slip

( ) Torn Page(s) _____   ( ) Weak or Loose From Cover_____

( ) Torn Margin_____   ( ) Torn Cover _____

( ) Loose Page_____   ( ) Loose Cover _____

( ) Worn Spine _____   ( ) Other _____

Date Received:_____

Date Repaired:_____

Could not be Repaired:_____

Replace   Yes   No   Title:_____

Figure 11.2 Mending Slip

Bindery Slip

ISSN:_____ ISBN:_____

Book or Journal Name:_____

Author:_____

Call Number:_____

Begin Volume: _____ Year: _____ End Volume: _____ Year: _____

Frequency: _____ Total Volumes: _____

Spine Lettering:_____

Cover Color:_____ Text Color: _____

Book:

Recase: _____ Mount Cover: _____ Pocket/Cloth: _____ Pocket/Paper:_____

Standard Book:_____ Custom Book:_____ Thesis:_____

Periodical:

Title Page:_____ Table Contents:_____ Index:_____ Front Cover: _____

Back Cover:_____ Ads:_____

Date Sent:_____ Date Returned:_____

Comments:

Figure 11.3 Bindery Slip

ADMINISTRATIVE POLICIES—COLLECTION EVALUATION

Conducting an evaluation of the collection requires a systematic method for collecting data. The two policies below use different methods. One policy uses the popular CREW method (Continuous Review, Evaluation, and Weeding) and the other uses a random sampling technique along with other quantitative and qualitative procedures. Both policies track the data needed properly to evaluate your collection.

Features of an Effective Policy

- Compares collection to standard lists;
- Uses circulation reports to assess usage;
- Evaluates Internet links on the library's Web site on a continuing basis;
- Compares the percentage of items that circulate against total holdings;
- Examines money spent per capita and the number of items per capita;
- Conducts an ongoing evaluation of holdings;
- Integrates weeding and evaluation and selection;
- Uses collection turnover statistics;
- Periodically reviews the entire policy;
- Examines interlibrary loan and reserve (hold) requests, which can be used to make selection decisions.

Benefits of Effective Policies

Evaluations arm you with vital objective information about how the community uses the library. Ongoing evaluations have important benefits that shape the collection and allow you to meet community needs as they change. By following a written plan of action covered in these policies you can expect the following results.

- Aids in the selection of material;
- Demonstrates the strengths and weaknesses of the collection;
- Highlights problem areas;
- Gives you a basis on which to compare data from your library to other libraries of similar size;
- Allows you to compare your collection against standard lists;
- Tells you what percentage of the collection accounts for most of the circulation, such as 20% of the collection accounts for 85% of circulation;
- Puts you in a position to respond to changes in your mission or in the community, by periodically reviewing your policy.
- Highlights the connection between interlibrary loan requests in a specific area and potential subject area deficiencies in your collection;
- Makes better budget decisions possible, based upon patterns and conclusions gleaned from the data;
- Requires Internet links to meet the same criteria of selection, such as authority and accuracy.

Policies

Washoe County Library System   Reno, Nevada

The collection needs continuous evaluation in order to be sure that the Library is fulfilling its mission to provide material in a timely manner to meet patrons' interests and needs. Statistical tools such as circulation reports, collection turnover rates, fill rates, reference fill rates, shelf allotments and volume counts are studied to determine how the collection is being used and how it should change to answer patron usage. The collection's holdings are also checked against standard bibliographic tools such as Public Library Catalog, Fiction Catalog, Children's Catalog, Best Books for YA, Books In Print and subject specialty catalogs and lists to be sure that the Library is acquiring recommended material. The material is examined for physical condition and frequency of use. Patron input and community surveys are also used in evaluating the collection. Through ongoing quantitative and qualitative methods, the Director, the Collection Development Librarian, Managers and staff monitor the collection to see that it is serving the public. Changes to the Internet sources are monitored to ensure that links are current and the sources listed are appropriate. Non-working menu items and other out-of-date data will be deleted

Eugene Public Library   Eugene, Oregon

Collection Assessment

The Eugene Public Library materials collection will be evaluated on the basis of the following criteria:

- # Items per capita
- $ Spent per capita
- # Magazine subscriptions per capita
- % Holdings in non-print formats
- % Annual growth or decline in total holdings
- Document delivery rate

All individual subject areas will be assessed according to one or more of the following criteria:

- % Holdings in a particular subject area compared to % of circulation from that area
- Comparison to standard lists
- Proportion of subject area in circulation at any given time
- Median age of publication
- Representation of diverse viewpoints
- Completeness of sets or series

- \# of interlibrary loan requests

- \# of reserves placed

- % Annual growth/decline

FORMS

Accurate record keeping saves you many headaches. You have all the information to make decisions regarding use and frequency of periodicals and newspapers, in-house use statistics for reports, number of times the staff shelves and reshelves material for productivity reports, and similar receiving information. You can easily find answers to questions by using these forms. They take care of the little details and allow you time to attend to other matters.

Benefits of Written Forms

- Saves time from looking for newspapers and periodicals you did not receive;

- Aides in selection when Request Slips provide usage information on newspapers and periodical you own;

- Combines Request Slips with in-house usage statistics for monthly reports;

- Enables you quickly to replace missing issues;

- Enables you to update the library holdings catalog when issues are missing, saving you time from repeatedly looking for the same missing issue;

- Quickly reports missing issues to subscription vendor or publisher;

- Helps you to manage day-to-day operations by giving you accurate and timely information about periodicals and newspapers.

Name:_____ Smart Money_____Expiration Date: November 2003

Subscription began: November 2001

Year:	Jan	Feb	Mar	Ap	May	Je	July	Au	Sept	Oct	Nov	Dec	Index
2001											x	x	ms
2002	x	x	x	x	x	x	x	x	x	x	x	x	ms
2003													

Frequency:_____ Department:_____

2001		Spring		Sum			Fall		2000

Figure 11.4 Monthly Periodical Check-in

Periodical and Newspaper Request Slip

Newspaper Name:_____

City:_____ Date: _____

Journals:

Title:_____

Volume:_____ Date:_____

Figure 11.5 Request Slip for Periodicals and Newspapers

	1	2	3	4	5	6	7	8	9	10	11	12	13	14	15	16	17	18	19	20	21	22	23	24	25	26	27	28	29	30	31
Jan																															
Feb																													×	×	×
Mar																															
Apr																															×
May																															
Jun																															×
Jul																															
Aug																															
Sep																															×
Oct																															
Nov																															×
Dec																															

Figure 11.6 Weekly Periodical and Newspaper Check-in

Daily Periodical and Newspaper Statistics Sheet

DATE   TITLE   RESHELVE   SHELVE

Figure 11.7 Daily Periodical and Newspaper Statistics Sheet

CHECKLIST

- Do you have retention and replacement guidelines to help with selection responsibilities?
- Have you established standards for mending material, such as not allowing the labor and repair cost to exceed the replacement cost?
- Prioritize bindery material when funds become available.
- Coordinate weeding, mending, retention, and replacement policies with the collection development policy.
- Combine evaluation with weeding and replacement.
- Will the Newspaper Statistics Sheet provide needed workload and productivity information?
- Will the Request Slip for Periodicals and Newspapers help you track usage?
- type of schedule do you want to make for evaluation and weeding?

Chapter 12

COLLECTION DEVELOPMENT

OVERVIEW

Defining your community's needs, understanding what material will meet those needs, and deciding how you will meet those needs, while maintaining and defending a balanced diverse collection, is the responsibility of the collection development policy. In these policies you will find the guidelines, standards, procedures, and criteria needed to build a vibrant collection your community will prize for all their information needs. Within this framework are the tools you use to establish selection goals, responsibilities, resources, criteria, chose formats, select material and when necessary, defend the collection. When used in conjunction with weeding and evaluation (see Chapter 11 on Collection Maintenance and Evaluation), you can establish and follow collection priorities creating a relevant and responsive collection.

Without written guidelines, there is no direction or purpose to the collection. Without standards, there is no protection against censors. Without criteria, any material, regardless of merit will be added to the collection. Without procedures, there will be no consistency in who selects, how they select, and from what resources they draw.

This chapter covers policies and forms in the following areas:

- Selection Objectives
- Community Assessment
- Selection Criteria
- Selection Responsibilities
- Selection Resources
- Selection Parameters and Priorities
- Limited or No Collection
- School Curriculum
- Internet and Electronic Resources
- Children's Department

- Controversial Material
- Labeling Material
- Patron Recommendations
- Challenges
- Challenge to Material Form
- Surveys
- Challenge Forms
- Patron Request Forms
- Administrative Policies

ADMINISTRATIVE POLICIES

Features of an Effective Policy

The collection development policy is one of the most important policies your library can develop. How you select, who selects, and why you select material will affect the library for years to come. By following written guidelines, you will build a strong framework out of which grows a robust information resource center for your area. Spur-of-the-moment selection criteria with improvised guidelines pushes the collection in different directions every time you order material. These policies contain the necessary features for establishing selection criteria, responsibilities, resources, and conduct a formal community assessment.

An effective policy possesses the following features:

- Supports the American Library Association's Library Bill of Rights, "Freedom to Read Statement," and "Freedom to View Statement";
- Promotes a balanced collection representing a wide range of viewpoints;
- Encourages patron suggestions;
- Recognizes financial limitations;
- Strives to meet the information needs of the community;
- Uses surveys, demographic, and census data to access community needs now and in the future;
- Considers relevancy, merit, reputation of author and work, accuracy, creativity, price, format, and reviews;
- Designates or delegates selection responsibilities;
- Uses a wide variety of review sources.

Benefits of an Effective Policy

- Communicates the library's commitment to the community;
- Protects the integrity of the collection by providing balanced and diverse information;
- Recognizes that financial limitations are factors in building the collection;
- Protects the library from censors;
- Uses traditional and non-traditional selection resources ensuring that a wide range of material is collected;
- Eliminates confusion when questions arise about material by placing ultimate responsibility;
- Makes possible three-, five-, and ten-year planning with the use of census and demographic data;
- Functions as an excellent public relations document to present to the community;
- Makes patrons feel they have input into the process when they can recommend items, which can translate into support for such things as a library bond package;
- Ensures that quality material is added to the collection;
- Provides consistency as librarians change;
- Makes discussions easier when there are differences of opinion;
- Establishes collection priorities, such as, print over non-print and unabridged over abridge;
- Priorities are used in conjunction with the evaluation process other collection priorities will be established such as areas that are deficient;

- Priorities define the scope of the collection such as, breadth over depth and general treatments over more technical material;
- Priorities help staff decide what formats to maintain, such as, no books-on-tape;
- Priorities follow general criteria then break them down into special criteria depending upon the material type.

Policies

Selection Objectives

Delaware County District Library   **Delaware, Ohio**

The objectives of the Library as factors in selection are as follows:

- To help people know more about themselves and their world
- To supplement formal study and encourage informal self-education
- To meet the information needs of the community
- To stimulate thoughtful participation in the affairs of the community, the country and the world
- To support educational, civic, cultural and recreational activities within the community
- To aid in learning and improving job-related skills
- To assist the individual to grow intellectually and spiritually and to enjoy life more fully.

Ohio County Public Library   **Wheeling, West Virginia**

The goal of the Ohio County Public Library is to select, organize, preserve, and make freely and easily available to all individuals in the community printed and other materials which will aid them in the pursuit of information, education, research, recreation, culture, and in the creative use of leisure time. The primary goal of collection development is to provide the best possible collection with the financial resources available The decision to select any item for the collection is based on demand, anticipated need, and the effort to maintain a wide and balanced collection.

The library patron is an important part of the selection process. An individual request from a patron for a title is usually honored if the request conforms to the guidelines outlined in this policy statement. The library has a suggestion box near the circulation desk and request forms at both the reference and circulation desks. Suggestions regarding services and other aspects of library operations are also encouraged.

The library strives to maintain materials representing all sides of an issue in a neutral, unbiased manner. Selection of materials by the library does not mean endorsement of the contents of views expressed in those materials. The existence of a particular viewpoint in the collection is an expression of the library's policy of intellectual freedom, not an endorsement of that particular point of view. The library provides service to all within the framework of its rules and regulations and does not knowingly discriminate in its material selection regarding race, creed, sex, occupation or financial position.

The Ohio County Public Library endorses the Library Bill of Rights, the Freedom to Read Statement, and the Freedom to View statements of the American Library Association, all of which are included at the end of this policy and are intended to be a part of this policy statement.

Community Assessment

Eugene Public Library   Eugene, Oregon

Eugene Public Library patrons are of all ages and interests, and Eugene's relatively high level of educational attainment ensures demand for materials on a wide variety of subjects. More than half the City's residents hold a library card, and more than 80% of the population use the library at least once a year. The Library offers bookmobile service to 17 stops and serves local nursing homes and homebound patrons. It is an active member of the Lane County Literacy Coalition and houses its own literacy project and director. As a member of OCLC, a nationwide bibliographic database service, and through cooperative agreements with other Lane County public libraries, EPL is able to provide interlibrary loan service for patrons with needs outside the scope of the collection. The children's division offers preschool programs and storytelling, puppetry and music programs for older children. Class visits are conducted on a regular basis to familiarize students of all ages with public library services. The current profile of the Eugene community is likely to change over the next ten years, and so will the demand for library services. There will be an increase in residents in the age 65 and older and 25–29 categories, and a decline in teenagers and young adults. These changes are expected to increase demand for recreational reading as well as leisure activity, medical and investment information. There will be a more ethnically and racially diverse population, particularly in Hispanic and Asian groups, and a consequent need for more foreign language materials, bilingual staff, literacy tutoring and cultural awareness materials. Increases in the number of small businesses should continue, and will create a greater demand for business reference service and materials on accounting, personnel management, marketing, travel and finance. The gap between the information-rich and information-poor will widen, increasing both the need for sophisticated reference service and a materials collection strong in basic life skills information. The need for children's materials will continue to increase because of the demands of well-educated parents, lack of other sources for this material in the community and the rise of home schooling.

Selection Criteria

Kokomo Public Library   Kokomo, Indiana

Popularity and patron requests will not be the only basis for selection. The selection of both books and nonbook materials follows the same criteria as listed below.

In terms of relevancy, the material:

> is timely or relevant for contemporary society

is representative of various contemporary points of view reflecting current conditions, trends, and controversies that are international, national, and local

interprets, documents, or illuminates the past

provides information on a particular subject

fosters a knowledge of self and an understanding of others

enables the individual to acquire knowledge for decision making

satisfies community interest in a subject

fulfills current or anticipated demand

features a local author or subject or

has reference or research value

In terms of merit, the material:

advances the individual's capacity for understanding the world in which s/he lives

stimulates aesthetic appreciation and imagination

is noted for literary or artistic quality

contributes to the enjoyment of life

is recognized as a classic in its genre

has gained the attention of critics and reviewers

has received awards or honors

reflects the competence and reputation of the author, director, illustrator,

creator, or producer, performer, and/or publisher

In terms of form and content, the material:

is accurate

is readable or understandable

is suitable for the intended audience, including special needs populations

provides documentation of source material

is included in bibliographies or recommended lists

contributes to a collection of classics or contemporary works or

is suitable and durable in format

No book or other material will be excluded because of the race, national origin, color, gender, personal history, or the political, religious, or social views of the author or creator. Judgment for selection is made on the material as a whole and not on a particular passage, page, scene, or other part alone.

Woodbridge Town Library   **Hartford, Connecticut**

The following are the criteria for materials selected for inclusion in the library's collection, whether through purchase or gift:

excellence of reputation of the work

opinion of critics and reviewers

authority and reputation of author

accuracy and timeliness

creativity and vitality

literary merit

appeal and relevance to community interests

format suitable for library use

suggestions by library users

price and availability of funds

relationship to other items in the collection

accessibility through transit holds or interlibrary loan

Selection Responsibilities

Library Director is Completely Responsible for Selection

Eugene Public Library   **Eugene, Oregon**

Ultimate responsibility for the EPL materials collection resides with the Library Services Director. The Head of Adult Services and Head of Children's/Extension Services are responsible for overseeing Collection management. Reference and children's librarians, the Assistant Head of Adult Services and the Head of Adult Services all have collection development responsibilities for specific subject areas and formats. All librarians have a professional responsibility to be inclusive, not exclusive, in developing materials collections.

Library Board Delegates Selection Responsibilities

Tippecanoe County Public Library   **Lafayette, Indiana**

The Library Board delegates to the Library Director the authority and responsibility for selection and management of all print, non-print and electronic materials, within the framework of this policy. Actual selection and management activities are shared among trained library staff who shall discharge this obligation consistent with this policy and established procedures.

Selection Resources

Tippecanoe Public Library   **Lafayette, Indiana**

The following sources are representative of the many aids used for selection of materials:

256

Professional Journals:

> Appraisal, Billboard, Booklinks, Booklist, Bookstore Journal, Bulletin of Center for Children's Books, CD Digest, Horn Book, Library Journal, New York Times Review of Books, Publishers Weekly, School Library Journal, Video Librarian, Voice of Youth Advocates

Other:

In addition, the following works may be consulted:

> Books in Print, Public Library Catalog, Fiction Catalog, General Periodicals, Children's Catalog, Junior and Senior High School Catalogs, Trade Journals and Other Authoritative Subject bibliographies

Selection Parameters and Priorities

Eugene Public Library   **Eugene, Oregon**

- Print over non-print materials. Videos are purchased very selectively, with an emphasis on classics, travel and "how-to" videos rather than popular films. Audiocassettes and abridged versions of books-on-tape may be added to the collection if donated, but will not be purchased. Musical scores will not be added to the collection. EPL is currently phasing out its record collection and adding compact discs.

- Currency. Collection emphasis is on up-to-date information. Older materials which remain accurate will be retained and replaced according to patron demand.

- General treatments over those which are specialized, scholarly, or primarily for professional use.

- Breadth over depth. In general, EPL will purchase single copies of a wide range of titles rather than multiple copies of the same title. Multiple copies may be purchased when they are warranted by public demand, or when the title is of local interest and may go out of print, or if it is the definitive title on a particular subject.

- Single-volume overviews over multi-volume works.

- Works of broad popular appeal that meet the needs of the independent learner over textbooks or other materials which meet curriculum requirements of the formal student.

- Materials written in English language, although a 1991 LSCA grant was used to provide materials for members of the Hispanic community.

- Unabridged editions over abridgments. Abridgments will be considered only if they retain the flavor and quality of the original.

West Hartford Public Library   **West Hartford, Connecticut**

The library provides access to information in a wide variety of print and non-print formats. Presently, books, newspapers, magazines, pamphlets, government documents, maps, videocassettes, audiocassettes, CD-ROMs, microfilm, and educational toys are included in the library's collection. In addition, the library purchases access to information through databases, information services and online services. In the future the types of materials acquired will change, as new technologies become available.

Bettendorf Public Library   Bettendorf, Iowa

Adult Fiction

The library provides a collection of standard and contemporary fiction titles as well as genre fiction for the intellectual enrichment, information, and entertainment needs and interests of the adult population of Bettendorf. Multiple copies of frequently used titles are provided. Large print and audio cassette and compact disc copies of some popular titles are also available.

Special Criteria (in addition to General Criteria)

- Collection's need to reflect minority as well as majority cultures

- Literary merit

Adult Nonfiction

The library maintains a collection of general interest nonfiction titles to provide for the information needs and browsing interests of library patrons. Materials for which there is heavy, temporary demand may be selected with less emphasis on the general criteria listed above.

Special Criteria (in addition to General Criteria)

- Suitability for intended audience (research-level books not purchased)

- Ease of use, including index, bibliography and illustrations

Periodicals

The library maintains a collection of magazines for informational and recreational reading. Most periodicals are retained for five years. Some titles for which indexing is available and for which there is heavy demand are maintained indefinitely in microform.

Special criteria (in addition to General Criteria)

- Available indexing (lack of indexing will not exclude a title if it meets patrons needs)

- Community interests as measured by surveys, purchase requests and interlibrary loan requests

- Availability of display shelving and storage space

Newspapers

Newspapers are selected to provide local, state, regional and national coverage. Local newspapers plus a selection of regional and national titles are purchased. Issues are retained for four to six months.

Deaf Services Collection

The library maintains a strong core collection of books, videos and periodicals in support of its ongoing outreach to the deaf community. This collection, which was developed with federal grant money, acts as a resource for other libraries in the Quad Cities and in the state of Iowa. New items are purchased on the recommendation of the Deaf Services Coordinator from the appropriate departmental budget.

Literacy Collection

The LIFE (Literacy Is For Everyone) collection consists of books, videos, kits, and periodicals serving the needs of adult new readers, literacy tutors, and adult basic education students.

- The Adult Services Manager selects new materials for this collection from the Adult Services budget based on the recommendations of local literacy providers and specialized selection tools.

Reference Materials

Reference materials provide timely and accurate information on a wide variety of topics. Because of method of use, rarity, or cost, they are maintained for in-library use only.

Special criteria (in addition to General Criteria)

- Currency of the material

- Thoroughness of coverage

- Importance of subject matter to the collection

- Ease of use (especially indexing)

Reference Materials in Electronic Format

Some reference tools are purchased in computer-based formats (CD-ROM, on-line, etc.).

Special criteria (in addition to General Criteria)

- Ease of use

- Timeliness of updates

- Licensing restrictions

- Technical support

- Hardware and software requirements

Pamphlet File

The pamphlet file is a collection of pamphlets, clippings from newspapers and magazines, pictures, maps and government documents that supplements both the circulating and reference collections.

Special criteria (in addition to General Criteria)

- Currency

- Format

Bettendorf Public Library   **Bettendorf, Iowa**

Iowa Collection

Nonfiction books about Bettendorf, Scott County and the State of Iowa are housed in a separate collection. These materials are selected and retained under the following criteria:

- The library attempts to be as inclusive as possible in obtaining books pertaining to the history, economic, social and cultural life of Bettendorf.

- The library makes no attempt to be inclusive in its collection of materials on Scott County or the State of Iowa.

- The library does not collect letters, papers, documents, photos, or other primary resource material of local interest other than books.

Limited or No Collection

New Castle-Henry County Public Library   **New Castle, Indiana**

AREAS OF LIMITED ACQUISITION

- Law and Medical Books. Only very general or basic reference books will be purchased in certain areas. The books are not to be too specialized or considered beyond the province of public service. These areas include law and medicine.

- Research Material. The New Castle-Henry County Public Library does not attempt to provide specialized material for scholarly research or for extensive genealogical investigation due to limited funds and the easy availability of large research collections in the Indiana State Library and the Allen County Public Library. This library does have, however, a responsibility to obtain and preserve materials connected with New Castle, Henry County, and Indiana.

- Textbooks. Textbooks will be considered for purchase only when they are the best or only sources on a topic for reference and research. The library is in no way obligated to provide textbooks for regularly assigned formal classroom or correspondence instruction.

PUBLIC SERVICE POLICIES

Features of an Effective Policy

These policies implement the selection objectives, criteria, and resources presented above. Collection priorities and parameters determine what actually makes it to the shelf, what electronic databases you subscribe to, and which Internet sites you highlight for patrons. No single library can offer everything for everyone. Priorities and parameters enable you to build the best collection for the money you have to spend. Selection is easier and the material chosen is better when you follow policies like these.

- Tolerates diverse philosophies, such as, a policy for supporting and not supporting school curriculum;
- Lists electronic resources and highlights helpful Internet sites;
- Identifies characteristics of highly controversial material and sets procedures for ordering this material;
- Does not automatically exclude a resource if it is controversial;
- Does not label or mark material for the purpose of restricting access;
- Recognizes special and changing needs of children;
- Supports purchasing popular children's series titles;
- Encourages use of nontraditional items in the children's area, such as puppets and learning tools;

Benefits of Effective Policies

- Makes budget allocations decisions easier when using set collection priorities;
- Explains to the community that the library cannot afford everything;
- Contains a thoughtful explanation of school curriculum policies for parents and students;
- Relies on special criteria, like in the Bettendorf example, which takes into account the uniqueness of different areas of collection priorities, such as information gleaned from surveys and interlibrary loan requests, and requests to purchase;
- Simplifies and makes the selection process more reliable, by basing decisions on established criteria thatcombine statistics from Request Slips for Periodicals and Newspapers (see Figure 11.5 in Chapter 11) and in-house use, for better indications of what to subscribe to each year;
- Makes it easier for the patron to find needed information quickly, by chooses preselected Web sites that are authoritative, accurate, and up-to-date;
- Provides a tremendous service for patrons by bringing everything on the topic together in one place, particularly those rare, but needed, special collections such as the Literacy and Deaf Services Collections;
- Fine tunes the collection so you can build a more responsive collection the community enjoys using, based on chosen collection priorities and parameters;
- Realizes that without a written policy you are selecting material without knowing why and will have no real knowledge of what the collection has
- Makes it easier to evaluate gifts and donations;
- Addresses the unique needs of a children's department.

Policies

School Curriculum

Does Not Support

Woodbridge Town Library   **Woodbridge, Connecticut**

The library is not designed to furnish material for curriculum study in schools, but to complement that study. The library is not always able to purchase or obtain through interlibrary loan multiple copies to meet the demands of the school reading lists. This is due to budgetary restrictions and high demand for these titles in other libraries. Textbooks will be purchased only when they constitute the best available source of information on a particular subject.

Does Support

Albert Wisner Public Library   **Warwick, New York**

Use of the Library by students of all ages is encouraged. The Albert Wisner Public Library makes every effort to work closely with the schools and teachers in our service area.

Teachers are encouraged to make use of the "Assignment Alert Form" which is provided for them annually at the beginning of the school year. The "Assignment Alert" allows the teacher to notify the Library, in advance, of upcoming assignments which will be given. When the Library receives an "Assignment Alert" from a teacher, librarians will: gather books from the library's collections to meet the needs of the assignment and place them on Temporary Reference or other libraries will be contacted in an effort to gather materials to support the assignment or librarians will request materials through the Interlibrary Loan process for individual students

Teachers are encouraged to visit the Library to determine the scope of our collections so that assignments can be given with full knowledge of the resources available in the community. Teachers are also encouraged to visit the Library to choose titles which most closely fulfill the needs of the assignment.

In the event that a student should use the Library and fail to find the materials necessary for the completion of an assignment, the librarian will provide him with a letter which verifies his effort and clarifies for the teacher the problem with the location of materials.

The Albert Wisner Public Library supports the schools' use of Summer Reading Lists for students. Each Spring, the Library contacts schools in an effort to obtain the current Summer Reading Lists. The Library makes every attempt to maintain a sufficient number of copies of the titles on the lists to meet the student demand. However, budget constraints limit the number of copies that can be purchased and students are encouraged to place titles on Reserve in the library so that they can be held for them upon return of the titles to the Library. It is important that students make every attempt to locate Summer Reading materials early enough so that the Library's Reserve system can be used.

Internet and Electronic Resources

West Baton Rouge Parish Library   **West Baton Rouge, Louisiana**

Electronic resources currently accessible through the Library's LAN include the following:

GALENET: An online information resource created by Gale Research, offering coverage of biography, literature, science, and other areas of study.

INTERNET: An unregulated worldwide information and communication network connecting thousands of other computer networks accessible through Microsoft Internet Explorer and Netscape Communicator.

LOUIS and LOUIS DATABASES: An online network for accessing the library catalogs of Louisiana's colleges and universities. Databases include indexes and abstracts from ERIC, Medline, PsycINFO, and Serline.

Electronic resources enable the Library to provide information beyond the confines of its own collection, making available material that could not otherwise be offered. However, users should be aware that some information may be inaccurate, outdated, or controversial. Use of these resources carries with it a responsibility to evaluate the quality and validity of the information accessed. Lawful use of electronic resources is the individual's responsibility.

Grand Island Public Library   **Grand Island, Nebraska**

Electronic databases selected by library staff, either as menu choices on computers or Internet links established by the library, are selected in accordance with the criteria for selection as outlined in the Collection Development Policy so that the information provided is as current, complete and accurate as possible. The Internet in general is a global entity enabling the library to provide information to patrons beyond the library's collection. It includes useful ideas, information and opinions from around the world. However, it also has a highly diverse user population and not all sources provide accurate, complete or current information. Therefore, the evaluative criteria used in library's Collection Development policy to determine purchases of written materials may not apply to all material accessed electronically. Patrons need to be good information consumers, and are encouraged to refer their inquiries to library staff members as the need arises.

Children's Services

Bettendorf Public Library   **Bettendorf, Iowa**

Children's Materials

> Children's materials are selected to meet the recreational, educational and cultural needs of children from infancy through age 12. Additional materials are selected to assist adult caregiverswith the changing needs of children. Multiple copies of frequently requested titles are provided.

Juvenile Fiction

> The library maintains a variety of children's fiction from the most distinguished in

children's literature to popular titles and new, enticing titles that will attract readers of many tastes and abilities. Popular series titles are purchased in response to patron requests.

Special criteria (in addition to General Criteria)

- Appropriate reading level and interest level

Picture Books

These books, in which illustration is as important as text, serve to introduce children to the world of books. The library includes a wide variety for adults to read to toddlers and preschoolers and for children to look at and use as they begin to read. This collection includes beginning readers, concept books, wordless books and board books as well as picture books.

Special criteria (in addition to General Criteria)

- Relationship of illustration to text

- Appeal of story and illustration to children

- Age appropriateness of art, text, topic

- Durability of format

Juvenile Nonfiction

The juvenile nonfiction collection contains general informational works, browsing items and subject-oriented materials on topics of interest to children preschool age through sixth grade. The library does not provide basic texts or materials needed in quantity for schoolwork. It does, however, purchase supplementary materials to enrich the resources available at area schools.

Special criteria (in addition to General Criteria)

- Suitability for intended audience

- Ease of use, including index, bibliography and illustrations

- Quality of illustrations, maps, graphics and photographs

- Usefulness of material for research

Parents' Shelf

Many of the materials in the Parents' Shelf collection are chosen for their usefulness in helping parents and other caregivers help their children understand and deal with the problems and situations of everyday life. These include both juvenile and adult titles. Additional materials are chosen to meet the needs of adults providing educational and recreational opportunities to groups of young children. Some duplication exists between this collection and the adult nonfiction materials.

Special criteria (in addition to General Criteria)

- Suitability for intended audience

Realia

The realia collection enables children to have hands-on experiences through the use of puppets and Learning-To-Go Kits. Puppets are selected as companions to children's literature rather than as toys. The Learning-To-Go Kits have topics that are mutually agreed upon by the staff of Youth Services and the Family Museum of Arts and Science. The kits have been designed to bring the resources and materials from each facility out into the community and into the hands of children. Some duplication of materials does exist within the general collection of library materials.

Special criteria (in addition to General Criteria)

- Durability of materials

- Ability to clean and disinfect

- Pieces large enough to avoid injury

- Appeal of author, genre, series for children

- Inclusion of material on recommended reading lists

Controversial Material

Kitsap Regional Library   **Bremerton, Washington**

When considering adding materials of a highly controversial nature, including those displaying explicit sex acts between humans, judgment is best applied by more than one person. Two or more appropriate staff members should preview controversial materials. The Collection Manager and the Director need to be actively involved before a selection decision is made.

The Branch Managers, as collection developers, identified characteristics often present in highly controversial materials. The characteristics are:

- depiction of explicit sex acts involving humans

- depiction of explicit violence

- either of the above when children are involved

- excessive use of objectionable language

- values in direct opposition to those of a large number of the Library's customers

- potential for being inflammatory

- content or presentation inappropriate for user age

- strong potential of adversely impacting the Library's ability to provide access to a wide range of information

Presence of these characteristics does not disqualify an item from addition to the Library's collection of materials. However, selectors are expected to be sensitive to their presence and to employ a team selection process when there is a great possibility that an item, having one or more of these characteristics, may be highly controversial.

Lucius Beebe Memorial Library   Wakefield, Massachusetts

Beebe Library does not promote particular beliefs or views. Rather, it provides a resource for the various opinions which apply to important, complex, and controversial questions, including unpopular and unorthodox positions. Language, situations, or subjects which may be offensive to some community members do not disqualify material which, in its entirety, is judged to be of value. Materials are not marked or identified to show approval or disapproval of contents, no materials are marked to restrict their use by ages, and no materials are sequestered except to protect valuable items from injury or theft.

It is the view of the Trustees that responsibility for the reading of children rests with their parents or legal guardians. The selection of materials for the adult collection is not restricted by the possibility that children may obtain materials their parents consider inappropriate.

In the interest of protecting the individual's right to have access to materials, the Library supports the following documents:

The First Amendment to the U.S. Constitution. The Library Bills of Rights—Adopted June 18, 1948, amended February 2, 1967, and June 23, 1980 by the American Library Association Council. The Freedom to Read Statement—Adopted June 25, 1953; revised January 28, 1972, January 16, 1991, by the ALA Council and the AAP Freedom to Read Committee.

Labeling Material

Tippecanoe Public Library   Lafayette, Indiana

Labeling and/or special shelving of materials may be used for some collections but will not be used for the purpose of restricting access or pre-judging content.

Richland Public Library   Richland, Washington

"Labeling" is an attempt to prejudice the reader, and as such, it is a censor's tool. If materials are labeled to pacify one group, there is no excuse for refusing to label any item in the library's collection. No sizeable group of persons would be likely to agree either on the types of materials that should be labeled or the sources of information which should be regarded with suspicion. Freedom is no freedom if it is accorded only to the accepted and the inoffensive. It is in the public interest for libraries to make available the widest diversity of views and expressions, including those that are unorthodox or unpopular with the majority.

Patron Recommendations

Pasadena Public Library   Pasadena, California

The library strongly encourages input from the Pasadena community concerning the collection. A suggestion for purchase procedure enables Pasadena citizens to request that a particular item or subject be purchased by the library. All suggestions for purchase are subject to the same selection criteria as other materials and are not automatically added to the collection. It is the library's intent that suggestions for purchase be used to help the library in developing collections which serve the interests and needs of the community. You can make a suggestion online.

Challenges

Ohio County Public Library   Wheeling, West Virginia

The Library Board considers all materials selected under this policy to be constitutionally protected under the First Amendment of the United States Constitution. If a patron claims that a particular item is not constitutionally protected, the burden of proof rests with the patron.

The Board of Trustees recognizes the right of individuals to question materials in the library collection. Whenever a patron objects to the presence or absence of any library material, the complaint will be given hearing and consideration. All complaints to staff members will be referred to the professional staff who will discuss the matter with the complainant. If not satisfied, the patron will be given a "Request for Reconsideration of Library Materials" form to complete. This completed form will be given to the Library Director who will then meet with the professional staff to evaluate the material in question and consider the merits of the completed request form. The professional staff will consider whether the material meets the selection criteria outlined in this policy. A decision will be made regarding whether or not to add or withdraw the material within a reasonable amount of time, with written reasons for the decision conveyed to the patron. If the patron is dissatisfied with the staff's decision or the written reply, he or she may appeal the decision to the Board at a regularly scheduled Board meeting. The Board, after receiving public testimony from the patron, other interested parties, and from the Director, will decide whether or not library policies have been followed and whether to add or withdraw the material in question.

Materials subject to complaint shall not be removed from use and circulation pending final action. If a court having jurisdiction over the library decides that any material in the collection is unprotected by the Constitution of the United States, such material will be removed immediately. Material under court consideration will remain available to patrons until a final ruling is made.

Tuscarawas Public Library   **New Philadelphia, Ohio**

Citizen's Request for Reconsideration of Materials

Format (Book, Video, etc.) ——————————.

Author (if applicable) ——————————.

Title (or URL) ——————————.

Publisher ——————————.

Your name ——————————.

Address ——————————Telephone ——————————.

——————————

Group you represent (if any) ——————————

Did you examine the entire work? ——————————.

If not, what parts?——————————

What do you believe is the purpose of this material?

———————————————————————

———————————————————————

Specifically, to what in the material do you object?

———————————————————————

What harmful effect do you feel might be/was the effect of your using this

material? ———————————————————————

Is there anything good or useful about this material? What?——————————

———————————————————————

What prompted you to use this item? ——————————.

For what age group would you recommend this item? ——————————.

What would you recommend to replace this item ——————————

———————————————————————

Signature——————————

We are sorry if you have been offended by any material in our collection. The Tuscarawas County Public Library subscribes to the Library Bill of Rights as adopted by the American Library Association June 27, 1967 and its subsequent amendments. This document reads, in part: "As a responsibility of library service, books and other library materials selected should

Figure 12.1 Challenge to Material Form

be chosen for values of interest, information and enlightenment of all the people of the community." We realize that everyone's tastes are different, and that it is our responsibility to provide materials on a multitude of subjects and viewpoints, in many styles.

The Internet makes available a wide variety of material, most of it useful and worthwhile, but some Internet sites are unsuitable for children and offensive to many adults. Unfortunately, we cannot filter out such sites without also eliminating access to many good resources. We have no control over Internet information, and we caution parents and others that objectionable sites do exist, although they are not usually accessible except by deliberate choice on the part of the browser. Library policy prohibits the use of sites which may reasonably be construed as obscene, and individuals who access such sites may lose their internet privileges.

If you honestly feel that a book or other item in our collection does not belong in the library of a free society, we invite you to fill out the form on the reverse side of this sheet and leave it at the front desk. The desk clerk will see that it is given to the library director, who will be in touch with you regarding your complaint.

The Tuscarawas County Public Library believes in the rights of a free press guaranteed by the Constitution of the United States of America. We further believe that the parents of a child are the only people who should be allowed to monitor the reading, watching or listening activities of that child. Conversely, we believe that it is every parent's duty to monitor his or her child's activity, and that this is not the prerogative of the library.

Figure 12.1 continued

Dayton Montgomery County Public Library   **Dayton, Ohio**

DAYTON & MONTGOMERY COUNTY PUBLIC LIBRARY

REQUEST FOR RECONSIDERATION OF INTERNET SITE

The library will only block Internet sites with sexually explicit images. If you wish to request that an Internet site be blocked by the library's filtering software, or that the existing block on a site be removed, please complete the form below and return it to the Director, Please note: your request will be forwarded to the Board of Library Trustees and it will become a matter of public record, including your name and address.

Requested by:_____ Date:_____

Address: _____

City: _____ State:_____ Zip:_____

Phone:_____

Representing:

Self: _____

Organization: _____

Have you read the library's Materials Selection Policy, _____ Yes _____ No

Uniform Resource Locator (URL) and site title:

_____

Please check the appropriate line below and explain your position:

_____ I am requesting that this site be BLOCKED for the following reason(s). (Use the reverse of this form and/or additional pages if necessary.

_____ I am requesting that the BLOCK on this site be REMOVED for the following reason(s). (Use the reverse of this form and/or additional pages if necessary.

Signature:_____

Figure 12.2 Challenge to an Internet Site

Dallas Public Library   **Dallas, Texas**

The XYZ Library welcomes the opportunity to discuss the interpretation and application of the library's material selection principles. So that the library will have an accurate understanding of your comments, will you please complete the following concerning the material in question and return it to us. Use additional pages as desired.

Author: _____

Title: _____

Publisher: _____

If a book, was it a paperback?

Patron's name: _____

Telephone: _____

Address: _____

City: _____   Zip Code: _____

1. Do you speak as an individual or as a representative of an organization? If you are with an organization, please identify it.

2. Did you read the entire publication? If not, which part?

3. What portion of the publication did you object to? Please cite the pages or sections?

4. Do you believe there is anything good about this publication?

5. Are you familiar with reviews of this publication?

6. Can you recommend a better publication of this kind?

Date: Patron's signature _____

Figure 12.3 Challenge to Printed Material

Dallas Public Library   **Dallas, Texas**

The XYZ Library welcomes the opportunity to discuss the interpretation and application of the library's material selection principles. So that the library will have an accurate understanding of your comments, will you please complete the following concerning the material in question and return it to us. Use additional pages as desired.

Author: _____

Title: _____

Publisher: _____

If a book, was it a paperback?

Patron's name: _____

Telephone: _____

Address: _____

City: _____   Zip Code: _____

1. Do you speak as an individual or as a representative of an organization? If

you are with an organization, please identify it.

2. **Have you seen or heard the material in its entirety? If not, which parts**?

3. To what in this material do you object?

4. Do you believe there is anything good about this material?

5. Are you familiar with reviews of this publication?

6. Can you recommend a better publication of this kind?

Date: _____   Patron's signature: _____

Figure 12.4 Challenge to Non-Print Material

FORMS

Benefits of Written Forms

- Adds quality material to the collection you would know about otherwise from patrons through the Patron Recommendation to Purchase Form (Figure 12.7);
- Makes patrons feel more involved when they can make suggestions;
- Tracks actual patron activity, such as how the library is being used and how often, through surveys;
- Monitors customer service satisfaction through surveys;
- Keeps you prepared when material is challenged with the proper forms quickly available to you;
- Ascertains if the person who challenges material has read, heard, or viewed the material in its entirety;
- Uncovers whether you are dealing with a group or individual challenging material;
- Gives the person time to consider the challenge when she or he takes the form home to fill out, and has to answer
- Have you, or have you not, read it?
- Does the material have some merit?
- Is there really a better resource and what is it?
- What specifically bothers you about the material and why?
- Why is it harmful?

Bozeman Public Library   **Bozeman, Montana**

We are interested in YOUR opinion about the services we provide, as we plan for the future of your library. Please take a moment to let us know how we're doing.

1. How often do you visit the Library? (circle one)

Weekly_____ Monthly_____ Per year_____ Other_____

2. Please give us your thoughts on the following areas of service:

                                   Excellent Good Just OK Needs attention No opinion

Circulation Desk
Information Desk
Children's Desk
ILL (borrowing books from other libraries)
BridgerNet Catalog
Computers Word Processing)
Internet Access
Adult Programs
Meeting Room
Children's Programs
Collections: Books
Magazines/Newspapers
Videos & CDs
Books-on-Tape
CD-ROM Databases
Reference Materials
Parking Hours
Phone Service
Special Delivery Service
Seating/Tables
Other_____

 4. Other comments? (Please use back of paper.)

THANK YOU! Please return to Circulation Desk, Information Desk or Children's Desk

Figure 12.5 Survey

- How often do you visit the library:

Daily_____Weekly_____ Monthly_____ Every 3 months_____ Every 6 months_____ Once a year_____ This is my first time_____

- Why do you visit the library:

Personal interests_____School assignments_____ Government information_____ Attend programs_____ Bring children_____ Recreational Reading_____ Bestsellers or popular material_____ Hobby_____ Personal health_____ Repair or make something_____

- Do you usually find what you were looking for:

More than 75% of the time_____

Between 50% and 75% of the time_____

Less than 50% of the time_____

- Please rate the following using a scale of 1–5.

1 is very unsatisfactory. 5 is very satisfactory.

Hours of operation: _____

Help finding material:_____

Help answering questions:_____

Ease of check-out:_____

Number of Internet stations:_____

Number of programs:_____

Adult Programs:_____

Children's Programs:_____

Number of copies of popular material:_____

Quality of children's material:_____

Quality of adult books:_____

Quality of videos:_____

Quality of CDs:_____

Quality of DVDs:_____

Quality of books-on-tape:_____

If you answered any of the above with a 1 or 2, please tell us how we can improve.

Thank you for filling out our survey so we can better serve your needs

Figure 12.6 Library Survey for Public Libraries

Richland Public Library   **Richland, Washington**
Recommendation for Purchase Form

Top of Form 1

Book_____Video_____ DVD_____ Book On Tape_____

Magazine_____ Music_____ CD_____Book on CD _____CD ROM_____

Please enter the Title, even if it is just "Newest Book"

Please enter the Author, if known._____

Publisher and Pub Date, if known._____

Where did you read about, hear about or see this material?

Patron Name_____

Library Card Number_____

Phone Number_____

If material IS purchased, shall we place a hold on this material for you?_____

Figure 12.7 Recommendation to Purchase Form

Bottom of Form 1

Date:—————————————

Title:—————————————

Author—————————————

Publisher:—————————————

ISBN:—————————————

Staff members name:—————————————

Date ordered:—————————————

Date received:—————————————

Accession number:—————————————

Figure 12.8 Staff Order Card

Bottom of Form 1

Name:_____

Library Card Number:_____

Daytime Phone:_____

E-mail:_____

Title:_____

Author:_____

ISBN (if known):_____

Material Type: _____Book _____Video _____Audio _____CD

_____DVD _____Book on Tape _____CD Book on Tape

_____Music _____Other Specify_____

Date contacted:_____

Accession number:_____

Would you like the book reserved for you when it comes in:_____

Figure 12.9 Patron Request to Purchase

CHECKLIST

- Selection objectives need to be compatible with the mission statement.
- What type of survey will give you the best information about your community?
- Write the selection criteria, responsibilities, and resources so you can defend the collection against challenges.
- Are there available funds to support local school curriculum?
- What type of collection do you want—broad and deep, general, broad and deep in selected areas or some other combination?
- Can any print resources be cut in favor of electronic resources?
- Do you have helpful Internet resources bookmarked on your computers or links to them from your Web site?
- In what subject areas do you not want to collect, such as genealogical materials?

Bibliography

GENERAL PRINT RESOURCES

Eberhart, George, comp. 2000. *The Whole Library Handbook: Current Data, Professional Advice, and Curiosa About Libraries and Library Services*. 3rd ed. Chicago: American Library Association.

Evans, G. Edward. 2000. *Developing Library and Information Center Collections*. Englewood, Colorado: Libraries Unlimited.

Evans, G. Edward, Anthony J. Amedeo, and Thomas L. Carter. 1999. *Introduction Library Public Services*. 6th ed. Englewood, Colorado: Libraries Unlimited.

Giesecke, Joan. 2000. *Practical Strategies for Library Managers*. Chicago: American Library Association.

Hill, Malcolm K. 1993. *Budgeting and Financial Record Keeping in the Small Library*. Chicago: American Library Association.

Katz, Bill, ed. 1988. *The How-to-do-it Manual for Small Libraries*. New York: Neal-Schuman.

Jones, Barbara M. 1999. *Libraries, Access, and Intellectual Freedom: Developing Policies for Public and Academic Libraries*. Chicago: American Library Association.

Larson, Jeanette, and Herman L. Totten. 1998. *Model Policies for Small and Medium Public Libraries*. New York: Neal-Schuman.

Ruoss, G. Martin. 1980. *A Policy and Procedure Manual for Church and Synagogue Libraries: A do-it-yourself Guide*. Bryn Mawr, Pennsylvania: Church and Synagogue Library Association.

Schuman, Bruce A. 2001. *Issues for Libraries and Information Science in the Internet Age*. Englewood, Colorado: Libraries Unlimited.

Stueart, Robert D., and Barbara B. Moran. 1998. *Library and Information Center Management*. Englewood, Colorado: Libraries Unlimited.

Weingand, Darlene E. 2001. *Administration of the Small Library*. 4th ed. Chicago: American Library Association.

GENERAL INTERNET RESOURCES

ACQWeb Nashville, Tennessee: Vanderbilt University. (September 2002) Available: http://acqweb.library.vandrebilt.edu/American Library Association.)

American Library Association. "Intellectual Freedom." Chicago, Illinois: American Library Association. (January 2002) Available: www.ala.org.

———. "Statements and Policies." Chicago, Illinois: American Library Association. (September 2002) Available: www.ala.org.

Arizona State Library, Archives, and Pubic Records. Phoenix, Arizona. (September 2002) Available: www.lib.az.us.

Berkeley Digital Library. "Libraries on the Web." San Francisco, California: University of California Berkeley. (August 2002) Available: http://sunsite.berkeley.edu/Libweb/Public_main.html.

Connecticut State Library. Hartford, Connecticut. (September 2002) Available: www.cslib.org.

Indiana State Library. "Indiana Public Library with Policies on the WWW." Indianapolis, Indiana.

(September 2002) Available: www.statelib.lib.in.us.

Library of Congress. "Library and Information Science Resource." Washington, D.C. (September 2002) Available: http://lcweb.loc.gov/global/library.

Massachusetts Regional Library Systems. "Policy Collection." Shrewsbury, Massachusetts. (September 2002) Available: www.cmrls.org.

Montana State Library. Helena, Montana. (September 2002) Available: http://msl.state.mt.us.

Municipal Research and Services Center of Washington. Seattle, Washington. (September 2002) Available: www.mrsc.org.

Nebraska Library Commission. Lincoln, Nebraska. (September 2002) Available: www.nlc.state.ne.us.

Northeast Iowa Library Service. Waterloo, Iowa. (September 2002) Available: www.neilsa.org.

Outagamie Waupaca Library. Appleton, Wisconsin. (August 2002) Available: www.ows.lib.wi.us.

State Library of Louisiana. Baton Rouge, Louisiana. (September 2002) Available: www.state.lib.la.us.

State Library of Ohio. Columbus, Ohio. (October 2002) Available: http://winslo.state.oh.us.

Texas State Library and Archives Commission. Austin, Texas. (September 2002) Available: www.tsl.state.tx.us.

Washington Library Association. Seattle, Washington. (August 2002) Available: www.wla.org.

CHAPTER 1: CIRCULATION

Print Resources:

Martin, Murray S. 1998. *Charging and Collecting Fines and Fees: A Handbook for Libraries*. New York: Neal-Schuman.

Internet Resources:

Albert Wisner Public Library. "Collection Development Policy." Warwick, New York. (September 2002) Available: www.albertwisnerlibrary.org.

Beloit Public Library. "Circulation Policy." Beliot, Wisconsin. Available: http://als.lib.wi.us/BPL.

Cleveland Public Library. "Library Services: Policy on Patron Guideline." Cleveland, Ohio. (November 2002) Available: www.cpl.org.

Cleveland Public Library. "Miscellaneous Policies: Rules Governing the Use of the Library." Fayetteville, North Carolina. (December 2002) Available: www.cumberland.lib.nc.us.

Grand Island Public Library. "Unattended Children Policy." Grand Island, Nebraska. (September 2002) Available: www.gi.lib.ne.us.

Huron Public Library. "Conduct Rules." Huron, Ohio. (November 2002) Available: http://library.norweld.lib.oh.us/Huron.

Indian River County Library. "Circulation Policies." Indian River, Florida. (August 2002) Available: http://indian-river.fl.us/library.

Kentucky Department for Libraries and Archives. "Customer Policy." Frankfort, Kentucky. (September 2002) Available: www.kdla.net.

Kentucky Department for Libraries and Archives. "State Library Circulation Policy." Frankfort, Kentucky. (August 2002) Available: www.kdla.net.

Los Angeles Public Library. "Borrower Services." Los Angeles, California. (August 2002)

Available: www.lapl.org.

Marion Public Library. "Circulation Policies." Marion, Iowa. (August 2002) Available: http://community.marion.ia.us/library.

Meadville Public Library. "Meadville Public Library's Circulation Policy." Meadville, Pennsylvania. (August 2002) Available: http://mplcatl.meadvillelibrary.org.

Muehl Public Library. "Circulation Policy." Seymour, Wisconsin. (August 2002) Available: www.owls.lib.wi.us/sey.

Neuschafer Community Library. "Article VI Circulation Policy." Freemont, Wisconsin. (September 2002) Available: www.owls.lib.wi.us/fpl.

North Judson Wayne Township Public Library. "Fees and Fines Policies." North Judson, Indiana. (April 2003) Available: www.njwt.lib.in.us.

Pittsfield Public Library. "Circulation Policy." Pittsfield, Maine. (August 2002) Available: www.pittsfield.lib.me.us.

Tempe Public Library. "Tempe Public Library Circulation Policy." Tempe, Arizona. (August 2002) Available: www.tempe.gov/library.

Wood Place Public Library. "Patron Complaint Form Concerning Library/Librarian." California, Missouri. (December 2002) Available: www.woodplace.libraary.org.

CHAPTER 2: REFERENCE

Print Resources:

Bopp, Richard, and Linda C. Smith, eds. 2000. *Reference and Information Science: An Introduction.* 3rd ed. Englewood, Colorado: Libraries Unlimited.

Internet Resources:

Appleton Public Library. "Reference and Reader's Advisory Policy." Appleton, Wisconsin. (September 2002) Available: www.apl.org.

Beloit Public Library. "Children's Services Policy." Beloit, Wisconsin. (September 2002) Available: http://als.lib.wi.us/BPL.

Cleveland Public Library. "Library Services: Cleveland Research Center." Cleveland, Ohio. (November 2002) Available: www.cpl.org.

DeKalb County Public Library. "Reference Materials and Services." Atlanta, Georgia. (September 2002) Available: www.dekalb.public.lib.ga.us.

Fort Smith Public Library. "Fort Smith Pubic Library: Policies." Fort Smith, Arkansas. (September 2002) Available: www.fspl.lib.ar.us.

Henderson County Public Library. "Research Service Fee Schedule." Henderson, Kentucky. (November 2002) Available: www.hcpl.org.

Lucius Beebe Memorial Library. "Reference Policy." Wakefield, Massachusetts. (September 2002) Available: www.noblenet.org/wakefield.

Memorial Hall Library. "Reference Services Policy." Andover, Massachusetts. (September 2002) Available: www.mhl.org.

Mt. Lebanon Public Library. "Confidentiality of Library Records." Pittsburgh, Pennsylvania. (April 2003) Available: www.einetwork.net/ein/mtleb.

Newark Public Library. "Reference Service at Newark Public Library." Newark, New Jersey. (September 2002) Available: www.npl.org.

Pasadena Public Library. "Reference Services." Pasadena, California. (September 2002) Available: www.ci.pasadena.ca.us/library.

Pittsfield Public Library. "Reference Policy." Pittsfield, Maine. (August 2002) Available: www.pittsfield.lib.me.us.

Wadsworth Public Library. "Confidentiality of Patron Records." Wadsworth, Ohio. (November 2002) Available: www.wadsworth.lib.oh.us.

Westerville Public Library. "Reference Services." Westerville, Ohio. (November 2002) Available: www.wpl.lib.oh.us.

CHAPTER 3: INTERNET

Print Resources:

Smith, Mark. 1999. *Neal-Schuman Internet Policy for Libraries.* New York: Neal-Schuman.

Internet Resources:

Alhambra Public Library. "Internet Policy at Alhambra Public Library." Alhambra, California. (December 2002) Available: www.alhambralibrary.org.

Carrollton Public Library. "Electronic Resources and Internet Policy." Carrollton, Texas. (December 2002) Available: www.cityofcarrollton.com/leisure/library.

Hobbs Public Library. "Public Computers Policy." Hobbs, New Mexico. (December 2002) Available: http://hobbspublib.leaco.net.

James Kennedy Public Library. "Internet Use Policy." Dyersville, Iowa. (December 2002) Available: www.dyersvillelibrary.org.

Liberty Pubic Library. "Computer/Internet Policy." Liberty, New York. (December 2002) Available: www.rcls.org/lib.

Manitouwadge Public Library. "Terms and Conditions for Acceptable Use of Public Internet Access." Manitouwadge, Ontario, Canada. (December 2002) Available: www.nwconx.net/~library-man.

Marion County Library. "Marion County Library Internet Acceptable Use Agreement." Marion, South Carolina. (April 2003) Available: www.marioncountylibrary.org.

Neill Public Library. "Internet Use Policy." Pullman, Washington. (September 2002) Available: www.neill-lib.org.

New London Public Library. "Internet Use Policy." New London, Wisconsin. (www.owls.lib.wi.us/npl.

Old Town Public Library. "Internet Policy Internet Acceptable Use Guidelines." Old Town, Maine. (December 2002) Available: www.old-town.lib.me.us.

Pasadena Public Library. "Internet Rules and Procedures." Pasadena, Texas. (December 2002) Available: www.ci.pasadena.tx.us/library.

Pikes Peak Library District. "Internet Use." Colorado Springs, Colorado. (September 2002) Available: http://library.ppld.org.

Queens Borough Public Library. "Internet Policy for Public Use." New York, New York. (September 2002) Available: www.queenslibrary.org.

San Antonio Public Library. "Internet Acceptable Use Policy." San Antonio, Texas. (December 2002) Available: www.sanantonio.gov/library.

San Francisco Public Library. "Internet Use Policy." San Francisco, California. (April 2003)
    Available: http://sfp14.sfpl.org.

Vancouver Public Library. "Public Internet Access Policy." Vancouver, British Columbia, Canada.
    (December 2002) Available: www.vpl.vancouver.bc.ca.

Winnetka-Northfield Public Library District. "Winnetka-Northfield Public Library District
    Policy for Access to Electronic Information Networks." Winnetka, Illinois. (December 2002)
    Available: www.wpld.alibrary.com

CHAPTER 4: MISCELLANEOUS ADMINISTRATIVE POLICIES

Print Resources:

Herring, Mark Youngblood. 1993. *Organizing Friends Groups: A How-to-Do-It Manual For Librarians*.
    New York: Neal-Schuman.

Dallas Public Library. 1995. "Program Evaluation Form." Dallas, Texas: Dallas Public Library.

Internet Resources:

Cumberland Public Library. "Miscellaneous Policies: Policy on the Use of Telephones."
    Fayetteville, North Carolina. (December 2002) Available: www.cumberland.lib.nc.us.

Fulton County Public Library. "Friends of the Fulton County Public Library." Fulton, Indiana.
    (April 2002) Available: www.fulco.lib.in.us.

Fulton County Public Library. "Policy on the Distribution of Tax Forms." Grand island,
    Nebraska. (September 2002) Available: www.gi.lib.ne.us.

Hurt/Battelle Memorial Library of West Jefferson. "Photocopying Policy." Columbus, Ohio.
    (September 2002) Available: www.winslo.state.oh.us.

Jasper County Public Library. "Facsimile (Fax) Machine Policy." Jasper, Indiana. (March 2003)
    Available: www.jasperco.lib.in.us.

————. "Microfilm/Microfiche Reader/Printer Policy." Jasper, Indiana. (March 2003) Available:
    www.jasperco.lib.in.us.

Middleton Public Library. "Canvassing." Middleton, Wisconsin. (April 2003) Available:
    www.scls.lib.wi.us/middleton.

Middletown Public Library. "Volunteers." Middletown, Ohio. (April 2003) Available: www.middle-
    townlibrary.org.

New London Public Library. "Staff Educational Development." New London, Wisconsin.
    (September 2002) Available: www.owls.lib.wi.us/npl.

Pend Oreille County Library District. "Continuing Education Policy." Newport, Washington.
    (November 2002) Available: www.pocld.org.

Pikes Peak Library District. "Access to Materials." Colorado Springs, Colorado. (September
    2002) Available: http://library.ppld.org

Public Library of Cincinnati and Hamilton County. "Petitions and Solicitations." Columbus,
    Ohio. (April 2003) Available: http://winslo.state.oh.us.

Public Library of Cincinnati and Hamilton County. "Photographing and Videotaping." Columbus,
    Ohio. (April 2003) Available: http://winslo.state.oh.us.

Richland Pubic Library. "Word Processing." Richland, Washington (November 2002) Available:
    http://richland.lib.wa.us.

Sno-Island Regional Library System. "Program Policy." Marysville, Washington. (November 2002) Available: www.sno-isle.org.

Tuscarawas County Public Library. "Copyright." Columbus, Ohio. (November 2002) Available: http://winslo.state.oh.us.

Westerville Public Library. "Reference Services." Westerville, Ohio. (November 2002) Available: www.wpl.lib.oh.us.

Old Worthington Public Library. "Fax." Columbus, Ohio. (April 2003) Available: http://winslo.state.oh.us.

—————. "Surplus Furniture and Equipment." Columbus, Ohio. (April 2003) Available: http://winslo.state.oh.us.

CHAPTER 5: MISSION STATEMENTS

Print Resources:

Public Library Association. 1979. *The Public Library Mission Statement and its Imperatives for Service*. Chicago: American Library Association.

Internet Resources:

Dayton and Montgomery County Public Library. "Library's Mission Statement." Dayton, Ohio. (April 2003) Available: www.daytonmetrolibrary.org.

Laramie County Library System. "Library Mission Statement." Laramie, Wyoming. (April 2003) Available: www.lclsonline.org.

Marshall Public Library. "Marshall Public Library Long-Range Plan: 1999–2003." Marshall, Idaho. (September 2002) Available: www.lili.org/marshall.

Morton Grove Public Library. "Morton Grove Public Library Strategic Plan: 2003–2005." Morton Grove, Illinois. (April 2003) Available: www.webrary.org.

Pikes Peak Library District. "Mission Statement for Pike Peak Library District." Colorado Springs, Colorado. (April 2003) Available: wwwlibrary.ppld.org.

Newark Public Library. "Reference Service Policies." Newark, New Jersey. (September 2002) Available: www.npl.org.

CHAPTER 6: GIFTS, MEMORIALS, DONATIONS

Internet Resources:

Charlevoix Public Library. "Gift Policy." Charlevoix, Michigan. (October 2002) Available: www.charlevoix.lib.mi.us.

Cook Memorial Public Library. "Gifts and Donations." Libertyville, Illinois. (October 2002) Available: www.cooklib.org.

Ely Public Library. "Ely Public Library Gift Policy." Ely, Minnesota. (October 2002) Available: www.elylibrary.org.

Hibbing Public Library. "Gift and Bequests Policy." Hibbing, Minnesota. (April 2003) Available: www.hibbing.lib.mn.us.

Highland Park Public Library. "Gift Policy." Highland Park, Illinois. (October 2002) Available: http://hppl.lib.il.us.

Irving Public Library. "Gifts, Memorials, and Other Donations." Irving, Texas. (April 2003) Available: www.irving.lib.tx.us.

Norfolk Public Library. "Norfolk Public Library System Sponsorship Policy and Procedures." Norfolk, Virginia. (April 2003) Available: www.npl.lib.va.us.

North Castle Public Library. "North Castle Public Library Gift and Donation Policy." Armonk, New York. (April 2003) Available: www.northcastlelibrary.org.

Oakville Public Library. "Tribute or Memorial Gift." Oakville, Ontario. (April 2003) Available: www.opl.on.ca.

Oskaloosa Public Library. "Gift Wavier." Oskaloosa, Iowa. (April 2003) Available: www.opl.oskaloosa.org.

Park Ridge Public Library. "Library Gift Form." Park Ridge, Illinois. (April 2003) Available: www.park-ridge.il.us/library.

Park Ridge Public Library. "Notice to Library Donors." Park Ridge, Illinois. (April 2003) Available: www.park-ridge.il.us/library.

Shawnee Library System. "Gifts to the Library." Caterville, Illinois. (October 2002) Available: www.shawls.lib.il.us.

Villa Park Public Library. "Gifts and Bequests Policy." Villa Park, Illinois. (April 2003) Available: www.villapark.lib.il.us/library.

CHAPTER 7: LIBRARY BOARDS

Print Resources:

Swan, James. 1991. *Working Together: A How-to-Do-It Manual for Librarians*. New York: Neal-Schuman.

Wade, Gordon S. 1991. *Working with Library Boards: A How-to-Do-It Manual for Librarians*. New York: Neal-Schuman.

Internet Resources:

Appleton Public Library. "Personnel Policy." Appleton, Wisconsin. (September 2002) Available: www.apl.org.

Jackson County Public Library. "By-laws of the Board of Trustees." Seymour, Indiana. (November 2002) Available: www.japl.lib.in.us.

Nebraska Library Commission Library Development Services. "By-laws." Lincoln, Nebraska. (November 2002) Available: www.nlc.state.ne.us.

Neuschafer Community Library. "Article VII – Personnel Policy for the Director." Freemont, Wisconsin. (September 2002) Available: www.owls.lib.wi.us/fpl.

Neuschafer Community Library. "By-laws." New London, Wisconsin. (September 2002) Available: www.owls.lib.wi.us/npl.

Ohio County Public Library. "OCPL By-laws." Wheeling, West Virginia. (September 2002) Available: htttp://wheeling.lib.wv.us.

Pasadena Public Library. "Library Commission." Pasadena, California. (September 2002) Available: www.ci.pasadena.ca.us/library.

Rockaway Township Free Public Library. "Rockaway Township Free Public Library Board of Trustees Meeting of February 14, 2000." Rockaway, New Jersey. (October 2002) Available: www.gti.net/rocktwp.

Texas State Library and Archives Commission. "Public Library Advisory Board Handbook." Austin, Texas. (November 2002) Available: www.tsl.state.tx.us.

Waverly Public Library. "Board of Trustees Library Policies." Waterloo, Iowa. (November 2002) Available: www.neilsa.org.

Wisconsin Department of Public Instruction Public Library Development. "Sample Wisconsin Public Library Board of Trustee By-laws." Madison, Wisconsin. (September, 2002).

CHAPTER 8: EXHIBITS, DISPLAYS, AND BULLETIN BOARDS

Internet Resources:

Anchorage Municipal Libraries. "Exhibits Policy." Anchorage, Alaska. (March 2003) Available: http://lexicon.ci.anchorage.ak.us/aml.

Chelmsford Public Library. "Art Exhibits Policy." Chelmsford, Massachusetts. (March 2003) Available: www.chelmsfordlibrary.org.

Cumberland Public Library. "Miscellaneous Policies: Distribution of Printed Materials Policy." Fayetteville, North Carolina. (December 2002) Available: www.cumberland.lib.nc.us.

David and Joyce Milne Public Library. "Exhibition Rules and Application Form." Augusta, Maine. (March 2003) Available: www.milnelibrary.org.

Gates Public Library. "Bulletin Board and Display Policy Gate Public Library." Rochester, New York. (December 2002) Available: www.gateslibrary.org.

Indian Valley Public Library. "Exhibit, Display, and Bulletin Board Policy." Telford, Pennsylvania. (December 2002) Available: www.ivpl.org.

Joplin Public Library. "Public Forum Areas." Joplin, Missouri. (December 2002) Available: www.joplinpubliclibrary.org.

Lithgow Public Library. "Lithgow Public Library Exhibit Policy." Augusta, Maine. (December 2002) Available: www.lithgow.lib.me.us.

Middleton Thrall Public Library. "Bulletin Board Usage Rules." Middleton, New York. (December 2002) Available: www.thrall.org.

CHAPTER 9: MEETING ROOMS

Internet Resources:

Austin Public Library. "Meeting Room Policy." Austin, Texas: Austin Public Library (December 2002) Available: www.ci.austin.tx.us/library.

Bernardsville Public Library. "Community Room Policy and Procedures." Bernardsville, New Jersey. (December 2002) Available: www.bernardsville.org.

Fayette County Public Library. "Fayette County Library Meeting Room Application." Fayetteville, Georgia. (December 2002) Available: www.admin.co.fayette.ga.us/public_library.

Fayette County Public Library. "Meeting Room Policy." Fayetteville, Georgia. (December 2002) Available: www.admin.co.fayette.ga.us/public_library.

Hershey Public Library. "Use of Meeting Rooms." Hershey, Pennsylvania. (December 2002) Available: www.hersheylibrary.org.

Jasper County Public Library. "Meeting Room Policy." Rensselaer, Indiana. (March 2003) Available: www.jasper.co.lib.in.us.

Lawrence Public Library. "Meeting Room Policy." Lawrence, Kansas. (December 2002) Available: www.lawrencepubliclibrary.org.

Lucius Beebe Memorial Library. "Meeting Room Policy." Wakefield, Massachusetts. (September 2002) Available: www.nobelnet.org/wakefield.

Mt. Lebanon Public Library. "Meeting Room Policy." Pittsburgh, Pennsylvania. (March 2002) Available: www.einetwork.net/ein/mtleb.

Washoe County Library System. "Facility Use Policy." Reno, Nevada. (September 2002) Available: www.washoe.lib.nv.us.

CHAPTER 10: FOUNDATIONS

Print Resources:

Clow, Faye. 1993. *Forming and Funding Public Library Foundations*. Chicago: Public Library Association.

Edie, John A. 1993. *First Steps in Starting a Foundation*. Washington, District of Columbia: Council on Foundations.

Internet Resources:

Chapel Hill Public Library. "Methods of Giving." Chapel Hill, North Carolina. (August 2003) Available: www.chapelhilllibraryfoundation.org.

———. "Gifts and Bequests to the Chapel Hill Public Library Foundation." Chapel Hill, North Carolina. (August 2003) Available: www.chapelhilllibraryfoundation.org.

Jacksonville Public Library Foundation. "About the Jacksonville Public Library Foundation." Jacksonville, Florida. (August 2003) Available: www.jplf.org

Kirkwood Public Library Foundation. "Contributions Form." Kirkwood, Missouri. (August 2003) Available: http://kpl.lib.mo.us/kwd/found.

———. "Kirkwood Public Library Foundation By-laws." Kirkwood, Missouri. (August 2003) Available: http://kpl.lib.mo.us/kwd/found.

———. "Conflict of Interest Questionnaire." Kirkwood, Missouri. (August 2003) Available: http://kpl.lib.mo.us/kwd/found.

———. "Investment Policy Statement." Kirkwood, Missouri. (August 2003) Available: http://kpl.lib.mo.us/kwd/found.

———. "Guidelines Conflict of Interest." Kirkwood, Missouri. (August 2003) Available: http://kpl.lib.mo.us/kwd/found.

Oakland Public Library Foundation. "What We Do." Oakland, California. (August 2003) Available: www.oplf.org.

Queens Borough Public Library. "Queens Borough Foundation." New York, New York. (August 2003) Available: www.queenslibrary.org/qlf/index.asp.

River Falls Public Library Foundation. "By-laws of the River Falls Library Foundation, Inc." River Falls, Wisconsin. (August 2003) Available: www.rfcity.org/library.

————. "Mission Statement of the River Falls Library Foundation." River Falls, Wisconsin. (August 2003) Available: www.rfcity.org/library.

————. "Statement of Activities." River Falls, Wisconsin. (August 2003) Available: www.rfcity.org/library.

Salem Public Library Foundation. "Securing the future of the Salem Public Library." Salem, Oregon. (August 2003) Available: www.splfoundation.org/

Wyoming State Library. "A Member's Guide: An Introduction to Public Library Foundations." Cheyenne, Wyoming. (August 2003) Available: www-wsl.state.wy.us/slpub/foundations.

CHAPTER 11: COLLECTION MAINTENANCE AND EVALUATION

Print Resources:

Dallas Public Library. 2003. "Humanities Department: Forms." Dallas, Texas: Dallas Public Library.

DeSoto Public Library. 1996. "Policy and Procedure Manual: Circulation Policies." DeSoto, Texas: DeSoto Pubic Library.

Slote, Stanley, J. 1997. *Weeding Library Collections: Library Weeding Methods*. Englewood, Colorado: Libraries Unlimited.

Internet Resources:

Eugene Public Library. "Collection Development Policy." Eugene, Oregon. (September 2002) Available: www.ci.eugene.or.us/Library.

Kitsap Regional Library. "Collection Development Policy Third Edition." Bremerton, Washington. (September 2002) Available: www.krl.org.

Memorial Hall Library. "Memorial Hall Collection Development Manual 2002: Circulating Collection." Andover, Massachusetts. Available: www.mhl.org.

Neill Public Library. "Collection Development Policy." Pullman, Washington. (September 2002) Available: www.neill-lib.org.

Pasadena Public Library. "Collection Development Policy." Pasadena, California. (September 2002) Available: www.ci.pasadena.ca.us/library.

Tippecanoe County Public Library. "Tippecanoe County Public Library Collection Management Policy." Lafayette, Indiana. (April 2002) Available: www.tcpl.lib.in.us.

Washoe County Library System. "Collection Development Policy." Reno, Nevada. (September 2002) Available: www.washoe.lib.nv.us.

CHAPTER 12: COLLECTION DEVELOPMENT

Print Resources:

Dallas Public Library. 1995. "Objection to Non-Print Material." In Policy and Procedure Manual. Dallas, Texas: Dallas Public Library.

Cassell, Kay Ann. 1991. *Developing Public Library Collections, Policies, and Procedures: A How-to-Do-It Manual for Small and Medium Sized Libraries*. New York:: Neal-Schuman.

Fitas, Elizabeth, ed. 1995. Collection Development Policies and Procedures. Phoenix, Arizona: Oryx.

Internet Resources:

Albert Wisner Public Library. "Collection Development Policy." Warwick, New York. (September 2002) Available: www.albertwisnerlibrary.org.

Bettendorf Public Library. "Collection Development." Bettendorf, Iowa. (September 2002) Available: www.rbls.lib.il.us/bpl.

Bozeman Public Library. "Bozeman Library Survey." Helena, Montana. (May 2002) Available: http://msl.state.mt.us.

Dayton and Montgomery County Public Library. "Request for Reconsideration of Library Material." Dayton, Ohio. (September 2002) Available: www.daytonmetrolibrary.org.

Eugene Public Library. "Collection Development Policy." Eugene, Oregon. (September 2002), Available: www.ci.eugene.or.us/Library.

Grand Island Public Library. "Public Access Computer/Electronic Databases." Grand Island, Nebraska. (September 2002) Available: www.gi.lib.ne.us.

Kitsap Regional Library. "Collection Development Policy Third Edition." Bremerton, Washington. (September 2002) Available: www.krl.org.

Kokomo Public Library. "Collection Development Policy." Kokomo, Indiana. (November 2002) Available: www.kokomo.lib.in.us.

Lucius Beebe Memorial Library. "Collection Development Policy." Wakefield, Massachusetts. (September 2002) Available: www.nobelnet.org/wakefield.

New Castle Henry County Public Library. "Collection Development Policy." New Castle, Indiana. (November 2002) Available: www.nchcpl.lib.in.us.

Ohio County Public Library. "Collection Development Policy." Wheeling, West Virginia. (September 2002) http://wheeling.lib.wv/us.

Pasadena Public Library. "Collection Development Policy." Pasadena, California. (September 2002) Available: www.ci.pasadena.ca.us/library.

Richland Public Library. "Material Selection Policy." Richland, Washington. (November 2002) Available: http://richland.lib.wa.us.

Tippecanoe County Public Library. "Collection Management Policy." Lafayette, Indiana. (April 2002) Available: www.tcpl.lib.in.us.

Tuscarawas County Public Library. "Citizen's Request for Reconsideration of Material." Columbus, Ohio. (November 2002) Available: http://winslo.state.oh.us.

West Baton Rouge Parish Library. "Electronic Resources Access Policy." West Baton Rouge, Louisiana. (September 2002) Available: http://pelican.state.lib.la.us.

West Hartford Public Library. "Materials Selection Policy." West Hartford, Connecticut. (November 2002) Available: www.west-hartford.com/library.

Woodbridge Town Library. "Collection Development and Material Selection Policy." Hartford, Connecticut. (November 2002) Available: www.woodbridge.lioninc.org.

INDEX

About the Author

Rebecca Brumley is a librarian in the Humanities Division of Dallas Public Library. Brumley also consults with libraries in who are devising or revising workable policy and procedure manuals. She spends much of her free time on local animal rescue efforts, reading, and tending to her beloved garden.